Setting France Ablaze

Setting France Ablaze

The SOE in France During WWII

Peter Jacobs

Pen & Sword
MILITARY

First published in Great Britain in 2015 by
Pen & Sword Military
an imprint of
Pen & Sword Books Ltd
47 Church Street
Barnsley
South Yorkshire
S70 2AS

ISBN 978 1 78346 336 7

A CIP catalogue record for this book is available from the British
Library

Typeset in Ehrhardt by
Mac Style Ltd, Bridlington, East Yorkshire
Printed and bound in Malta
By Gutenberg Press Ltd

Pen & Sword Books Ltd incorporates the imprints of Pen & Sword
Archaeology, Atlas, Aviation, Battleground, Discovery, Family
History, History, Maritime, Military, Naval, Politics, Railways, Select,
Transport, True Crime, and Fiction, Frontline Books, Leo Cooper,
Praetorian Press, Seaforth Publishing and Wharncliffe.

For a complete list of Pen & Sword titles please contact
PEN & SWORD BOOKS LIMITED
47 Church Street, Barnsley, South Yorkshire, S70 2AS, England
E-mail: enquiries@pen-and-sword.co.uk
Website: www.pen-and-sword.co.uk

Contents

Acknowledgements

Many excellent books have been written about the Special Operations Executive over the years. One of the first, and, in my opinion, still one of the best, is *Inside SOE* by E. H. Cookridge, written in 1966 as the 'first full story of SOE in western Europe during 1940–45.' But it was following revelations of German successes in France, made during the late 1950s, that led to the commissioning of an official history of the SOE in France. Written by Professor M. R. D. Foot, himself a former member of the SOE, his superb and authoritative book *SOE in France* was also published in 1966.

As part of the Government Official Histories series, the aim of Michael Foot's book was to produce a history in its own right, compiled by a historian eminent in the field, who was afforded free access to all relevant material in the official archives. But *SOE in France* came under the spotlight when it was published and immediately prompted controversy. The names of many agents, some of whom were still alive at the time, were suddenly propelled into the public domain; whether they wanted to be or not. As a result, a number of pages were rewritten and the second impression, with amendments, was published in 1968. Nonetheless, *SOE in France* is an authoritative piece of work, stretching across 500 pages, and remains *the* source of reference for historians, researchers and authors alike, and provides a starting point for us all.

Since then, there have been numerous books written about agents of the SOE, particularly in recent years since the public release of personnel files. Many are about the female agents and one of the best is *Odette* by Penny Starns. In addition to Penny's great book, I pay particular tribute to many others: Squadron Leader Beryl E. Escott for *The Heroines of SOE*; Robyn Walker for *The Women Who Spied For Britain*; Russell Braddon for *Nancy Wake*; Susan Ottaway for *Sisters, Secrets and Sacrifice*, a book about Eileen and Jacqueline Nearne; Shrabani Basu for *Spy Princess*, the story of Noor Inayat Khan; Sarah Helm for *A Life in Secrets*, the story of Vera Atkins and the lost agents of SOE; and to R J Minney for, perhaps, starting the ball rolling with his legendary book *Carve Her Name With Pride* about Violette Szabo. As for the male agents, I can think of no better books than *No Cloak, No Dagger*, written by the former SOE agent Benjamin Cowburn, *The White Rabbit* by Bruce Marshall about Tommy Yeo-Thomas, and *No Banners*, the story of the Newton brothers, by Jack Thomas. All these, and many more, are excellent books and so anyone wishing to learn more about a specific individual should take the time to read them. A comprehensive bibliography at the end of this book will help guide the reader to specific areas of interest.

I must also thank the staff at The National Archives at Kew. Books like this would never be possible without the help and support given by all the staff at this marvellous facility; it really is a national treasure. There are so many who work tirelessly to help us all at Kew but I must single out Paul Johnson at the image library for his particular help and understanding. Similarly, I would like to offer my collective thanks to all the staff at the Imperial War Museum, Air Historical Branch and the Special Forces Club. All have provided much help over the years with access to files and other material as well as many images, some of which you will see in this book.

In addition to these formal institutions and establishments, there are also more and more websites becoming available. Run by enthusiasts they provide a wealth of knowledge and amongst these I include John Robertson's Special Forces Roll of Honour website (specialforcesroh.com), Nigel Perrin's website (nigelperrin.com), where much detail can be found about many SOE agents, and other websites such as the Tempsford Memorial Trust (tempsfordmemorial.co.uk). On a similar theme, I would also like to thank all those who contribute to the online SOE Forum, particularly members such as Steven Kippax, Mark Seaman and Martyn Cox. These and others contribute daily on a multitude of subjects relating to the SOE in order to share their knowledge and to ensure that the work of the SOE is never forgotten. From their contributions, and those of other members, I continue to learn so much.

During recent years I have been fortunate to spend time with descendants of some of those who served with the SOE in France and I am grateful to them all for providing me with material and images to help tell stories such as this. I have also been pleased to spend time across the Channel in France and, during the course of my research, I have continued to learn so much from the French people. But one community, above all others, has been of immense value to me and so I must say a special thank you to the people of Querrien in Brittany. They have made me so welcome during my visits and many have contributed personal accounts or articles, as well as many images, some of which I am pleased to be able to share in this book.

Finally, I wish to pay a personal tribute to the men and women of the SOE who bravely went into the field. Without their courage there would be no stories to be told. My personal thanks also go to the management and staff at Pen and Sword, particularly Laura Hirst for all her work behind the scenes, to enable this story to be told.

Introduction

Courage comes in many different forms, especially during war, but all those who went into Nazi-occupied France with the Special Operations Executive during the Second World War displayed courage in abundance. They came from all walks of life and were there for varying reasons, but they all went into the field in the knowledge they would probably receive no recognition for what they did and knowing that their lives could be cut short in a most miserable way. But who were these people and why did they do what they so bravely did? Besides, who or what was the SOE anyway?

Considered to be Britain's fourth armed service during the Second World War, the Special Operations Executive, the SOE, was formed in 1940 after the fall of France when the British prime minister, Winston Churchill, wanted to hit back at the enemy in Nazi-occupied Europe in whatever way he could. SOE operations would, he felt, divert vital enemy resources to counter acts of aggression but Churchill also realized that any act of aggression, no matter how small, would help raise the morale of those under occupation. In Churchill's own words he instructed the SOE to 'set Europe ablaze' but the new organization was to be kept separate from existing military and intelligence organizations, and was required to work closely with the many resistance movements in occupied Europe, with F Section (F for French) being responsible for SOE's operations in France.

The SOE gained little support from within Whitehall during its early years but by the time the Allied landings in north-west Europe took place on 6 June 1944, D-Day, it had reached a peak strength of nearly 13,000 people with F Section having established circuits all across France, most of them led by British-trained agents, to pave the way for the liberation of Europe.

Until that point, the Nazi occupation had turned France into something of a nation of slaves. Millions had been deported or compelled into forced labour and the Germans had plundered the French countryside to feed their own forces and population back home. Every day, convoys headed east, taking with them animals, land produce, raw materials and textiles, leaving the French cold and hungry. A black market had inevitably appeared as some profited from collaboration with the Nazis, but for the vast majority of the French there were endless queues with many basic products – such as coffee, butter or soap – considered luxuries beyond their reach. Furthermore, many had been kicked out of their homes to make way for the occupying forces who seemed to have spread across the towns and communities like a bad rash while blackouts and curfews, involving the prohibition of road traffic at certain times, had all but ended ordinary day-to-day life. Many of those who chose to resist the occupiers and their rules were arrested, often denounced to the Germans by so-called friends. Then, in turn, many of those arrested would stop at nothing to secure their own freedom by the denouncing of others.

And so it was against this background that SOE operatives went into Nazi-occupied France. They all accepted the hardship and risks, yet they went on to perform great deeds of bravery. Sadly, though, many were caught and after suffering brutal torture at the hands of their captors, followed by the horrors of the concentration camps, most had their lives brought to a sudden and tragic end.

The courage and initiative displayed by SOE's agents during the war has earned the organization both admiration and respect. Yet it is important to understand from the outset that only those who were actually there know the truth behind what went on at the time. It is imperative for authors not to fall into the trap of making simple accusations or to question individuals about the decisions they made more than seventy years ago. We are seldom in possession of all the facts. Furthermore, there was clearly some degree of carelessness reflected in the treatment of SOE's records at the end of the war. As the organization was wound up, there simply was not the staff nor, it would seem, the appetite, to work through the bundles of paperwork to retain records of everything that had gone on. Much of the material simply disappeared, either intentionally or otherwise, and so there are often gaps, which has led to much post-war speculation about some individuals and events.

But we have to start somewhere and using the files that have been released to the public at the National Archives, backed up by personal accounts where they are known to exist, enough has survived to be able to tell the stories of these incredibly brave people. I suspect, however, that some serious questions will always remain. We may never know, for example, whether the SOE's headquarters in London was infiltrated by the Germans, as has been suggested, and we may always wonder just how much those in London knew about the infiltration by German intelligence officers of SOE's radio networks in France. And we can only speculate about whether agents were deliberately dropped into enemy traps to continue playing a game of bluff and double-bluff in order to distract the enemy's resources and attention away from the real issue – the Allied landings in Europe.

Inevitably, there are occasional discrepancies between versions of the same event and where these exist I have ultimately had to go with what has either been historically the most consistent version of an event or to offer a more recent explanation where new and reliable information has come to light. If these have any errors then I can only apologize in advance.

As general guidance to the reader, I have mostly ignored the ranks of the agents as these were often irrelevant in the field and, at times, are known to have changed. Also, I have stuck with the agent's real name rather than the codename or operating name because these also changed from time to time, particularly for those returning to France for further missions. In the case of the female agents, I have used their first names as this was how they were to be later become better known, for example, Odette or Violette rather than Sansom or Szabo. The spelling of names can vary between sources, particularly those either French or German. For example, Joseph Antoine France Antelme is also known to have his surname spelt as Anthelme; in this case, I have gone for the more consistent Antelme. Also, the different spellings of a surname can add to confusion; Raoul Kiffer is also known to have his surname spelt as Kieffer. In the latter spelling he could easily be confused with the German intelligence officer bearing the same surname, Hans Josef Kieffer, and so I have stuck with Kiffer to avoid any confusion. Variations also occur in the spelling of places in France, such as Lyon/Lyons and Marseille/Marseilles, but, again, I have tried to be consistent by using the spelling used in authoritative pieces of work, such as M. R. D. Foot's

SOE in France, and so I have gone with Lyons and Marseilles; I hope the reader will understand should a variation be unfamiliar.

There are times in the book when I have dwelt on certain individuals, such as the Newton brothers, Noor Inayat Khan, Tommy Yeo-Thomas and Violette Szabo. This is not favouritism but it allows individual stories to be told within the overall big story and provides a valuable insight into what life was like in the field at the time and the quite extraordinary courage displayed by so many. But there is not the space to dwell too long on certain, and, at times, debatable, areas such as the demise of Francis Suttill's PROSPER circuit, an event that triggered the deaths of many agents who had become tangled in its web, or the treacherous Henri Déricourt affair, something that is well documented in more authoritative works.

Finally, it is important to understand that this is not a history of the SOE. Nor was it ever intended to be. The story focuses on the SOE operatives and their associates in the field rather than on the organization itself. On the SOE monument in London, situated on the Albert Embankment and overlooking the Houses of Parliament, it states that the SOE sent 470 agents into France. Unfortunately, there is not the space to mention them all but I believe it is important to tell the stories of these remarkably brave men and women whenever the opportunity arises. I am privileged to be able to do just that. Enjoy the book!

Peter Jacobs

Chapter 1

SOE and France – The First Year

In fact, rather than fiction, it is rare for so many remarkable accounts of bravery and personal endurance, coupled with political fascination, double-dealing and betrayal, to be part of the same story. But that is the story of the Special Operations Executive, Britain's most secret service of the Second World War that formed in 1940 after the fall of France. From that moment on its men and women bravely waged war in Nazi-occupied Europe until hostilities came to an end, and by the time the organization was wound up the SOE had enriched the nation's history with heroic legends.

But the SOE was never a popular department in Whitehall. While its origins stem from intelligence departments and a series of papers and discussions during the last days of Neville Chamberlain's term as Britain's prime minister, it had seemingly been thrown together in something of a hurry by his successor, Winston Churchill, after just two months in office.

The SOE was born on 19 July 1940, just a month after France had surrendered, when Churchill drafted a brief memorandum for his War Cabinet tasking the new organization 'to co-ordinate all action by way of subversion and sabotage against the enemy overseas'.[1] Or, as Churchill would later put it to his rather peevish Minister of Economic Warfare, Hugh Dalton, who had been given political responsibility for the new organization, 'to set Europe ablaze'.

Dalton, for one, believed that conducting war from within would be better achieved by civilians rather than professional soldiers, a view shared by many politicians. Churchill never fully disclosed why he did not entrust control over the SOE to the eagerly outstretched arms of the service chiefs, but he must have decided from the outset to keep a close personal eye on

---

1. Cookridge, *Inside SOE*, p.3.

what was his own brainchild, and, as things would turn out, it was perhaps fortunate that the service chiefs did not own the SOE.

Churchill's initial direction had been brief and very simple but in a later and fuller conversation he elaborated his directive. The SOE, he explained, was to be a secret organization to carry out two key tasks: to create and foster the spirit of resistance in Nazi-occupied countries; and, when appropriate, to establish a nucleus of trained men who would be able to assist in the liberation of those countries when the time came.[2] The second task could probably best be achieved by committing, or at least instigating, acts of sabotage in-country. These acts were initially and deliberately intended to be small, risking reprisals by the Nazis if instigated too quickly.

While the direction had been clear, there was no blueprint to follow and there were no rules. The men and women of the SOE would simply have to make things up as they went along, and if the SOE was to be successful then secrecy would be the key.

As an organization, the SOE sat equally alongside Britain's armed forces as a fourth service, although it would never be seen in Whitehall as truly a fourth armed service. The dominant figure in the organization was the executive director, a post briefly held by Sir Edward Spears and then, from the end of August 1940, Sir Frank Nelson. Nelson would later be replaced in 1942 by his deputy, Charles Hambro, who, the following year, would hand over, in turn, to his deputy, Major General Colin Gubbins, and it was Gubbins who would become the power behind the SOE during its key years of the Second World War.

The SOE initially made use of offices at a requisitioned hotel in Caxton Street but when accommodation became too cramped it set up its main headquarters in a greyish five-storey building at 64 Baker Street. For a long time its very existence remained unknown, even to high-ranking service officers. Those attached to the organization from other departments were discouraged from referring to it by its official name in private conversations; they tended to refer to the SOE as simply 'The Org' or 'The Old Firm' or 'The Racket'. If the organization had to be referred to in official

2. Foot, *SOE in France*, p.14.

correspondence then the designation 'Inter-Services Research Bureau' was adopted to allay unwelcome curiosity.[3]

As its numbers grew, SOE spread its operations to other countries but, for a number of reasons, France always offered the best opportunities to foster sabotage and subversion. It was just across the Channel and so could be supplied and re-supplied with relative ease. There was no shortage of places where agents could be dropped or picked up and the terrain in many parts of the country, particularly the rolling hills and dense woodland, proved ideal for conducting guerrilla warfare. Furthermore, French-speaking agents could be found without too much difficulty and, once on the ground, it was hoped they would be able to merge into the local population with credibility and ease.

The main body for organizing French subversion was F Section (F standing for French), initially launched by Leslie Humphreys in the summer of 1940. F Section took up residence in Baker Street but, when the building became full, the various departments spilled out to neighbouring buildings.

The fall of France resulted in the resignation of the French government and it was left to a First World War hero, Marshal Philippe Pétain, to sign a humiliating armistice with Germany. Under its terms, France was essentially left with an unoccupied zone in the south of the country, to the south of the Loire and inland from the Atlantic coast, called the *Zone Libre* (free zone), and administered from the town of Vichy by the French premier, then Pierre Laval, while the Germans occupied and governed the northern zone, the *Zone Occupée* (occupied zone), from Paris.

This arrangement gave those in the south a certain feeling of independence and freedom but many ardent patriots owed their loyalty to Pétain. Consequently, there was initially no organized underground resistance, certainly nothing comparable to what there was in Poland at the time.[4] Furthermore, the fact that the south was unoccupied did not mean the SOE would have freedom to operate in this region; far from it. The Vichy police and security service guarded its integrity but it did mean there were few

---

3. Cookridge, op. cit., p.29.
4. Wilkinson & Astley, *Gubbins & SOE*, p.84.

Germans around, although operating in Vichy France would not be without its difficulties.

The legitimacy of Vichy France and Pétain's leadership was immediately challenged by the exiled, and at that time little known, French officer, Brigadier General Charles de Gaulle. De Gaulle had served under French Prime Minister Paul Reynaud as the Under-Secretary for National Defence and War. He had unsuccessfully opposed surrender, advocating instead that the government should remove itself to North Africa and carry on the war as best it could from there.

From London, de Gaulle claimed to represent the legitimacy and continuity of the French nation. He set about building what became known as the Free French Forces from personnel outside France and used the BBC to broadcast his message to the French people at home to continue to resist Nazi occupation and to work against the Vichy regime.

But de Gaulle's period of exile in Britain would never be without its problems. In his dealings with the British, and later the Americans, he would always insist on retaining full freedom of action on behalf of France and this would constantly put a strain on his dealings with the Allies. Churchill, for one, was often frustrated at de Gaulle's patriotic egocentricity.

De Gaulle tried to insist that no SOE operations should be undertaken, either in Nazi-occupied France or the Vichy-controlled south, without his approval. But this was something the SOE was not prepared to do and so de Gaulle would continue to operate his own secret intelligence service in France and only consult the SOE if it was to his advantage to do so.

And so it was against this background that the SOE prepared to undertake operations in France, but it was still some way off being ready to fight a subversive war. The early weeks of its existence soon turned into months as discussions continued about what the SOE's role should actually be. Even by the early winter of 1940, some four months after it had been set up, the SOE was still puling in its cradle.

This was not because of any lack of enthusiasm amongst those working hard to make sure the new organization would succeed, far from it, but is more a reflection on how that enthusiasm needed to be channelled during its early months. There was a determination to conduct operations as soon as possible but an early attempt to land two agents on French soil by a motor torpedo boat during October had proved unsuccessful, and an attempt to insert an agent near Morhaix during the following month, this time by air, also proved unsuccessful when the agent refused to jump.[5]

In this latter case, the agent was returned to his unit, as would always be the case in such circumstances, but this was the only recorded refusal to jump during the SOE's operations.[6] There was, however, some joy towards the end of the year when five agents were transported by a submarine provided by the Royal Navy to seize a French fishing vessel near the Ile de Groix, just off the Atlantic coast of France near Lorient, to observe procedures being used by enemy U-boats when entering and leaving the harbour.[7]

While the agents had succeeded in gathering intelligence and sailed the fishing boat back to Falmouth, this kind of mission was far from the type of subversive activity that the SOE had been intended to perform.

While F Section had been feeling its way, de Gaulle's organization had been busy building in France and had now established an intelligence circuit under the quite brilliant and resourceful Gilbert Renault, codenamed 'Colonel Rémy'. There were others, too, who responded to de Gaulle's appeal. One was Pierre Brossolette, a gifted academic, who instead of pursuing an academic career had become a journalist in the years building up to the war and had used his newspaper columns to denounce both fascism and communism. He was also a popular voice on radio and his views on the rise to power of Adolf Hitler had led to him being blacklisted by the Nazis. Then, in 1939, he was fired from his radio station after publicly opposing the Munich Agreement while on air. After war broke out he joined the army but after the armistice the Vichy regime forbade him from teaching and so he and his wife ran a bookstore in Paris. It was not long before the bookstore became a hub of intelligence for French acts of resistance where documents such as factory plans, which could be used for bombings, were exchanged unnoticed.

5. NA HS 7/211, SOE War Diary, Oct – Dec 1940.
6. Foot, op. cit., p.138.
7. Richards, *Secret Flotillas*, p.307.

It was not long before Brossolette was approached by his friend, Agnès Humbert, an art historian and ethnographer who had become outraged when the Nazis removed her books from her library and had granted German soldiers free entry into the museums at the Palais de Chaillot in Paris. She and a group of like-minded intellectual and academic colleagues had also heard de Gaulle's broadcast and formed the *Groupe du musée de l'Homme* (translated as the group of the museum of man), which became acknowledged as being the first resistance group in occupied France.

It was early days of Nazi occupation but these pioneers soon built a highly diffuse underground network. Their action spread rapidly with the creation of a clandestine newsletter, *Résistance*, with editorials holding no illusions on Pétain and the Vichy government. With Brossolette producing the newsletter and co-ordinating contacts between more groups, he was taken on by Renault as the press and propaganda manager of what had become the most important information agency in France, the *Confrérie Notre-Dame* (Notre-Dame Brotherhood), amongst the first agencies of de Gaulle's intelligence service, the *Service de Renseignements* (SR) and soon to become the *Bureau Central de Renseignements et d'Action* (BCRA), headed by the former French Army officer Major André Dewavrin ('Colonel Passy').[8]

The Gaullists were impatient for liberation of their country and anxious to commence operations against the Nazis but with few resources they would generally have to rely on the British, and specifically on the SOE, when it came to inserting and recovering their agents to and from France.

The SOE would have to accept the existence of de Gaulle but the fact was that by early 1941 the SOE had not achieved anything when it came to action against the enemy. Indeed, when the Air Ministry asked the SOE to disrupt specialist Luftwaffe bombers performing an early form of target marking for the nightly blitz against London from their airfield at Meucon in Brittany, the SOE had to turn to de Gaulle and Dewavrin to provide French parachutists as F Section had no one ready at the time.

The mission, given the codename SAVANNA, highlights the differences of opinion between the SOE and the RAF during the early months. It should have taken place in February 1941 but senior RAF commanders insisted that

---

8. Rémy, *The Silent Company*, p.62.

the agents be dropped in uniform, believing there to be a vast difference in ethics between the time-honoured operation of the dropping of a spy from the air and this entirely new scheme for dropping men whom the RAF considered assassins.[9]

By the time these differences of opinion had been sorted, the opportunity had passed; the moon period in February had waned and the weather during early March was poor. In the end, the mission commenced on the night of 15 March when five French soldiers parachuted from a converted RAF Whitley bomber into southern Brittany[10]. Rather than attempt to break into the airfield to destroy the bombers on the ground, the plan was to kill the crews instead. It was understood they were accommodated some distance away and travelled to and from the airfield by bus but, as it turned out, the intelligence was poor. The Luftwaffe crews travelled to and from the airfield in cars, with no more than two or three crew members in the same vehicle at the same time, and so the mission was abandoned.

Keen to ensure the trip was not entirely wasted, the leader, Captain Georges Bergé, dispersed the men to carry out various reconnaissance tasks. Bergé went to Paris and then on to Nevers and Bordeaux with another member of his team, a man called Forman, before they made their way in early April to a rendezvous point farther south on the Biscay coast near the town of les Sables d'Olonne where they joined a third member of the team, Joel Letac, to be picked up by a Royal Navy submarine and returned to England.[11]

The submarine tasked with the pick-up, HMS *Tigris*, was commanded by the experienced Lieutenant Commander Howard Bone. Having surfaced a couple of kilometres off the coast in the dark of the night, a young SOE officer, Lieutenant Geoffrey Appleyard, and a Free Frenchman, Maître André Desgranges, landed ashore in separate collapsible canoes, called

---

9. Foot, op. cit., p.140. (Taken from SOE file marked secret & personal and dated 1 February 1941).
10. RAF bombers modified to carry SOE operatives included the Armstrong Whitworth Whitley, Vickers Wellington and Handley Page Halifax. Modifications included the addition of a hole in the fuselage floor for the operatives to jump through rather than having to use the aircraft's normal side entrance/exit doors.
11. Foot, op. cit., p.141.

folbots, to pick up the agents. All went well until one of the canoes, that of Desgranges, was torn by an unseen rock and holed, rendering it useless for the return. The two men then crawled up and down the beach to find the signal lamp of the agents whom they were to pick up but no light was seen, and so they reluctantly gave up the search to return to the *Tigris* before daylight.

In the event the agents could not be picked up on the first attempt, arrangements had been made for a further attempt a few nights later. Once again the *Tigris* surfaced only to find sea conditions were rough. Observing the shore from the submarine, Appleyard was convinced he could see a light flashing out to sea. Bone was not convinced but Appleyard was determined to go ashore to find the agents. Bone reluctantly agreed but warned him the submarine would have to leave no later than 3.00am.

The plan was the same as before but the rough sea soon swept the canoe of Desgranges away before he could even board it, leaving Appleyard to proceed alone. Paddling two kilometres in a rough sea was physically exhausting but he eventually made it to the shore. Working his way quietly along the beach he searched for the agents but he saw no flashlight. As time was getting short he became less quiet and soon he was calling out as much as he dare and flashing his torch in a last attempt to attract their attention. Just at the point he was about to abandon all hope, his signal was answered. He had found the agents.

The folbot was only designed for two and there was only time to carry out one run to the waiting submarine. The best Appleyard could do was to take two of them with him at the same time, and even that was risky because of the weight in the flimsy craft and the rough sea, and so the decision was made to leave Letac behind. It took a monumental effort to paddle the canoe back out to sea and then find the submarine. The heavy swell constantly threatened to capsize the canoe but the combination of hard paddling and continuous bailing out meant they reached the submarine just at the point when it was about to leave. Even the journey back to England was eventful. The skippers of Royal Navy vessels were expected to carry on as normal once agents had been picked up and, in this case, the crew of the submarine had spotted an enemy oil tanker. With the heavy sea continuing to cause problems, the *Tigris* ended up fighting a surface engagement lasting an hour and a half, which only ended after the tanker was sent to the bottom by a torpedo after the gunners had knocked the tanker's defensive armament out of action.[12]

Although SAVANNA had achieved nothing directly, it proved that the concept of subversive operations by inserting agents into France and then being able to extract them, was viable. Furthermore, Bergé had taken back with him much useful information. He found that he had been able to move around France with relative ease, particularly when using the railway network, and the intelligence that he had gathered provided the SOE with useful information about conditions inside France. Things like curfew rules and conditions, information on identity documents required, and how to get around on a bicycle without attracting attention, were all vital to know for the months and years ahead.

SAVANNA had also proved to be important for another key reason. It was clear from Bergé's report that de Gaulle enjoyed immense popularity in France, so much so that the SOE formed RF Section to work specifically with de Gaulle's Free French National Committee and its secret service in London. And so in the spring of 1941 RF Section was established in a small terraced house in Dorset Square, just across the road from Baker Street, under its first head, Eric Piquet-Wicks.

RF had little contact with F Section; it was not supposed to. Only much later, after Piquet-Wicks had left during 1942 to be replaced by James Hutchison as RF's head, did the Free French gain concessions from the British government to independently operate their secret service and networks in France. F Section, therefore, remained separate to RF but not anti-Gaullist; it would simply work independently. In any case, the two sections would pursue different aims. RF agents were to carry out direct forms of operations in France, mainly sabotage, to trigger events that, with Allied help, would ultimately remove the Germans and Vichy French. F Section's objectives were more limited than RF's and laid down by the SOE chain of command to suit outline directives from the British chiefs of staff.[13]

12. Appleyard, *Geoffrey*, pp.59–61.
13. Foot, op. cit., p.41.

Not surprisingly, there would always be friction between F and RF, as there was with the SOE and the other services as a whole, but eventually both sections simply accepted the existence of each other and there were countless examples of good co-operation between the two. There was also DF Section, originally a branch of F Section, tasked with providing clandestine communications links to and from Europe by land and sea, principally by running escape lines across France into the Iberian and Breton peninsulas.

Encouraged by all that had gone on with SAVANNA, the SOE agreed to undertake a second operation, this time against the Pessac power station on the outskirts of Bordeaux. Although F Section was keen to conduct the raid, codenamed JOSEPHINE B, the reality was that it still had no one trained and ready to go at the time. It therefore fell to RF Section.

On the night of 11/12 May 1941, three Free Frenchmen, including Forman who had recently returned from SAVANNA, were dropped near Bordeaux from a Whitley. Having hidden their explosives near the power station, the three reconnoitred their target but for a number of reasons the attack did not take place; mainly because it was considered too difficult to find a way in, the night patrols were believed to be too frequent and they had been unable to obtain any bicycles to make their escape. The three then missed the rendezvous with the submarine due to take them back to England. Dismayed, they set off for Paris where Forman managed to meet up again with Joel Letac who had remained in France having been unable to get off the beach during SAVANNA.

It was Letac's determination not to give up on the raid on Pessac that resulted in him accompanying the JOSEPHINE group back to Bordeaux. A further reconnaissance and a casual conversation with the gate keeper at the power station revealed there were not the night patrols that had initially been feared.[14] Having then obtained a small lorry, the four set out for the power station late on 6 June but the lorry broke down. The following night they tried again, this time using bicycles. After locating the explosives they had hidden nearly a month before, Forman scaled the boundary wall before

14. There appear to be variations in the accounts as to what happened during the raid and so the account is taken from M. R. D. Foot's *SOE in France*, pp.144–5 and taken from the SOE file.

opening a gate to let the others in. It took just thirty minutes for the raiders to place an explosive charge and incendiary device on each of the eight main transformers before making their escape. Just as they reached their bicycles all the charges went off, leaving behind them chaos and confusion. It took several months for repairs to be carried out and damage to the power station had its effect on the local electric railway system, while work carried out at the submarine base in Bordeaux, and at other factories nearby, had been severely disrupted. The saboteurs eventually made their way out through Spain.

But however successful SAVANNA and JOSEPHINE B had seemingly been, they were not contributing to the SOE's overall strategy of organizing sabotage within France or building up clandestine methods of resistance that could one day be used to support an Allied landing. Harsh as it may sound, most of SOE's first year had been wasted in disputes about what it ought to be doing. But F Section had just made its first real move towards doing what it ought to be doing when its first agent parachuted into France on the night of 5 May 1941.

Chapter 2

First Agents

The challenge faced by those charged with recruiting and training SOE agents was almost insuperable. No precedent had been set in any conflict fought before and there was a huge amount to do, not only in the recruitment and training of agents but also in the establishment of research stations for the production of specialized equipment, such as radio sets light enough for one man to carry, and to produce the forged identity papers required by the agents once in the field.

It took a special kind of person to become an SOE agent in France. First and foremost, it would mean a perfect knowledge of the French language. This meant far more than just being able to speak the language as the agent would have to appear native to the operating region to avoid attracting attention. A new identity, with a lifelong story, was required that could be passed off at any time, even if under extreme stress. Strength of character, power of leadership, organizational skills and intelligence were all amongst the more obvious personal attributes needed as the agent would be required to recruit helpers and couriers, and they would have to train patriots in the handling of weapons and explosives, and to carry out sabotage, until they were capable of being formed into more specialized groups.

Volunteers came from all walks of life – city financiers, journalists, university lecturers and from a range of businesses to name just a few. The recruiting officers had no set rules when selecting candidates and had to rely mainly on their personal judgement.

Before anyone could be dropped into France they would have to be trained as best as possible to give every chance of success, and so a tough training programme, both physically and mentally, was put together. Those who came from outside the armed forces, as many did, were given a commissioned rank and number in one of the three regular services, usually the Army.

Preliminary training was carried out at Wanborough Manor near Guildford in Surrey. Built in 1527 and owned by the earls of Onslow since the seventeenth century, the manor had been taken over by the First Aid Nursing Yeomanry, the FANYs, during the war as an ideal location for the training of SOE recruits. Those destined for France were joined by others from different nations recruited by the various sections of the SOE. Although the recruits were subjected to some military drill and had to attend many lectures on a variety of subjects, the atmosphere resembled more of a country house than a military establishment, although their behaviour and reactions were closely monitored. It was not unusual for their behaviour to be assessed when under the influence of alcohol and in their rooms during the night just in case they talked in their sleep, and if they did in what language they spoke.

The training at Wanborough Manor provided an opportunity to weed out any unsuitable candidates. Just because a candidate interviewed well during the selection process it did not mean they would be reliable or careful when out in the field. Having passed preliminary training, all recruits were given a course in physical toughening in Scotland and parachute training at RAF Ringway in Manchester, where they completed a handful of jumps, as well as any other specialist training required.

Eventually the student was sent to SOE's Finishing School at Beaulieu, the ancestral home of the barons Montagu in Hampshire. It was there that agents were given their final grooming to mould themselves into their new identities. They were also taught the elements of clandestine operations and security: how to identify or find a 'safe house'; how to establish contacts; how to use 'letterboxes' at specified addresses; how to communicate with the French Resistance; how to prepare dropping zones (DZs) and the reception of other agents; the use of false documents; and, above all, how to avoid detection and capture. There was also simulated interrogation. Short of being brutally manhandled, agents received treatment that had all the genuine flavour to frighten and bewilder them into telling something that should have been kept secret. Then afterwards, over a drink, the agent was debriefed on any mistakes made and how to behave if ever facing the real thing.[1]

---

1. Cookridge, op. cit., p.78.

There was much to learn and the final part of the course involved a four-day exercise combining all that the agent had been taught, typically by carrying out a reconnaissance of a target and working with other agents to simulate its destruction, having laid dummy explosives. Throughout the four days the agent would be watched and assessed by a number of observers, none of whom would be known to the agent. With all training complete, the agent was finally sent to one of SOE's many holding schools where they would wait until being called to London for their briefing immediately prior to their insertion into France; this could be anything from a few hours after arriving at the holding school to several weeks.

There were several ways of clandestinely inserting agents into France. Much would depend on resources available from the Royal Navy or RAF at the time, and this would clearly affect when and where drops or pick-ups could be made. France's extensive coastline, stretching from the English Channel and round the Atlantic coastline to the Mediterranean, meant there were several options when it came to putting agents ashore but the quickest method was to be dropped from the air to avoid a long and hazardous sea passage. It was all a matter of where the agent needed to be and when, and what resource could be made available.

So, who was the first agent from F Section to be inserted into France? In his book *SOE in France*, the SOE's official historian, M. R. D. Foot, makes reference to the SOE war diary for March 1941 that includes a laconic remark under a 'French Section' heading that states 'After a second failure to land the Brittany Agent, the operation was successfully carried out on the night of the 27th.'[2] But because there is nothing else recorded, it is generally accepted that the first F Section agent inserted into France, and certainly the first to be parachuted into the country, was 29-year-old George Bégué, a radio operator, who was dropped into unoccupied central France on the night of 5/6 May 1941.[3]

Born in Périgueux in the Dordogne, Bégué had mastered the English language, and met his wife, while studying engineering at university in

---

2. NA HS 7/214, SOE War Diary, pp.394 & 440 and Foot, op.cit., p.147.
3. Although George Bégué is considered to be the first F Section agent to be dropped into France, he was preceded by others from the BCRA and RF Section.

England. After war broke out he was assigned to liaison duties with the British forces in France and had then been fortunate to escape back to England during the evacuation at Dunkirk. Bégué then joined the Royal Signals, becoming a sergeant, but soon met Thomas Cadett, a former journalist and Paris-based war correspondent working for the BBC, who, by then, was working with F Section.

Bégué had been recruited into the SOE under the alias 'Georges Noble' and after a short training course at Wanborough Manor he was parachuted into France with a transmitter in a suitcase; his task was to set up a radio communications network and to meet the next agents to be inserted into the country. He had come down some twenty kilometres north of the town of Châteauroux and made his way through the night to the country home of the notable leftist French politician Max Hymans (Frédéric), a friend of Cadett and a member of the French Resistance.

Hymans was initially sceptical of Bégué but soon learned to trust him and gradually introduced the new arrival to others in Châteauroux. Having then found suitable lodgings where he could erect his radio antenna, Bégué made the first transmission to the SOE from France on 9 May.

Although the radio sets used by the SOE in those early days were small enough to be fitted into suitcases, they were very heavy and so it made moving around difficult. It was also risky to transmit for any length of time as the radio transmissions could be detected by listening posts and direction-finding vans. It would not be long before the Germans became more aware of SOE radio operators, also known as pianists, being sent into the field and transmitting information back to London, and so their techniques for the detection of transmissions quickly improved.

Lengthy transmissions would clearly increase the risk of capture for the radio operators and so it was Bégué who was behind the suggestion that the BBC should transmit messages at pre-determined times, although the messages would be coded to indicate when and where agents or supplies would be dropped over the next twenty-four hours. It would take a while to set up such a system and so, for now, Bégué had to continue alone but this idea would eventually reduce the amount of transmissions that a radio operator would need to make from the field. Although some were initially sceptical of the idea, because the Germans would also be able to listen in to the BBC broadcasts, provided that the enemy were not aware of what each message meant then the system worked exceedingly well for the rest of the war.

Over the next few nights three more agents were dropped in, all met on arrival by Bégué. One was Pierre de Vomécourt who arrived on the night of 10/11 May. A French army liaison officer with the British Expeditionary Force, de Vomécourt had escaped to England aboard a British warship during the fall of France. Keen to continue the fight against the Nazi occupiers of his country, he evolved a plan for clandestine resistance and sabotage actions in France and volunteered to return to his country to organize them. He had first put his idea to de Gaulle but was told that his actions would merely provoke German reprisals and thus create hostility against his own freedom movement.[4] De Vomécourt had then turned to the British but the War Office told him there were no plans to send agents and saboteurs into France. He was advised, therefore, to join the British Army as a private and maybe get a commission later but this was not at all what he had in mind. After kicking his heels for a while, he became aware of the SOE and so became one of the first agents to be recruited by F Section.

Under the codename of 'Lucas', Pierre de Vomécourt promptly made his way to his younger brother Philippe's house on an estate at Brignac, near Limoges. He was relieved to learn that his wife and children, whom he had left behind almost a year ago, were well in his Paris apartment. Philippe de Vomécourt also offered his services to the SOE, as did his older brother, Jean.

During the next few days, the three brothers set about dividing France up into sections in which each would operate. Jean lived on an estate at Pontarlier near the Swiss border, in the occupied zone, and so he would set up an escape route into Switzerland for British aircrew, while Philippe (Gauthier) would remain in the unoccupied zone and set up a network from his home. Pierre, meanwhile, would base himself at his house near the Bois de Boulogne in Paris where he and Bégué and a third man, Roger Cottin (Albert), who had been parachuted into France three nights after Pierre de Vomécourt, would operate as a group in the occupied north of the country to create a network of supporters who were hostile to the Nazi occupation.

---

4. Cookridge, op. cit., p.99.

These first two SOE networks, otherwise known as circuits, were set up in the early summer of 1941 by Pierre and Philippe de Vomécourt. Called AUTOGIRO and VENTRILOQUIST respectively, they were F Section's first two major activities in France. Helped by several friends, and often using their own money to fund activities, the brothers set up safe houses and places to store arms and ammunition, as well as finding suitable locations where supplies could be dropped by air.

The first drop of supplies, consisting of just two containers, was arranged by Bégué and was dropped from a Whitley at Château Bas Soleil near Brignac, close to Philippe's house, on the night of 13 June. Drops would not always be straightforward and this was certainly true for this first known drop. For two nights the reception committee had waited for the drop but no aircraft turned up. On the third night an aircraft arrived overhead but did not drop and it was finally on the fourth night that the drop took place. Even then, one of the containers landed outside the prepared zone and more than a kilometre away. On that night there were only two in the reception committee – Philippe and a young man called Gabie – and so the two men were left to drag the heavy containers across a stream and up a steep hill to the house before they could be hidden in the cellar.

The following day there was much speculation as to what the aircraft overhead had been. As gossip and rumours about a possible drop started to spread, de Vomécourt cleverly reported to the local *gendarmerie* (military police) post that he, too, had heard an aircraft overhead and suggested it best if his fields could be searched to make sure there were no signs that paratroopers had come down on his land. The search, of course, revealed nothing and the *gendarmes* went away satisfied that de Vomécourt could not have possibly been involved.

The supplies dropped that first night included tommy guns, revolvers, knives and a small amount of explosives.[5] But Bégué had not found it easy to set up the drop. Although he had received transmissions each night confirming that an aircraft was coming, it had not proved to be the case and had, in the end, meant too many wasteful transmissions and put him at significant risk.

---

5. Ibid, p.123.

The end of the SOE's first year of existence coincided with Hitler's decision to turn on the Soviet Union. It meant that Britain was no longer fighting alone and it was now time for the SOE to revise its strategy for the next period of the war. Dalton envisaged a threefold aim: subversive propaganda using agents; sabotage; and the building of secret armies. For this latter point he proposed to assemble 3,000 Frenchmen in small sabotage groups by the autumn of 1942 and by the same date to have armed 24,000 of the French Resistance. But there remained concerns amongst the service chiefs that arms and supplies dropped from the air would fall into the wrong hands, and so to allocate precious resources to support the SOE could, according to them, prove wasteful.

While the top-level wrangling went on in the corridors of Whitehall, F and RF Sections went about their business but many of the minor operations carried out ended up being dogged by troubles, largely due to the problem with communications. One example was a planned attack against the airfield at Mérignac in September. Two agents were dropped into the south-west of the country to carry out a reconnaissance of the base but were unable to pass back details to an assault party because their radio transmitter had been damaged during the drop. Other problems had occurred due to the limited number of radio channels available, putting the existence of agents at great risk, and because it would take until October for the BBC transmissions of messages to be up and running.[6] There were further problems, too, such as the arrest of an agent dropped into the Vichy south to set up three circuits, and the arrest of an agent dropped into Normandy because he was instantly recognized and arrested for a previous offence.

But not everything was going against plan and one agent, 34-year-old Jacques Vaillant de Guélis, who was dropped into the Vichy south during August, would achieve much during his brief stay in France. He had been an interpreter the previous year with the British Expeditionary Force and although he had been captured, de Guélis had then managed to escape and, after being recommended to the SOE, was taken on by F Section as a briefing officer.

---

6. Cowburn, *No Cloak, No Dagger*, p.52.

De Guélis had agreed to go into the field and was parachuted into France on the night of 6 August with another agent, Georges Turck (Christophe), a French architect, to join the de Vomécourt brothers. During his month in France, de Guélis carried out numerous minor tasks, such as collecting specimen documents and papers, and conducted a reconnaissance of suitable landing sites around the mouth of the River Rhône for future insertions and pick-ups. He also succeeded in recruiting some of the first local agents in the south of France so that they could then be put in touch with London. Most significantly, though, he prepared the way for the first resident woman agent that SOE put into France, an American citizen by the name of Virginia Hall.

Although Virginia would be the first woman to be based in France, she was not, in actual fact, the first woman to have been involved with the SOE in France. That honour goes to a young Chilean actress, Gigliana Gerson, the wife of another agent, Victor Gerson, who had made a three-week visit during May–June 1941 for the purposes of 'sight-seeing', before returning to England via Spain with various pieces of information relating to travel across France, including details about bus and train movements, and how to move between the occupied and unoccupied zones.[7]

Nonetheless, 34-year old Virginia Hall, with her reddish hair, calm personality and strong American accent, became the first female F Section agent sent into France. A talented linguist, particularly in French and German, she was extremely intelligent and had been educated at some of the best schools and colleges in America and Europe. But a shooting accident before the war had resulted in her losing the lower part of her left leg, although she quickly adapted to life with an artificial limb. She had been in France when war broke out and working in the south of the country with the Ambulance Service but, horrified by the signing of the armistice, she had made her way to Britain, via Spain, where she volunteered for service with the SOE. As a citizen of the United States, which, at that stage, was not at war, Virginia knew that her American nationality would allow her relative freedom to move around in France.

---

7. NA HS 7/216, SOE War Diary, May 1941.

Leaving Britain at the end of August under the codename 'Marie', Virginia travelled to France by a commercial route under the identity of Marie Monin, a correspondent for the *New York Post*. She would spend the next fifteen months in Lyons as the organizer and courier of her HECKLER circuit, and would very soon become the focal point for F Section agents operating in the unoccupied zone.

Chapter 3

First Lysander

H aving arranged Virginia Hall's contacts in Lyons, it was time for Jacques de Guélis to leave France. His departure was planned for the night of 4/5 September 1941 and it would be the SOE's first pick-up by a Lysander from the recently-formed Special Duties Flight of 138 Squadron, based at Newmarket racecourse.

The pick-up was organized by George Bégué but, as he and de Guélis were preparing to leave Châteauroux during the early evening, members of the local *gendarmerie* turned up at the hotel for a routine check of identity papers. As the two Frenchmen were being held for checks, the Lysander, flown by Squadron Leader John Nesbitt-Dufort, commander of the flight, was already at Ford airfield in West Sussex where it was being refuelled for the crossing and picking up the agent for the outbound flight.

Nesbitt-Dufort's passenger for this first drop was Gerry Morel who was being sent into the field to make contact with friends and encourage them to form groups that could carry out sabotage raids when suitably armed by the British. An insurance broker by background, and fluent in English and French, Morel had been captured at Dunkirk. He had been too ill to make the last evacuation but had then been released by the Germans who believed he did not have long to live. Morel would never fully regain full health but, having made something of a recovery, he was keen to continue the fight against the Nazis and so made his way to Britain via a lengthy route of Spain, Brazil and Portugal where he finally made himself known to British Intelligence in Lisbon. He was then recruited by the SOE but his health prevented a parachute drop into France and so Gerry Morel was about to become the first agent to be inserted into the field by Lysander.

It made obvious sense to make best use of scarce resources and so the Lysanders would rarely cross the Channel without any passengers. The biggest advantage of delivering agents in this way, rather than by a parachute drop, was that it ensured pinpoint accuracy. The Lysander, with its short take-off and landing capability, and its robust fixed undercarriage, was ideal for such a role as it could operate from unprepared fields. Despite its appearance, the aircraft was aerodynamically advanced. Its cruising speed was only around 200mph, half the speed of marauding night fighters, but its wings were fitted with slotted flaps and automatic slats which reduced the aircraft's stalling speed to around 70mph. The high-wing monoplane gave the pilot an excellent view downwards on both sides, and the Mk III variant used by the special flight had been suitably modified for clandestine operations. The little stub wings, to which bombs could be attached, had been removed, as had the air gunner's gun mounting and other equipment; a fuel tank had been fitted to increase the aircraft's operational range, and a short steel ladder had been fixed to the rear cockpit on the port side for agents to get in and out of the aircraft quickly. The aircraft had also been painted matt black in the misguided hope that it would be impossible to see at night. Transit heights varied according to the weather conditions but were usually at around 3,000 to 7,000 feet, but when approaching the enemy coastline it would be even lower to avoid detection by radar and make the aircraft less visible to any ground defences. Agents were required to sit on a wooden seat facing the tail. It gave them an excellent view and during transit they were to act as rear lookouts in case any enemy night fighters were seen. Although the aircraft had no guns to defend itself, the Lysander would prove extremely manoeuvrable should it be necessary.

With Nesbitt-Dufort on his way, de Guélis and Bégué finally managed to get away from the hotel as soon as the check of identity papers was complete. They then cycled as quickly as they could to the field, nearly twenty kilometres to the north-east of Châteauroux, to get ready for the pick-up. By the time they arrived they could hear the sound of the aircraft approaching as they laid out the lights.

While de Guélis and Bégué were preparing the landing site, Nesbitt-Dufort was approaching the field. Lysander operations were, in the main, governed by the moon period. The pilot needed moonlight to navigate and to find the small fields that served as landing grounds. The field designated as the landing ground needed to be away from roads, railways and inhabited buildings. It also had to provide enough space for the Lysander to be able to land and then take off again, ideally with 600 yards of flat ground offering more than one direction to the pilot so that the aircraft could land whatever the direction of the wind. But finding a field that met these criteria was not always possible and so the Lysander pilots learned to make do with whatever field had been provided.

The normal procedure once they could hear the sound of the aircraft in the distance was for the reception committee to run out into the field to operate the torches they had already set in position and pointing downwind. The torches were tied to stakes in the ground and their position meant that when illuminated they formed the letter 'L'. First of all one member of the reception team flashed the code letter for the landing. Once this was acknowledged by the pilot, others switched on their torches so that all three could be clearly seen by the pilot, with the long arm of the 'L' into wind to give the pilot the direction of approach. The idea was for the pilot to land along the length of the 'L' and then turn off along the short part of the 'L' and stop at the light.

In his haste to get to the field and lay out the lights as quickly as he could, de Guélis had picked the wrong field. Meanwhile, Nesbitt-Dufort had arrived overhead the correct field, which he could identify from the aerial photograph with him, but could see no signal from the ground. Faced with no alternative, he started circling overhead to see if anyone turned up.

For both the pilot and agent, this was not ideal. The aircraft, if seen from the ground, was now vulnerable to attack by small arms fire. Furthermore, the enemy would know that a drop or a landing was imminent, which would put those on the ground at risk as well. But delays were occasionally inevitable, for a number of reasons, and so the Lysander pilots would have to get used to loitering for as long as they dared until the amount of fuel left on board dictated when the pilot would have to abandon the mission and return home.

In this case, Nesbitt-Dufort circled the landing ground for fifteen minutes. He was just at the point of leaving when he saw a flash from the ground to the right and a short distance away. It was signalling the letter 'G', the correct code to indicate the field was in safe hands. As he approached the flashing light he could see a series of lights indicating a flare path but, to the pilot, it looked too small a field in which to land. Nonetheless, Nesbitt-Dufort expertly touched down in the field. It was a bumpy surface and would not usually have been considered suitable but Nesbitt-Dufort brought the aircraft to a halt just before reaching a line of trees.[1]

The patience, observation and flying skill on the part of John Nesbitt-Dufort meant this first Lysander mission was a success; de Guélis was picked up and Morel dropped off. The journey back had its moments too. It started with the take-off as there was barely enough room for the Lysander to get off the ground and the bumpy surface made the whole experience one not to forget. Using every possible inch of space, and again with great flying skill, Nesbitt-Dufort just managed to get the aircraft airborne but not without clipping the trees and collecting telephone wires, as well as causing a blinding flash after hitting high tension cables as the Lysander limped into the air. Then, during the transit home, they had to avoid two patrolling night fighters before they arrived back over the south coast of England to find that fog had formed over much of West Sussex. Furthermore, the impact with the high tension cables on take-off had put his radio out of action. Fortunately, the landing lights could be seen at Tangmere and they were both soon back on the ground.

Meanwhile, back across the Channel in France, Morel had made a hasty getaway into the countryside. A *gendarme* had arrived to see what all the noise was about and so Bégué had left to return to Châteauroux on his own.

As things were to turn out, Morel's mission was less of a success than had been hoped. Although he managed to make a decent start, he was betrayed after just six weeks and arrested by the Vichy French. He was imprisoned at Périgueux before his health deteriorated once again and so he was moved to Limoges prison hospital. He then had a major abdominal operation but, before he had time to recover, he took an opportunity to escape. He was met by a friend of Philippe de Vomécourt and after staggering through a snowstorm during the night, Morel was passed on to Virginia Hall who saw him on to an escape line across the Pyrenees and eventually made it back to England.[2] Morel then became the operations officer for F Section, a post he held until the summer of 1944. Although his health was ruined, he showed great personal courage planning countless operations for agents in the field.

---

1. Verity, *We Landed by Moonlight*, p.40.
2. Foot, op. cit., p.156.

Chapter 4

Worrying Times

Just two nights after Morel's insertion and the departure of Jacques de
Guélis, six more agents were on their way to France. They were to be
dropped from a Whitley of 138 Squadron on the night of 6/7 September
at Argenton-sur-Creuse, to the south of Châteauroux, in the largest single
drop to date.

For agents going into France the build-up was generally much the same.
After being briefed in London they were driven to a large country house
close to the airfield at Tempsford. They were then fitted out with clothing
for the jump and issued with weapons, emergency rations and other items
that might prove useful, such as maps for the appropriate area. They were
also issued money (typically 100,000 francs), worn in a belt against the body,
and offered the 'L' pill ('L' standing for lethal), a glass capsule covered
in rubber and containing cyanide. This could be concealed in the mouth
and would cause death within minutes if it was crushed and the cyanide
swallowed. Whether to take the 'L' pill or not was a matter of personal choice.
Everything was then checked for one final time to ensure the agent was not
carrying anything obviously from Britain. Pockets were searched to look for
any tell-tale signs; cigarettes, photos, letters, bus tickets, cinema stubs and
so on. Identity cards and other forged documents were then checked for one
last time before being taken to the waiting aircraft in a car with blinds drawn.

The six agents, in flying suits, parachute harnesses and packs, struggled
on to the aircraft. They could only take with them what they could fit into
their packs and flying suits. Only the wireless transmitter, which was being
taken into France by the one radio operator amongst the group, André
Bloch (Draftsman), who was heading for the occupied zone to settle in the
suburbs of Paris, had its own special packing. It hung in a bag from the roof
of the fuselage directly above the exit hole in the floor; at the point of drop it

would be attached by strops to Bloch's rigging so that both he and his radio transmitter would drop together under the same parachute.[1]

In addition to Bloch, there was Victor Gerson (Vic), the husband of the Chilean actress Gigliana, the first woman to have gone into France for the SOE, and 37-year-old Ben Cowburn (Benoit), about to undertake the first of his eventual four missions.

Born in Lancashire, Cowburn had gone to Paris with his parents when aged eight. He had then attended a British school in France and later studied electrical engineering before joining an American company building distillation plants for oil refineries all over France. With a great knowledge of the oil industry, and fluent in French, Cowburn was a great addition to the SOE.

Also to be dropped that night were Michael Trotobas (Sylvestre), a British-born officer of the Manchester Regiment who had been raised and educated in England and France, the French Count Jean du Puy (Denis) and George Langelaan (Langdon).

Having boarded the aircraft, the six took their positions and tried to get as comfortable as possible along the floor of the fuselage. The RAF despatchers helped as much as they could and once airborne provided light refreshments for those who could stomach them. During the transit there was little opportunity for the men to move at all and there were no windows to let in any light. The dimness of the fuselage lighting soon became total darkness as all internal lights were switched off to cross the Channel.

With so many inside the fuselage for such a large drop, conditions on board were unpleasantly cramped and quite nauseating for those not familiar with the smell and movement of an aircraft. The constant drone of the engines was difficult to ignore but some did manage to doze off for a few minutes of sleep. As they crossed France into the unoccupied zone, the exit hole in the fuselage was uncovered. The agents were positioned in their nominated order for the jump with the radio operator, Bloch, being the first. He could now see the ground below. There was no blackout and, being a Saturday night, there were signs of normal French activity below. They were now getting close to the drop zone, evident by the increased level of activity inside the aircraft.

1. Cowburn, op. cit., p.9.

To ensure drops were as accurate as possible, they were made from low level and typically only 500 feet above the ground, too low for the agent to have time to open the parachute and so the bag containing the chute was tethered by a static line attached inside the aircraft. As the agent dropped, the static line was pulled taut and the pack containing the parachute was held back so that the canopy deployed just beneath the aircraft.

Bloch sat at the exit hole with his feet dangling through. Cowburn would be the second to jump and so he took his position opposite Bloch. They could now see the ground rushing by below. A red light indicated it was nearly time to jump and then the sound of the engines changing pitch indicated they were levelling out at the required height for the jump. The despatcher raised his hand and the red light turned to green.

The next thing the agents knew was the rush of wind and the sudden jerk as their canopies deployed. Some drops were termed 'blind', meaning agents would not be met on arrival by a reception committee, but on this occasion the agents were met by Bégué, Hymans and the local farmer, Octave Chantraine, where the drop was being made. Because there were six agents to drop, they had to be dropped in two groups, three at a time; otherwise they would have become too spread across the ground.

With the six agents safely on the ground, they were fed and briefed at the farm before going their separate ways. Bloch headed off to Paris as planned. Gerson would become a frequent traveller between England and France and would go on to set up the SOE's biggest and most successful escape line, known as the Vic Line, which ran until the liberation of France. Cowburn was to travel around as much of France as he could to determine which establishments were producing oil for the Nazi war effort so that attacks could be planned in the future. The targets had proved too small for RAF bombers to hit and so the SOE had been asked to take over from where Bomber Command had left off.[2] As things would turn out, SOE's response, though prompt, was equally ineffective. Cowburn would return to Britain six months later, via Spain, with much useful information but the reality was that the oil establishments were too well guarded, and so very few important sites were even damaged. Trotobas was to look at the possibility of later

---

2. Frankland & Webster, *Strategic Air Offensive Against Germany 1939–45* Vol 1, pp.158–69.

setting up a new circuit in Lille. Du Puy would go north to the occupied zone and operate from his home at Courléon, and Langelaan would remain in the local area but would be arrested by French police just a month later while waiting to meet Bégué at a restaurant in Châteauroux.[3]

Eight more agents were inserted during this period, arriving in two separate groups. The first four – Francis Basin (Olive), Robert Leroy, Robert Roche and Emile George Duboudin (Alain) – were dropped on the beach at Barcarès, north-east of Perpignan on the Mediterranean coastline of France, on 19 September. They were dropped by HMS *Fidelity*, a clandestine vessel posing as a Spanish and Portuguese freighter, which was equipped with small landing craft for dropping off and picking up agents and escaped prisoners from the Mediterranean coastline. It marked the end of a lengthy voyage for the four agents, a journey that had lasted seventeen days of riding heavy waves of a fierce storm and dodging U-boats, and once ashore the four headed off on their separate missions in Bordeaux (Leroy), Marseilles (Roche), Lyons (Duboudin) and the Riviera (Basin).

Francis Basin, in particular, would enjoy much early success. He was travelling under his own name and used the cover story of being a former French soldier with no intent of joining the Free French. Having been born and raised in Provence, he was back in a part of France that he knew well. His task now was to go to Cannes to liaise with a man known as Carte, whose real name was André Girard, a well-known painter by profession, who had set up his own CARTE network of resistance groups at Aix, Cannes and Nice. Girard also ran an effective intelligence circuit, capable of transmitting far across Europe, with his contacts spreading far and wide across the Vichy south as well as deep into the occupied zone. Within the next few months Basin would recruit a number of remarkable men and women, enough to set up thirty SOE *réseaux* stretching from Cannes along the Mediterranean coast to Marseilles and as far north as Grenoble. Setting up his headquarters in Cannes, and using the villa of a colleague, Basin formed a group known as 'Network Olive'.[4]

---

3. Foot, op. cit., p.157.
4. Cookridge, op. cit., p.151.

The second group of four inserted around this time – Jack Hayes, Clément Jumeau, Jean Le Hamzat and Daniel Turberville – were less fortunate. They were dropped near Bergerac in the Dordogne on the night of 10/11 October and received by Jean-Pierre Bloch but one, Turberville, was arrested the following day. The Vichy police then set a trap and caught the other three while trying to make contact with Turck at his supposed safe house at the Villa des Bois near Marseilles. Within ten days of being dropped, all four had been captured and put in the Béleyme prison at Périgueux where conditions were degrading and humiliating, where hygiene and sanitation were non-existent, where food was unspeakably bad, and all this combined with vermin and disease. Jack Hayes and Clément Jumeau would later escape and be given further missions with the SOE, although Jumeau would be captured again during 1943 and after a torrid time in squalid conditions and solitary confinement, died of pulmonary tuberculosis.[5]

The same trap that had caught Jumeau and his three colleagues during October 1941 then caught others around Marseilles, including Robert Roche. On one of the agents was found the name of a local garage owner in Châteauroux called Fleuret, whose premises had become a general rendezvous point for agents as well as being a place to collect and drop off bicycles. Fleuret was immediately arrested with another agent, Jean Bouguennec, who happened to be visiting the garage at the time. Next to be pulled in was Michael Trotobas and so it went on. These arrests then led the Vichy police to a number of French associates of the SOE and then finally, on 24 October, to the seemingly indispensable George Bégué.

It was a classic case of too many agents being given the same safe house and the only agent to escape the Villa des Bois debacle was Victor Gerson. Although an attempt was clearly made to snare him too, Gerson did not like the look of the villa. His sixth sense kicked in and he headed off to Spain.

Of a total of about twenty agents who had been inserted into France, most were now in various prisons and would end up at Mauzac, the Vichy concentration camp in the Dordogne, although some would escape the following year through the assistance of Virginia Hall.

---

5. Grehan & Mace, *Unearthing Churchill's Secret Army*, pp.90–1.

Some of these arrests might have been avoided but the fact was that many agents arriving in France during these early insertions did not know fully what to expect when it came to living in the country. Even those who had left France just over a year ago, before the occupation had set in, found the France they had returned to was very different to the one they had left; even in the south. At that early stage, little was known about how best to get about to avoid arousing suspicion. There were few motor vehicles on the road and so the best form of transport was the bicycle. It was also important to quickly become familiar with the use of food ration cards and the black market in order to avoid drawing attention to themselves. They had to make sure the faked ration cards produced in London would actually work in France and they soon learned that items such as cigarettes could not be obtained without a tobacco card. When travelling by train between towns and cities, they found there to be fewer services running and there were numerous plain-clothed observers seemingly watching every move.

To cross the demarcation line required a pass but these could not easily be obtained. The border between the two zones was guarded heavily by the Germans and so it was important to learn how to cross in other ways. There was already an established smuggling trade from one side to the other to which the French authorities were known to turn a blind eye, and other unofficial methods included travelling hidden inside a vehicle or train, or crossing the border on foot with a guide; this option, of course, cost money. The penalty for an illegal crossing was imprisonment and there was always the possibility of being shot by the German guards.[6]

In the occupied zone, the Gestapo (an abbreviation of *Geheime Staatspolizei*, the German Secret State Police) already had a reputation for inflicting various tortures on captives to force information out of them. They were in a different league to the Vichy police in the south and were difficult to spot. They did not wear uniforms and were known to be mingling amongst the crowds – at railway stations, bars and restaurants – and so could be anywhere at any time. It was a risky business.

While this early run of arrests might be considered unfortunate, it was a serious blow to the SOE in France, a defeat even. Back in London it was

---

6. Cowburn, op. cit., p.29.

understandable that questions were being asked by the new head of F Section, Maurice Buckmaster, a former reporter with a French newspaper and a senior manager with the French branch of the Ford Motor Company, who would now lead F until its end, ably supported by his assistant, Vera Atkins.

Buckmaster had useful and extensive contacts in France, and knew the country well. He was keen to communicate better with his agents in the field but the number of F agents now left operating in Vichy France was down to single figures: Virginia Hall, known as 'Marie of Lyons'; Francis Basin and Dr Levy (a Jewish physician known as 'Louis of Antibes' who had been recruited by Jacques de Guélis during his time in France) were operating an embryonic circuit in Antibes on the Mediterranean coast, called URCHIN; an agent called Jean Bardanne (a well-known Marseilles journalist with the codename 'Hubert'); George Duboudin, who was struggling to form sabotage teams around Lyons, and the de Vomécourt brothers.[7] Elsewhere, Robert Leroy was still operating in Bordeaux, but alone, while Ben Cowburn continued to operate independently backwards and forwards across the demarcation line.

Cowburn was spending an increasing amount of time in Paris and was gradually being drawn into what was fast becoming the whirling vortex of AUTOGIRO. He had helped André Bloch arrange a supply drop for Pierre de Vomécourt in the Sarthe but the radio operator's days were numbered. On 12 November a transmission made by Bloch at le Mans was intercepted and tracked by a German direction finder. It is believed he was arrested the following day and, three months later, André Bloch was executed, having kept silent throughout his captivity.

The noose was now tightening for those operating in France. While 1941 had seen its first agents inserted, there remained the fact that, so far, little sabotage had actually taken place, apart from some damage caused to the railway network and the odd train wrecked here and there. As the year drew towards a close, F Section was still very much in its 'heroic stage' with only a handful of agents in the field and battling against an enemy who now seemed to hold all the trump cards.

---

7. Foot, op. cit., p.158.

Chapter 5

A French Agent, an English Agent and a German Agent 'La Chatte'

A ndré Bloch had been the only radio operator in the occupied zone at the time of his arrest and so it now left AUTOGIRO, and everyone else in the zone for that matter, without a quick means of making contact with London; the only way now was through the Vichy south, which could take several days.

The counter-espionage war was now moving to another level as the Germans had used reprisals for the first time towards the end of 1941 when forty-eight citizens of Nantes were shot in revenge for one assassinated German colonel. Sadly, reprisals such as these would be unavoidable during the hard years ahead but they often helped recruiting for the French Resistance rather than hinder it. In his book *SOE in France*, M. R. D. Foot states that for every Frenchman or Frenchwoman whom reprisal executions frightened into acquiescence, a score were shocked into opposition – in their hearts at least – and so became ripe for recruiting.[1]

With Bloch out of the frame, and with F Section having no further drops planned for the rest of the year, Pierre de Vomécourt decided he could wait no longer for a new radio operator. He and Roger Cottin had both tried desperately to convey a message to London, urging the despatch of another pianist, but their efforts had proved fruitless. He had thousands of potential resisters waiting to be armed, if only the SOE could provide them with the arms and ammunition, and so he decided to find a radio operator for himself.

Through a trusted contact, de Vomécourt had heard of the existence of a group of former Polish intelligence officers who had missed the evacuation of Polish army units when France had fallen and had set up a number of radio posts, and were now in regular contact with London.

---

1. Foot, op. cit., p.160.

The group he had been put in touch with was the Franco-Polish *Interallié* espionage network based in Paris, which had been created by Captain Roman Czerniawski after the fall of France. He had been sheltered by a French widow and, with her late husband's clothes and, most importantly, his identity papers, Czerniawski became Armand Borni overnight. Having initially been set up in Paris, *Interallié* had soon grown into a large network of over a hundred people across fourteen locations in the occupied zone.

Eagerly but cautiously, and posing as a 'Monsieur Lucas', de Vomécourt approached the group and recruited one of its leaders, a 33-year-old Frenchwoman called Mathilde Carré, to become his pianist. On the face of it, there was no obvious reason for de Vomécourt to worry. The *Interallié* network was well known to London and Mathilde Carré was one of its most trusted members.

Operating under the cryptonym 'Victoire', but also known as 'Lily' and often referred to as '*La Petite Chatte*' (the small cat) for her feline predatory and stealthy propensities, Mathilde quickly demonstrated her ability to transmit and receive messages from London. An early transmission to test her reliability and trustworthiness, asking for more money to be sent to France, had been welcomed in London as proof that there were still agents operating in France, and when the money later arrived, de Vomécourt was satisfied she was capable of performing her duties and could be trusted.

However, the signals had arrived at F Section in London via British Military Intelligence and what those in Baker Street could not possibly have known at the time was they had been cunningly crafted and transmitted by a German radio operator of the *Abwehr* (German military intelligence). In Paris, de Vomécourt had no idea either, nor was there any reason why he should have done, but the fact was that Mathilde Carré, along with Roman Czerniawski, had both earlier been arrested.

The man behind the arrests was Hugo Bleicher, a *Feldwebel* (equivalent rank to sergeant) in the *Abwehr*, who would go on to become the Nazi's notorious spy-catcher in France. He was forty-two years old and had been recruited into the *Abwehr* because of his knowledge of French and Spanish, and because he had impressed during the early phase of identifying members of the *Interallié* network; it was Bleicher, then serving at a field police station in Cherbourg, who had sent the initial report suggesting that a local woman was possibly working for a British spy, which had then triggered an investigation that eventually led to the break-up of the network.

Bleicher was ruthless in his pursuit of anyone in France who opposed the German occupation. Having arrested the key members of *Interallié*, he decided to work on the two women, Mathilde Carré and Renée Borni, the young widow who had given Czerniawski his new identity. It soon became clear that Renée Borni knew very little – she had been kept distant from the true identity of key individuals – and so Bleicher decided to concentrate on Mathilde Carré instead.

After interrogation and the threat of death, she agreed to turn double-agent and reveal names of agents operating in France that were known to her and, one by one, members of *Interallié* were rounded up. Within three days, the network that had given such good service to the British for more than a year was disabled. Then, with the co-operation of some of its former members, the *Abwehr* decided to pose as *Interallié* and continue transmissions with London as if nothing had happened.

It was not just *Interallié* that the *Abwehr* wanted. They saw the network as a way of getting into the heart of the SOE. And so a fake *Interallié* cell was set up at the home of a wealthy businessman under an *Abwehr* officer supported by a small staff. Mathilde Carré had then moved in with Bleicher but continued to act normally as Victoire and so all messages between de Vomécourt and the SOE were now passing through Mathilde and were, therefore, known to Bleicher.

Mathilde Carré was not the only one to be turned; others had been turned too. Bleicher's usual ultimatum to those under arrest was either to work for him or be turned over to the Gestapo. One of these was Raoul Kiffer, previously the trusted chief of *Interallié*'s D Sector. It was Kiffer's arrest in Cherbourg on 3 November that had triggered the events leading to so many arrests and from then on, under the name of 'Kiki', Kiffer would become one of the Germans' most useful informers.[2]

And so it was against this background, and completely unknown to him, that de Vomécourt met several times with Mathilde. During one meeting, he and Cottin were even introduced to Hugo Bleicher, who was posing as Jean

---

2. Cookridge, op. cit., p.132.

Castell, a supposed member of the Belgian Resistance. After one exchange of messages, de Vomécourt found out that he was ordered to go to London. The *Abwehr* hoped that by doing so he would report favourably on the service he was getting from *Interallié*.

De Vomécourt was to be picked up by Lysander on 16 January 1942 from a field just outside the village of Laas near le Mans. On the day of the pick up, he travelled with Cottin, Mathilde and Castell (Bleicher) through heavy snow showers in a car driven by another supposed member of the Belgian Resistance but was really another feldwebel in the *Abwehr*. They all spent the night huddled together in the car, half-frozen, waiting for the Lysander to arrive. But it never came. The bad weather had made it impossible to pick him up and so he would now have to wait for two weeks until the night of 30 January.

On the night of the re-scheduled pick up, de Vomécourt and the others made the journey for the second time, this time to a field near Estrées-Saint Denis. But, once again, the aircraft failed to show up. There was now suspicion on both sides. Bleicher was not convinced that it had been the weather that had caused the two abortive attempts but felt that London had become suspicious. He also suspected Mathilde Carré of playing a double game.

De Vomécourt, meanwhile, had already become suspicious of her and so decided to provide a test of his own. He asked Mathilde if she could provide him with some forged documents and when she arrived the following day with a near-perfect collection of identity passes and papers, all supplied through Bleicher, his suspicion turned to a feeling of certainty, particularly when she also gave him a photograph of a man and asked him if he knew who it was. The photograph was of Michael Trotobas, who had dropped into France back in September and who the *Abwehr* was now anxiously trying to identify; thus it had become clear that Mathilde Carré could not be trusted. But, for now, de Vomécourt decided to keep playing the game, albeit very carefully.

The Germans also hatched a plot to determine exactly who Mathilde Carré was working for. They felt that if she could go to London with the man they knew as 'Monsieur Lucas' (de Vomécourt) she could find out more about F Section. If she was genuinely working for the Germans she would return to Paris with important information about its organization under the cover that she was to continue her work for the SOE once back in the field. Furthermore, arranging a pick-up with London would also give the Germans a chance to observe the processes and procedures for how SOE pick-ups were conducted. All Bleicher needed to do now was to persuade Mathilde to go.

Mathilde was now meeting with de Vomécourt and Cottin on a regular basis but she was already worried that they were suspicious of her. It was now that de Vomécourt decided to question Mathilde outright as to how she got the genuine passes and identity cards, and to determine once and for all whether she was, as he suspected, working for the Germans.[3] It was at that point that Mathilde Carré tearfully confessed all.

Once he knew, de Vomécourt could have got out. He could even have planned to kill Mathilde but instead he decided to use her. She had been an Allied agent, had then become a double-agent, and his plan now was to turn her back again. While maintaining her contact with the Germans, his plan was for her to transfer loyalty back to the Allies and enable him to outwit the *Abwehr*. It was an extremely risky option but such was his hold over her, albeit temporary, he was confident he could pull it off. He then briefed Cottin and Cowburn, after which de Vomécourt and Mathilde started to put together a plan.

As the Germans were working on the idea of sending Mathilde and Monsieur Lucas to London together, the two built on the idea. At the beginning of February messages were sent to London demanding the two be picked up, stating that the Gestapo were now hot on their tail and their lives were in danger. London replied, stating that a pick-up by air was not possible but that a naval motor torpedo boat would be sent instead. The pick-up was eventually arranged for the night of 12 February and would take place at a remote cove near Locquirec on the northern coast of Brittany.

The evening before the pick-up was due to take place, de Vomécourt, Mathilde and Cowburn made their way to the Gare Montparnasse and left Paris on the night train for Brest. They knew that travelling in an adjacent carriage were two members of the *Abwehr* who were to shadow them; Bleicher had briefed Mathilde before they had left Paris and she had now told the others.

---

3. Ibid., p.138.

The plan, as far as the Germans knew, was that de Vomécourt and Mathilde would board the MTB for England while Cowburn was to meet two new agents coming ashore; they were being sent by the SOE to probe and report on the reliability of the AUTOGIRO circuit. However, the real plan was that all three agents were to board the MTB and, keeping the two new agents on board, would all return to England. Once in London, the story would be told in full and the British would then send false information to Bleicher via the radio network. Cottin, meanwhile, would remain in Paris. This was the most risky part of the plan because of the danger Cottin could suddenly find himself in. But keeping him in France, and carrying on as usual, would dispel any suspicions within the *Abwehr* that Mathilde had been found out and had changed sides. If all went according to plan then the tables would have well and truly turned on the Germans.

The Germans had arranged for all coastal patrols to be kept clear so that the MTB could safely make the rendezvous with the agents. It had been a long but trouble-free journey from Paris but, at midnight, de Vomécourt, Mathilde and Cowburn arrived at the beach where the pick-up was due to take place. In Benjamin Cowburn's book *No Cloak, No Dagger,*[4] he describes his recollection of the events on the beach that night in full, but to anyone observing what happened it would have looked, at times, more like a pantomime act than a serious attempt to recover agents off a beach.

The first part of the attempted recovery seemed to go much as planned. The agents could hear the muffled sound of the MTB as it approached in the distance. Although they could not see it, the MTB came to rest just off the shore. Cowburn had been instructed to start signalling out to sea from the beach at midnight and to continue flashing his lamp at regular intervals, which he did. Nothing happened and so Cowburn continued the routine for about half an hour. He could then make out a dark shape on the water's edge. He went forward and could soon make out the unmistakeable shape of someone approaching. Passwords were successfully exchanged and the two men introduced themselves.

The newcomer was one of the two new agents expected. He explained that the MTB was anchored out in the bay and that he had been dropped

---

4. Cowburn, op. cit., pp.83–6.

off by dinghy farther along the beach. The dinghy had now returned to the MTB to pick up the second agent and their equipment.

Cowburn and the agent were then joined by de Vomécourt and Mathilde. As they stood at the water's edge looking out into the darkness at sea, the water was lapping at their feet. The tide was on its way in and the sea was progressively becoming rougher as a storm was starting to brew. After a while they could make out the shape of a dinghy coming ashore, bobbing up and down as it approached the beach. They could then see a second but the waves were making it difficult for both dinghies to land, and so the four agents waded into the surf to help.

Two men climbed out of the dinghies, the second agent and a naval officer, Lieutenant Commander Ivan Black. De Vomécourt informed the navy officer that there needed to be a change in the plan and that they all needed to go immediately to the MTB. But as they all tried to clamber into the two dinghies, they felt the full force of the breaking waves. In an instant both dinghies were turned upside down. Everyone was now in the water, and so too was the luggage containing the equipment meant for the two new agents. In what was now a quite bizarre scene, Mathilde Carré, still in her fur coat, had taken the appearance of a rather sodden and bedraggled cat.

The struggle against the force of nature lasted for nearly an hour. Two naval seamen had managed to get one of the dinghies righted but could not get close enough to the beach to land, and soon disappeared into the darkness. Cowburn would later describe the dinghies as 'absurd little things that were about as seaworthy as an inverted umbrella'.[5]

The naval officer, Black, had managed to signal the MTB and a larger rowing boat was sent towards the beach but by now the sea had become rougher still. There was no chance of those left ashore swimming out to the boat that was tossing to and fro violently in the rough sea without a hope of making it ashore. It then also disappeared back into the darkness.

The six left on the beach were now left wondering what they should do. All attempts to get off the beach that night had failed. De Vomécourt decided that he, Mathilde and Cowburn should remain in the vicinity together, so that Mathilde could discreetly contact the Germans, while the others hid

5. Ibid., p.85.

in the woods. They could all then meet up again the following night and hope the MTB would return. Any Germans observing the events would have witnessed the storm and so it would not be difficult for Mathilde to explain why they had been unable to get away.

The two groups parted as planned. By the following morning the storm had died down. While de Vomécourt and Cowburn waited in a café, Mathilde went to the local barracks to make contact with the Germans. When she returned, she informed the others that the naval officer, Ivan Black, had been captured but, as yet, the two others ashore had not been found.

The two agents – a 45-year-old former English teacher in Paris called Claude Redding and his 28-year-old radio operator, G. W. Abbott, a former travel agent – had, in fact, both stumbled across an isolated farm during the night and decided to hide in the barn. In the morning they made themselves known to the farmer, who then promptly notified the Germans. The Germans also recovered their suitcases that had gone overboard when the dinghies had capsized and had washed up on the beach. When opened they revealed a mix of radio equipment, weapons, ammunition and money.[6]

The Germans were keen to try the whole pick-up idea again that night but, despite a long night of waiting, the MTB did not return. The three agents decided to give up and return to Paris but returning to the city would further delay their escape from France, and the more time spent in Paris would only increase the likelihood of their own plan to dupe the Germans coming unstuck. It was an extremely high-risk game they were playing and they could all be arrested at any time. And so de Vomécourt decided it was time for them to split, to give them more chance of informing London what was going on; he and Mathilde would return to Paris while Cowburn was to make his way to the unoccupied zone to contact de Vomécourt's brother and then make his way back to England from there.

The three caught the Paris express together but instead of going all the way to the capital they got off at le Mans, the cover story being that de Vomécourt wished to speak to some of his contacts there, which would be entirely believable given his circuit had connections in the Sarthe region, before returning to Paris.

---

6. Cookridge, op. cit., p.141.

The following morning Cowburn took a train for Tours and then another for Bordeaux. He was followed initially but it appears he managed to give his shadow the slip while changing trains. Besides, he had no intention of going all the way to Bordeaux. He got off during the dead of the night at Angoulême, caught a slow train later and then got off at Montmoreau before finally crossing the demarcation line on foot using a pathway at Ribérac in the Dordogne that he had used once before.[7] He made his way to Philippe de Vomécourt and from there to Lyons where he met up with the trusted Virginia Hall. With her help, Cowburn crossed the Pyrenees during the harsh winter weather and finally reached Spain. Having reported to British officials in Madrid, he was taken to Lisbon and flown to England.

By the time Cowburn reported back to Baker Street, Pierre de Vomécourt and Mathilde Carré had already arrived in London. They had continued their journey to Paris as planned and she had reported back to Bleicher. Through instructions given to her by de Vomécourt, Mathilde told Bleicher that she and Monsieur Lucas should still be allowed to go to London together as planned but this time they intended to return to France with a senior officer in the British Intelligence.

The Germans took the bait and other than showing concern for the well-being of the two agents dropped off in France, the British had no reason to suspect that the Victoire line of communication was anything other than genuine. The Germans had retained the upper hand and after a series of messages between the fake *Interallié* cell and London, during which the SOE was given assurance that the two new agents were safe and well, a further attempt to pick up de Vomécourt and Mathilde was planned for the night of 19/20 February, only this time it was to take place at Point de Bihit. Once again the MTB arrived but de Vomécourt and Mathilde had not been able to make it to the rendezvous point in time. They had taken a wrong turning and had been signalling out to sea from the wrong beach. Then, finally, on the night of 26/27 February, the pick-up took place, again using the Point de Bihit for the rendezvous. This time, de Vomécourt and Mathilde were accompanied by Bleicher to make sure they were in the right place at the right time. At last,

---

7. Cowburn, op. cit., p.89.

the combination of a near-full moon, a calm sea and everyone being on the right beach meant the pick-up went according to plan.

Back across the Channel and waiting on the jetty at Dartmouth was Buckmaster. They all travelled to London together and during the long train journey de Vomécourt briefed Buckmaster on the truth behind the Cat. The British now knew the *Interallié* cell was controlled by the *Abwehr* and transmitted that de Vomécourt and Mathilde had arrived safely in London as they had been expected to do. Unknown to the Germans, the British would continue to play the game for several weeks.

Just a month after he arrived in London, de Vomécourt was on his way back to France to pick up the threads of AUTOGIRO. There was no radio operator ready to accompany him and so, on the night of 1 April 1942, and with the new codename of Sylvain, he dropped blind and alone next to his brother Philippe's estate near Limoges. He then made his way to Paris to meet up again with Roger Cottin. His return had been kept quiet. As far as Bleicher was concerned, he and the *Abwehr* were still waiting patiently in Paris for his return, although they had apparently written Mathilde Carré off as a bad risk.

Since de Vomécourt had left France, Cottin had seemingly been left alone but this did not turn out to be the case. Although Cottin had always been careful to try to avoid being picked up, by using various aliases and different addresses, one of the Gestapo's many French informers had been shadowing him. Just three weeks after de Vomécourt had returned to France, he was spotted visiting Cottin. First the Germans arrested Roger Cottin and then, on 25 April, Pierre de Vomécourt, after the Frenchman had been lured to a café.

De Vomécourt's arrest soon led to others, including Noël Burdeyron (Gaston) who had arrived in France the previous July with his radio operator. The pianist, however, was arrested soon after his arrival back in France when he was recognized by a local policeman. Burdeyron had then decided to lie low at his home in Normandy, after which he had carried out some useful sabotage missions, including singlehandedly derailing a German supply train, but his luck had now run out. Also arrested during this latest round-up was Jack Fincken, who had been dropped during

January to help de Vomécourt, and Jean du Puy, who had been in France since early September.[8]

And so the AUTOGIRO circuit was snuffed out before it had ever really got properly alight. The arrests of de Vomécourt and Cottin were kept quiet from the British, although word did eventually filter through to Baker Street some weeks later.

De Vomécourt was beaten mercilessly but the Germans were unable to extract any new information from him. In some ways, the timing of his arrest was fortunate for Pierre de Vomécourt as it meant he would survive his captivity. At that stage of the war, agents such as he, Cottin and the two agents captured on the night of de Vomécourt's first attempted pick-up, Redding and Abbott, were treated relatively humanely as prisoners of war. De Vomécourt would eventually end up in Colditz Castle and be released at the end of the war.

Back in London, Mathilde Carré had not been informed about de Vomécourt's return to France. She was questioned at length by the British, during which she told all that she knew about the *Abwehr* in Paris, naming all those she had come into contact with and providing a list of codes given to her by Bleicher. The arrests of de Vomécourt and Cottin meant that her usefulness had come to an end. She ended up in Holloway Prison and at the end of the war was handed over to the French authorities. It took more than three years for her to be put on trial but eventually, in January 1949, she was sentenced to death, although this was later commuted to a prison sentence of twenty years. She was released in 1954, having served twelve years in captivity since her arrest in London, after which she lived in France under an assumed name. She later published her memoirs in which she denied many claims that had been made against her and her activities during the war, after which she disappeared from public life. Mathilde Carré died in 1970.

In his book *No Cloak, No Dagger*, Ben Cowburn describes Mathilde Carré as a 'strange, unbalanced woman', and suggests she, on her own admission, was responsible for the betrayal of about sixty or seventy men, of whom about fifty were known to have been executed. However, when she did decide to

---

8. Foot, op. cit., p.174.

turn against the Germans, she seems to have done so wholeheartedly in spite of the enormous risk involved. Cowburn then goes on to describe how he met Hugo Bleicher, by chance, in Paris after the war. They had both been called as witnesses during a trial involving a case of treason, with which, at that time, Bleicher was assisting the French authorities. Cowburn approached Bleicher, telling him that he was the agent known to the *Abwehr* as Benoit. The German replied 'Ah! You escaped.' He then looked at Cowburn almost pleadingly and asked, 'Tell me, I beg of you, La Chatte, is it true she was double-crossing me?'[9]

It proved beyond doubt that the British bluff had succeeded but the final collapse of AUTOGIRO during April 1942 had left F Section without any organized circuits in France at all.

9. Cowburn, op. cit., pp.101–2.

Chapter 6

Establishing Circuits

The disabling of AUTOGIRO had been a massive blow for the SOE. It had left F Section on the defensive and with hardly a useful agent in France. Jean Bardanne had been arrested and Robert Leroy, who had been operating alone in Bordeaux, had now left France and had returned to England via Spain, while Francis Basin and George Duboudin, both still in France, were unable to conduct active operations against the enemy.

Virginia Hall, meanwhile, was still in Lyons but she had been forced to keep a lower profile for the time being at least. The United States had now entered the war and so she had to be more careful when moving around. Although she had remained untouched so far by the Germans, she could sense danger and now was not the time to raise her head above the parapet; she had, however, managed to get word to London about the arrests and probable demise of AUTOGIRO. The only agent causing the enemy any problems at all was Philippe de Vomécourt, who persisted in disrupting the rail network whenever he could.

While its few agents were struggling for survival in France, it was decided back in London to formulate a better plan for the construction of circuits in France. Agents were to be inserted to form a group of three; an organizer to lead the circuit, a radio operator to provide the link between the circuit and others, including London, and a courier to make sure everything arrived in the right place at the right time. Circuits would have to be kept small if they were to survive for any length of time. And so it was for the organizer to decide its membership to prevent the circuit from being infiltrated or blown.

It was also time to introduce a man into France who is still remembered today as an emblem of the French Resistance – Jean Moulin, codenamed 'Max' but also known as 'Rex'. Acting on the authority of de Gaulle, Moulin was parachuted into the Alpilles with two colleagues in early January 1942 to unify the various resistance groups in France. It was the first time RF

Section had dropped agents into the unoccupied zone and it was a mission that, for Moulin, would last more than a year. It was he, more than any other man, de Gaulle included, who succeeded in welding the rival fragments of the French Resistance into, more or less, a coherent and disciplined body.

The harsh winter conditions meant there were few insertions during the early weeks of 1942 but the first Lysander drop of the year highlights the extreme hazards faced by the pilots, not just from the enemy but also from the weather. John Nesbitt-Dufort, who had successfully carried out the first Lysander pick up of the war, had dropped off his passenger, an agent called Simon, late in the evening of 28 January near Issoudun to the north-east of Châteauroux. His two passengers for the return journey, Maurice Duclos and Roger Mitchell, quickly boarded the aircraft and the take-off went without incident. But the weather encountered during the flight back to England was so bad, with severe icing, that Nesbitt-Dufort was forced to turn back. He eventually made a forced landing in a field south of the demarcation line but a ditch running across the field caused the undercarriage to break off, tipping the Lysander up on its nose. All three managed to vacate the aircraft, after which the pilot set it alight. Nesbitt-Dufort had found himself in the unenviable position of being on the ground in France. He was taken to a safe house but, with no identity papers, he could not risk moving around and so spent the next thirty days waiting to get back to England. He was eventually picked up by one of the squadron's Avro Ansons on the night of 1/2 March, more than a month after he had first taken off for France.

One agent who had been on his way to join AUTOGIRO before it collapsed was Marcel Clech (Bastien), a radio operator and former Breton taxi driver. He should have been inserted in Brittany during February while Pierre de Vomécourt was still active but many things had gone awry that month and so he was eventually dropped off by submarine along the Riviera coast in April. Having made his way to Lyons to meet up with Virginia Hall, Clech found out that AUTOGIRO had collapsed and so he made his way to Tours instead.

Clech's submarine drop from Gibraltar had been arranged by Peter Churchill (Raoul), a pioneer of inserting agents into France. Aged thirty-three, Churchill had been born in Amsterdam and educated at Malvern and Caius College, Cambridge, where he read modern languages. Bilingual in

French and fluent in Spanish, Italian and German, he had initially been commissioned into the Intelligence Corps but with France being a second country to him, he was just the type of man the SOE was looking for and so Churchill had joined F Section in April 1941.

For his first mission in early 1942, Churchill had landed by submarine near Antibes, a part of the coastline he knew well from his holidays before the war. He had been put into France to provide guidance for all circuit organizers in the south-east of France and was also there to ensure the equitable distribution of funds and to organize an inter-circuit courier service, as well as to supervise the provision of dropping grounds and safe houses for each zone.[1]

Much of Churchill's time was spent gathering intelligence and keeping his ears to the ground. His work involved plenty of travel and dangerous liaison activities, and these included evaluating the CARTE circuit established by André Girard.

It had been Francis Basin's URCHIN on the Côte d'Azur that had first brought the important work of CARTE to London's attention. Girard had established important links, particularly with senior French military officials, and he boasted a network of thousands of trained soldiers. While Girard had made every effort to help Basin, whom he greatly respected and was prepared to co-operate with, his relationship with Churchill was never more than diplomatic. Nonetheless, the British agreed to send Girard more agents, weapons and other supplies.

Churchill also met up with Duboudin, who had recently set up the SPRUCE circuit in Lyons and, like Girard, was in need of supplies and a radio operator. Churchill had taken with him a large amount of French currency, some two million francs, and so the money was distributed between the SOE operatives in the area. Half was split between Basin, Duboudin and another agent, Ted Coppin (Olivier) in Marseilles, while the largest share, about a million francs, went to André Girard.[2]

With his first mission successfully complete, Churchill made his way home through Spain. At that stage of the war it was considered relatively safe to insert agents into the Vichy south by sea and so for Churchill's second

---

1. NA HS 9/315, SOE Personnel File, Captain Peter Churchill.
2. Cookridge, op. cit., p.157.

mission, in April 1942, he delivered two young SOE radio operators to the Riviera. One, 27-year-old Edward Zeff (Georges 53), was destined for Lyons to join SPRUCE, and the other, 25-year-old Isidore Newman (Julien), was to join URCHIN.

The two pianists, each with their radio sets, were delivered safely ashore by canoe where they were met by a reception committee. Churchill then made the return journey, taking with him to London Emmanuel d'Astier de la Vigerie, the founder of the resistance group *La Dernière Colonne* in Clermont-Ferrand (later to be known as *Libération-sud*), which had being carrying out sabotage attacks at train stations as well as distributing propaganda leaflets and the underground newspaper *Libération* throughout the region.

Opportunities for the SOE to conduct active sabotage were still extremely limited at this stage, although a three-man team, dropped into France near Paris by RF Section during early May, attacked a main radio station transmitter near Melun that was being used to jam RAF communications. It took the raiding party three days and nights to reach the transmitter and to reconnoitre it before they successfully set their charges on the main pylons, putting the radio transmitter out of action for two weeks.[3]

While isolated acts of sabotage were good at this stage, it was also important to develop new circuits across France. Having a circuit in the north, particularly in and around Paris, was always high on London's priorities and so it was necessary to understand the extent of the arrests relating to AUTOGIRO and to find out if anyone had somehow managed to survive.

At that stage it was believed that Noël Burdeyron might have escaped the chain of arrests and so a young army officer, 24-year-old Christopher Burney, one of a number of former commando officers recruited by the SOE, was sent into France to find out. Burney had previously lived in France and spoke idiomatic French without an accent. On the last night of May 1942 he parachuted into France under the codename of Charles. He was dropped near le Mans with another agent, William Charles Grover-Williams (Sebastian), a former Bugatti racing driver in his late thirties and

---

3. Foot, op. cit., p.204.

winner of the inaugural 1929 Monaco Grand Prix, who could also speak excellent French.

Burney's mission was to make his way to Normandy and try to find Burdeyron through a friendly house in Caen. Assuming the Frenchman had not been captured, Burney would then act as his assistant but, having made his way to Caen, he found the house was under surveillance and then found out that Burdeyron was in prison. Rather than return to England via Spain, Burney decided instead to try to set up his own circuit. However, he would soon be captured and, after brutal interrogation, sent to Buchenwald.[4]

The largest concentration camp on German soil, Buchenwald was run by some of the SS's most sadistic officers and had some of its most brutal thugs as guards. Its cocktail of miserable conditions, hard work, hunger and typhus, made it one of the worst of all the camps with prisoners from all over Europe; Jews, non-Jewish Poles, political prisoners, the mentally ill and physically disabled were amongst those kept there with many unashamedly used as guinea pigs for the sake of 'biological research'. Several SOE operatives would end up there but few would survive.

Meanwhile, Charles Grover-Williams had arrived in Paris to find that AUTOGIRO was, as had been feared, no longer in existence. With the help of some good contacts and friends from his pre-war motor racing days, including Jean-Pierre Wimille and Robert Benoist (Lionel), a former world champion now in his late forties, Grover-Williams put together a small group of reliable members called CHESTNUT, to operate from the Benoist estate at Auffargis near Rambouillet in the south-west suburbs of the city.[5]

The three former racing drivers used their wives and one or two close friends to act as couriers. In many ways they were the perfect operatives in and around Paris. They were well known to the Germans, respected even, because of their motor racing prowess and were able to move around with relative freedom, and without suspicion.

The work of the racing drivers was good but F Section needed a larger central circuit, based on the workings of AUTOGIRO. Pierre de Vomécourt had initially been identified for this key post but his arrest, and that of Roger

---

4. Ibid., p.175.
5. Ibid, p.176.

Cottin, had put paid to Buckmaster's plans. Not wishing to abandon the idea altogether, Buckmaster decided to send Ben Cowburn back into France.

Cowburn had only recently returned to London following the Cat affair but was keen to volunteer for his second mission, and so he was sent back into the field with Edward Wilkinson (Alexandre) to form a new circuit called TINKER in the Indre. But Paris would be a dangerous place for Cowburn to be and so the idea was that he would introduce Wilkinson to his Paris contacts and, after Wilkinson had established a new foothold in the French capital, Cowburn would then leave to work in the unoccupied zone.

Cowburn and Wilkinson got on extremely well. Wilkinson, an officer in the RAF, had been born in America and spoke French fluently. On the night of 1/2 June 1942 the two men boarded a RAF Halifax for the trip across the Channel where they were to be dropped in the 'safer' unoccupied zone before making their way north.

They were the only two to be dropped that night and so they were able to make themselves as comfortable as possible on the aircraft. Compared to Cowburn's insertion nine months before, when he had been one of six agents on board a Whitley, it would be a luxurious transit. But that was as good as it got. After a transit which took far longer than it should have done, the two agents were finally given the signal to jump. It was to be a blind jump and so there would be no one to meet them on the ground.

Unfortunately for Cowburn and Wilkinson, instead of being inserted near Bellac as planned, they came down well to the north-east of Limoges and some seventy kilometres from where they should have been dropped. The two had become separated in the darkness of the night and, despite looking for each other at daybreak, they were left to make their own separate ways to meet up again a couple of days later at a pre-arranged rendezvous point for 'lost' agents at a café in Tarbes.

Eventually reunited, they made their way to Lyons to meet up with Virginia Hall to find a radio operator. She found them Denis Rake (Justin) who had only recently arrived in France. He was unable to travel immediately to Paris, and so Cowburn and Wilkinson left Lyons together, while Rake stayed behind to get hold of a transmitter and to then make his own way north a few days later.

With Cowburn and Wilkinson having arrived in Paris, it soon became obvious that Rake was overdue. Cowburn decided to return to Lyons to see what had happened. It turned out that Rake had been unable to get across the demarcation line while trying to get to Paris to join up with them.

Cowburn decided to remain in the south while Virginia Hall set about making a new plan to get another radio operator and transmitter to Paris. Besides, he had work to do finding new targets and delivering small quantities of sabotage equipment.

Carrying explosives, incendiaries, guns and ammunition in suitcases over long distances was risky business. While a suitcase at a crowded railway station may not have stood out, the weight of one full of weapons and explosives would have certainly attracted attention if the person carrying it was stopped or if the suitcase was handled by someone else. Agents, therefore, had to take care when handling such luggage and not stand out to anyone observing stations. Using porters was certainly not a good idea and once on a train it was important to ensure the heavy luggage was stowed somewhere where it would not need to be moved or attract any attention.

During this time Cowburn spent a lot of time with Virginia Hall, the lady known only as Marie. He could instantly sense how everyone had come to depend on her when it came to sorting things out. Everybody seemed to take their troubles to her but she was always willing to help, particularly when it came to helping agents new in country; she would feed them or give them her ration cards, help make contacts for them and even do their washing.[6] In her book *The Heroines of SOE*, Beryl E. Escott describes Virginia as 'a grossly overworked spider in the midst of a gradually growing web' while the SOE historian, M. R. D. Foot, in *SOE in France*, acknowledges the immense contribution of Virginia Hall, stating that 'without her indispensable work about half of F Section's early operations in France could never have been carried out at all.'

It was while he was back in Lyons that Cowburn met up with Wilkinson again after Wilkinson had decided to leave Paris and travel back to the unoccupied zone. With him was Rake, who had eventually managed to

---

6. Cowburn, op. cit., p.112.

get across the demarcation line but was now back in Lyons to collect a transmitter.

Within a few days a spare set had been found. Wilkinson and Rake set off again for Paris, taking with them Richard Heslop (Xavier), one of a new batch of agents to have recently arrived in France, who was on his way to Angers in the occupied zone. Because Heslop had yet to experience the crossing of the demarcation line, Wilkinson offered to take him along but, soon after, they were all arrested.

There are two versions of the circumstances behind their arrest. One is that they were all arrested during a night stop at Limoges. Rake was in the hotel alone and his unease and overly anxious appearance during a routine check of papers by the Vichy police did not go unnoticed. Rake was detained and when Wilkinson and Heslop went to join him at the hotel, they walked straight into the trap.[7] The other version, that of Rake, was that he was waiting in his hotel room when two Vichy police barged in, dragging with them Wilkinson and Heslop.[8]

Either way, they were all arrested. Although Rake and Wilkinson kept to a story of having only just met, they were both searched and their identity cards examined more closely. Although ostensibly issued in different towns, they were made out in the same handwriting. Furthermore, they were both carrying a lot of currency and a closer examination of their notes showed them to be numbered in a consecutive series. With hindsight these will seem basic errors but when the identity cards were being forged and money was being issued, it was never intended for these two agents to have ever been together in France. They had gone into the field separately, and each with a different mission, and so it was simply bad luck that they had been picked up at the same time.

It was now the middle of August 1942 and Cowburn would have to continue operating alone. He met two drops on Chantraine's farm near Châteauroux, which had been arranged before Rake's arrest and contained equipment and explosives to carry out sabotage missions. He also persuaded some of his contacts to contaminate machinery in a local aircraft factory

7. Ibid, pp.116–7.
8. Grehan & Mace, op. cit., p. 195.

and supervised an attack against high tension lines around a power station, which succeeded in cutting off power for a few hours. But there was only so much that one man could do and so, on the night of 26/27 October, Ben Cowburn was picked up by Lysander near Mâcon and returned to England.

While Cowburn had been operating in the Indre, another attempt to supply a successor to AUTOGIRO in or near Paris had taken place. Raymond Flower (Caspar), a 30-year-old chef who had worked in the French hotel business, was dropped at the end of June near Tours. Flower was to make contact with Marcel Clech to find out what had happened in Paris and to then set up a small circuit in the Loire valley.

Flower and Clech never seemed to get on with each other. They were soon joined by Pierre Culioli, a diminutive young army officer who had helped a number of RAF aircrew escape to Spain. Culioli was now being hunted by the Gestapo and so he had absconded to Tours under the alias Pierre Leclair. Culioli had contacts and proved to be an enthusiastic and efficient agent but his initial admiration for Flower diminished rapidly, feeling that his leader was treating his stay in France more like a holiday than anything else. While his criticism may have been harsh, Baker Street had also begun to wonder about Flower's suspended animation.[9]

Now that more agents were being inserted into the unoccupied zone, all of whom seemed to end up passing through Lyons, it was important to co-ordinate SOE's activities. It was already proving difficult to differentiate between agents being sent into France for specific purposes and those who were there for general subversion. SOE activities were starting to overlap with large resistance organizations, such as the COMBAT network, which boasted several thousands and worked with F Section circuits as well as with RF. And so a young linguist, Victor Hazan (Gervais), was sent from London to meet with all the circuit organizers in the Vichy south. In reality it would prove to be an impossible task for anyone. Voluble agents, such as Philippe de Vomécourt and Francis Basin, shouted him down while secretive ones, like George Duboudin, kept well out of his way. While he could not achieve what

---

9. Cookridge, op. cit., p.198.

he had been sent to do, Hazan was, however, able to prove useful in training new recruits in the use of British weapons and explosives.[10]

Amongst others to arrive in Lyons at this time was 25-year-old Alan Jickell (Gustave), a half-French wharf clerk from Cardiff, who was sent in to manage the reception of weapons and their storage, and Duboudin's assistant, 35-year-old Robert Boiteux (Nicholas), a strong, energetic and voluble half-Jewish London-born Frenchman, a former boxing champion, and known as 'the Bond Street hairdresser' because of his previous occupation.

Boiteux had been lucky to escape arrest by the Vichy police on the night of his insertion near Mâcon when the agent he jumped with, Robert Sheppard (Patrice), landed on the roof of the *feldgendarmerie*. The chase was on from the start but Boiteux had managed to make his escape, although he and Duboudin would not get on and so Boiteux would end up running SPRUCE.

June 1942 also saw the arrival in France of Alfred and Henry Newton, known in Baker Street as 'The Twins'. Of all the high adventure tales that have to do with the activities of the SOE, few can rival the story of the Newton Twins.

10. Foot, op. cit., p.191.

Chapter 7

The Twins

Peter Churchill had not been long back in England from his second
mission when he was summoned to Buckmaster's office in Baker
Street and told he was wanted for a mission of a specialized nature.
Buckmaster explained that he had been asked by the Chiefs of Staff if he
had someone who could tackle a rather tricky proposition and, having
informed the chiefs that he did have someone in mind, Buckmaster was
then instructed by Prime Minister Winston Churchill to approach the agent
about the mission.[1]

With such direction from the very top, Churchill (Peter Churchill that is)
did not hesitate to volunteer for the mission. During his briefing he found
out the Chiefs of Staff had ordered the destruction of a radio station at Saint-
Assise that was being used by the German naval command for directing
U-boats in the Atlantic. Allied convoys were being attacked on a regular
basis and the only radio transmitter considered powerful enough to transmit
over such a long distance was the one at Saint-Assise. Destroying the radio
station, even for a matter of days, would break down communications for
long enough to give the Royal Navy enough time to hunt down the packs
of U-boats and save the lives of many British and Allied seamen. Peter
Churchill's task was to take two highly trained demolition saboteurs to
France and blow up the radio station.

The two saboteurs chosen by Buckmaster were Alfred and Henry Newton.
Although they were known in Baker Street as 'The Twins', the Newton
brothers were, in fact, born ten years apart with Henry, aged thirty-eight,
the elder of the two. They were the sons of a former Lancashire jockey who
had been a trainer in France and had lived there with his family for many
years. Before the war, the two brothers had become well known in Europe as

---

1. Cookridge, op. cit., p.159.

cabaret artists called the Boorn Brothers (Boorn being their mother's maiden name) and both had married in France with Alfred, who was married to a German-born dancer, having three young sons.

The brothers, their parents and their families had all lived together in Cendrieux, an isolated hamlet near Périgueux in the Dordogne. After the German invasion they had become trapped in France and so Alfred and Henry Newton organized what was, perhaps, the first underground movement in the unoccupied zone. There was little, in reality, that two men could achieve but most of their villagers were neither convinced Vichyites nor Gaullists, and so the brothers set about preventing them from becoming lulled into the constant Vichy-German propaganda. Twice a day the Newtons met a trusted group of men and women in a barn and passed on to them information about the war that they had picked up from listening to the BBC's Home Service on a hidden receiver. Then the couriers would hurry away on bicycles to their villages nearby where others waited their turn to further spread the news.

The bush telegraph worked well and the news spread far and swiftly. The results were astonishing with news travelling more than 100 kilometres. More schemes were then hatched, including minor acts of sabotage such as putting sugar in the petrol tank of an enemy vehicle, as well as gathering and storing weapons and explosives that had been left abandoned by the French army. Gradually the Newtons created impalpable opposition to the Vichyites and occupying forces. They knew that other groups were working on similar lines but it was too early to think about attempting to join forces; that would have to wait.

Unfortunately, though, their moonlight bicycle excursions and numerous early morning 'fishing trips' caught the attention of the Vichy police and one morning they were summoned to Périgueux where they were interrogated by two Vichy officials. There had been nothing to detain them and so the two brothers were released home on 'forced residence', meaning that each morning they were required to report to an official who was given responsibility for their good behaviour.

The Newtons had no intention of remaining in Cendrieux. Satisfied their family members were safe, and having formed the nucleus of a valuable resistance group, they planned to make their way to England.[2] But it was then that the family received a letter from the American Consulate-General in Marseilles, urging all British civilians residing in the unoccupied zone in France to make arrangements to leave the country at the earliest possible date. Negotiations were taking place with the Vichy French for the repatriation of British subjects under and over the military age.

This news upset everything the brothers had planned and so they decided to remain where they were for now to continue their subversive activities with renewed vigour. The Germans had put pressure on the Vichy French to take a much stronger stance against any subversive activities and so the brothers were again summoned to Périgueux, only this time they were put in front of a military tribunal. Their 'trial' took place in a makeshift hut on a patch of waste land near the cattle market and turned out to be more of a farce than a serious session in court. At the end the Newtons were told they were sentenced to undergo disciplinary labour at a nearby camp called Chancellade but, again, the situation turned into farce when they were issued with work passes to work on local farms instead.

Then, suddenly, and without any notice, they found their families had gone. They had been evacuated by the Red Cross and were on their way to Spain and then Lisbon, from where they would sail to England.

The brothers decided that it was now the time to make their way to England. They soon managed to escape from Chancellade at night through a combination of forged passes and a sleepy sentry, and made their way to Marseilles and then Perpignon before crossing the Pyrenees. Having finally arrived in Spain they were arrested for illegally entering the country without passports and sentenced to fifteen days at the Miranda de Ebro internment camp amongst many other nationalities – Poles, Czechs, Dutch, Danes, Belgians, Norwegians, French and even Greeks and Arabs – all trying to make their way to Britain. They were eventually released at the end of 1941 and taken to the British Embassy in Madrid, and it was there a military attaché gave them the devastating news that their entire family – their parents, wives and Alfred's three young children – had been killed when a German U-boat sank the mercy ship they were sailing on for England.

---

2. Thomas, *No Banners*, pp.28–31.

From that moment on, the Newton brothers were consumed with a passion for revenge on the Nazis.[3] They made their way to Gibraltar to wait for a passage back to England and by the time they arrived in Liverpool after a long sea passage on board the Royal Navy destroyer HMS *Hesperus*, they only had one thought between them – vengeance on the Nazis.

The brothers were met on arrival by an army sergeant and escorted by train to the War Office in London. It was January 1942 and bitterly cold with the capital covered in snow. They were met by a man dressed in a lounge suit, an army captain. He knew about the brothers and their loss, and asked them what their plans were now that they were back in England. The brothers then brought the captain up to date with their activities over the past couple of years and informed him they intended to seek revenge, Henry's words being along the lines of 'Give us a couple of tommy guns and a bunch of hand grenades. We know bloody well what we're going to do'.[4]

With that the army captain gave them both instructions to go to Portman Square to meet with an army major, Lewis Gielgud, the brother of the English actor John Gielgud and a recruiting officer for F Section. The Newtons were as blunt with Gielgud as they had previously been with the captain, even suggesting they should be allowed to land back in France with a commando unit where they could inflict as much damage on the enemy as possible. This amused Gielgud but, as he explained, if they were to be allowed to do so then, at best, they might kill a few Germans but then they were almost certain to be killed themselves. Gielgud went on to explain that the two brothers were too precious for that to be allowed to happen and that, with their courage and ability, they could contribute to the war in a far better way. And so the two Newton brothers were recruited by the SOE. Gielgud had clearly recognized that he had recruited two men who would shirk no task, however dangerous or difficult, and they were considered perfect to be trained as saboteurs.

The brothers now lost their true identities. Given the surname of Norman, Alfred became 'Arthur' and Henry became 'Hubert', with the codenames 'Artus' and 'Auguste' respectively, and together they simply became known as 'The Twins'.

---

3. Thomas, op. cit., inside front jacket.
4. Ibid, p.94.

Although other brothers worked within the SOE, the Newtons were the only brothers known to operate together as a team. For the next few weeks they were trained, first at Wanborough Manor, where Alfred was more adept at learning than his brother,[5] and then in Scotland for their physical commando-style training, followed by parachute training at Ringway and finally their specialist sabotage training at Brickendonbury Manor in Hertfordshire.

The Twins were put through their paces but both proved incredibly tough. As the weeks passed they became experts in creating mayhem and sudden death. They learned how to handle weapons and explosives of all types with much of their training focusing on the destruction of buildings and machinery. They were taught how to take almost any manufactured article – whether it be a bicycle, hairbrush or a matchbox – and convert it into a piece of equipment to maim and kill. The Twins were then commissioned with the rank of second lieutenant and after some leave were summoned to Baker Street with Peter Churchill to be briefed on their special mission.

Having been briefed on the radio station at Saint-Assise, the three went off to plan their attack. The Twins were excited by the idea, particularly as they both felt they had a personal score to settle with the *Kriegsmarine* (the German Navy). They had about ten days to put together a plan and were given every possible assistance, using aerial reconnaissance photos of the site, seemingly taken from every possible angle, a scale model of the site and surrounding terrain, and calculations of the amount of explosive required to bring down one of the transmitter pylons.

Churchill and The Twins headed off to Surrey, where they tried out various combinations of explosive charges on a steel bar, and then Sussex, where timbered columns with mocked-up screw jacks were erected to bear some resemblance to Saint-Assise. For ten hectic days and nights they planned and rehearsed the operation, placing the charges and setting the pencil time-fuses with precision.

The raid was planned for 28 May 1942 but then, and without warning, came the news that it was cancelled. The Twins were livid. They were told the Germans had heard that a raid was about to happen and had strengthened

---

5. NA HS 9/1096/8, Personnel File, A. W. O. Newton.

their defences with more troops spread across the entire area. It appears the Germans were waiting for them. They simply would not have stood a chance and any attempt to mount the raid would have been almost certain suicide. The Twins were, nonetheless, determined to go ahead and give it a try but in the end their request was denied.

A story later emerged that a member of the French Resistance and a couple of his friends had been cycling past the radio station at Saint-Assise. They had been carrying explosives hidden in the frames of their bicycles and when they left their bicycles against one of the radio masts to go for a walk, the explosives had blown up and damaged the mast. Within minutes the station had become surrounded by Germans and the area cordoned off. No one would be able to get anywhere near it.[6]

Whether this farcical reason for the cancellation of the raid was true or not is unknown, but The Twins would have to be patient and wait for another opportunity to return to France. They did not have to wait long, just a matter of a few weeks in fact, before they were again summoned for briefing at Orchard Court.

This time they were to go into France to work for a man known as Gauthier (this was Philippe de Vomécourt) in the Lyons area to act as sabotage instructors and to train members of the resistance groups how to handle British weapons and teach them guerrilla tactics. They were given their new identity papers, forged of course, and something of a rather muddled brief, but they were told they would be working with a radio operator, codenamed "Celestin", and that all three of them were to be dropped on the same night.

Inside the car waiting to take them from their briefing was Celestin, or, to give him his real name, Brian Stonehouse, a tall and young *Vogue* fashion artist. Also in the car was F Section's operations officer, Gerry Morel. They all then headed off for what would be The Twins' last meal in England before heading across the Channel the following night.

It was now approaching the end of June and that night the BBC transmitted its list of coded messages to various reception committees across France. Amongst them was *Les durs des durs arrivent* translated as 'the toughest of the tough are arriving', to indicate the imminent arrival of The Twins. The message had been

---

6. Cookridge, op. cit., p.161.

sent in response to an earlier message from Philippe de Vomécourt complaining about the standard of two earlier agents sent to him. In that message he had said *'Petits Suisses trop nous. Envoyez des durs'*, translated as 'Swiss cheeses are too soft. Send tougher ones'. And so tougher ones were on their way.

The first attempt to drop The Twins and Stonehouse was unsuccessful after the Whitley they were travelling in had to turn back due to an intercom failure inside the aircraft. The following night the three climbed aboard a RAF Wellington and this time were more fortunate, although their aircraft had to circle for forty minutes over the Loire while the crew tried to identify the correct drop zone. Finally, some people were spotted on the ground cycling along a road towards the field and flashing torches into the air. Because of the aborted attempt the previous night, the reception committee of two men and two women had not been aware that the drop had been re-scheduled for that night, but they were now on their way to the field, having been woken by the sound of the aircraft overhead.[7]

The Twins and Stonehouse came down in a field near Tours. A German guard post was known to be just a kilometre or two away and so the three new arrivals were quickly led away. They had been briefed to expect their circuit organizer – Philippe de Vomécourt – to meet them at the drop zone and that they were to be accommodated at the Château le Breuil, but there was no sign of de Vomécourt and the château was considered unsafe. They were taken instead to a barn with no light and no water. It had not been the arrival they had expected.

After being instructed to leave their suitcases and money behind, which none of them were particularly happy about, they made their way on foot to the railway station at Loches. They had been told that they could either catch a train to meet with de Vomécourt in Limoges or meet with his assistant, Joseph (real name J. M. Aron), in Lyons. At this point the three agents decided to split. Stonehouse would go to Limoges and meet with de Vomécourt while The Twins would go to Lyons and meet with Aron.

For the next three days the Twins waited in a small café in Lyons at the specified times for their contact to show up. But no one came. They could

---

7. NA HS 9/1096/8, Personnel File, A. W. O. Newton (Mission Report dated 28 April 1945).

not risk checking into a hotel as they did not know which were considered safe. They were also without any food coupons and did not know the black market restaurants yet, and so they lived on a few sweets and chocolate they had brought with them from England. Every night they took the train to Avignon for somewhere to sleep and to keep warm before returning to Lyons again the following morning.

With no change on the fourth and fifth days, The Twins considered what to do next. If no contact was made soon they agreed that Henry would make his way to Paris to meet up with former friends while Alfred would return to England via Spain to brief London on what had happened and to find out what they should do next. Then, on the sixth morning, and quite by chance, they spotted an SOE agent they recognized from England. It was Alan Jickell, a man known to them only as Gustave.

It would normally be forbidden, and dangerous, for agents to make contact with each other in this way but The Twins felt they had no alternative. They approached him and explained what had happened. Jickell explained that he was working with a circuit in Cannes and would get word to London informing them that they had been found safe and to seek instructions for what they should do next. Jickell then found them somewhere safe to stay.

Those back in Baker Street were aware that The Twins had yet to make contact with their circuit but were somewhat surprised to find out that they had managed to make contact with another circuit in Cannes. It was at this point that The Twins met with Virginia Hall in Lyons and, finally, de Vomécourt – seventeen days after they had landed in France. But it soon became obvious that de Vomécourt had no time for them. It was arms and money he wanted and not more of London's incompetents.[8] Equally, The Twins had no time for de Vomécourt. In fact, since their shambolic arrival in France, they had become increasingly despondent with the whole set-up.

For the next couple of weeks, Alfred and Henry worked separately on different tasks. While Henry went off to check out the suitability of a small airfield near Vierson close to the demarcation line, Alfred went off to Marseilles to take charge of a nascent group that he was told numbered

8. Foot, op. cit., p.192.

around 2,000 men, all waiting to be trained and armed. He arrived to find only a handful of dockers.

Although tough, the Newton Twins were by no means stupid. They finally managed to settle down at le Puy in the Haute Loire but found organization to be practically non-existent and considered much of what their colleagues were pretending to do a sham. They were also being steadily outmanoeuvred by some who did not hesitate to invent and spread infuriating rumours to their discredit, and had managed to isolate them from Stonehouse.[9]

However, the Twins were soon doing a sound job of organizing and training a couple of hundred reliable men of what became their own GREENHEART circuit. They had recruited *gendarmes* at Saint-Paulian, the firemen at Saint-Puy and many other notable individuals from the local area. They had also built up a fleet of cars and other vehicles for use, and a way of getting hold of, or forging, identity papers and other key documents, as well as ration books and tobacco cards.

The brothers worked harder than ever, with little sleep, as they cycled round the countryside looking for suitable drop zones, checking on military posts and establishments, and looking for industrial targets to attack. Relaxation was usually spent teaching some new recruit how to silently dispose of a German soldier. It was not long before the members of their circuit were thoroughly schooled in how to kill and how to commit arson and acts of sabotage such as train derailment.

There were tangible results too. For example, the entire output of six-ton trucks from a factory in Lyons was sabotaged. They had been 'greased' in key areas with a mixture containing paraffin and a high proportion of pumice and steel powder, while the engines were 'treated' with a concoction that gummed up and corroded every component. After seemingly running normally for a short time, the trucks would then seize so badly that they were to be of no further use. There were other acts, too, such as blowing up a Gestapo staff car, killing its occupants instantly, blowing up a railway bridge and attacking a train carrying enemy anti-aircraft guns and their crews. The Twins also provided Virginia Hall with complete *gendarme* uniforms

---

9. NA HS 9/1096/8, Personnel File, A. W. O Newton (Mission Report dated 28 April 1945).

to help resistance members escape from a prison at Castres.[10] Then, on 12 November, as the Germans were moving into the unoccupied zone, The Twins spotted two German radio trucks. They quickly got some explosives, made two charges and later that evening attached them to the trucks; the subsequent explosions wrecked both.

The Twins now made another useful contact, a man known to them as 'Colonel Lucien' (Raymond Bizot). They travelled the area, building up the Maquis as they went. Unlike other resistance groups, they kept no records of their circuit, its members and their activities to prevent any information from ever falling into enemy hands; everything was committed to memory. When someone was arrested The Twins simply went to ground but they, too, had now become wanted men, although the Germans had little information on either to go on.

Frustratingly, The Twins felt they were getting little support from back home. Air drops that had been planned never took place. They also had no way of communicating directly with London; they were isolated from Stonehouse and every message had to go through Lyons and Virginia Hall who then passed them to the radio operator of another circuit for transmission. They felt isolated and had no money. Although Virginia did what she could to help, they even went as far as to sell off some plots of their own land in France to raise money for their cause.

For several months The Twins waged their own private war on the Nazis, just as they had always intended to do. Eventually, though, the lack of money, the lack of arms and explosives, and the lack of direct radio link with London, forced them to abandon their work. Through their colleague, Alan Jickell, they made contact with an escape line with the plan to return to England via Spain.

But, even then, people could not be trusted. The Twins had caused a certain amount of intrigue amongst many throughout their time in France and, unfortunately, before they could make their escape, they were betrayed by a Nazi informer called Robert Alesch, the former Abbé of Saint-Maur and known as the Bishop.

---

10. Ibid.

In April 1943, the night before Jickell was due to collect them from their safe house in Lyons and take them on to Perpignon, The Twins were having dinner with their two most trusted French friends when their room was stormed by the Gestapo. Not surprisingly, they did not go down without a fight, but they were heavily outnumbered and it took several minutes for them to be overpowered.

The Twins were then imprisoned and brutally tortured by the infamous Gestapo chief, Klaus Barbie, the so-called 'Butcher of Lyons', although this only resulted in them hating the Nazis even more. The Twins would never give anything away. They were transferred to the notorious Fresnes prison, in the suburbs of Paris, the following month. Life there was awful. The prison was overcrowded, with prisoners doubled up in tiny cells, and for the inmates life was as basic as it gets: an iron bed, a sheet and a blanket with a toilet pan, limited exercise and poor food. It was barely enough to keep them alive. Most of the day was spent working, such as sewing or peeling potatoes, or recovering from the interrogations carried out at the Avenue Foch, where the buildings numbered 82–86 were being used by the counter-intelligence branch of the SS, the *Sicherheitsdienst* (SD), under the senior German intelligence officer in Paris, Hans Josef Kieffer, with most of the interrogations and torture of F Section agents taking place on the third floor at number 84.

For The Twins it was a gruesome existence but still the brothers remained silent. In January 1944 they were moved to the concentration camp at Buchenwald along with other F Section agents. They later described just how horrible their journey to the camp had been with more than a hundred men packed into a goods wagon, without water, for three days.[11]

During the bitter months that followed they were put into gruelling working parties but somehow both managed to survive, even though Henry contracted double pneumonia. As the war approached its end, agents were being shot but The Twins managed to hide in what was known as the 'Little Camp', a horrifically overcrowded and disease-ridden compound within the overall camp. By repeatedly changing their numbers and identities within

---

11. NA HS 9/1096/8, Personnel File, A. W. O. Newton (Mission Report dated 28 April 1945).

the camp they were able to escape execution. Finally, a month before the end of the war, the camp was liberated by the Americans. The Twins were two of only four surviving British agents left in the camp.[12]

The Twins had survived against all the odds, although the loss of their family would always be felt. After arriving back in England at the end of the war, both Newton brothers were appointed Members of the Order of the British Empire for their mission and for the extreme courage and bravery they had shown after capture.

---

12. The two other surviving agents were Christopher Burney and Maurice Southgate.

Chapter 8

Women Enter the Fray

After his experience of working with Raymond Flower and Marcel Clech, Pierre Culioli would have been forgiven for giving up on the SOE and going off to join the French Resistance instead. He might well have done had it not been for the arrival of Yvonne Rudellat, the first female specifically recruited by F Section and sent into occupied France to conduct subversive warfare.

Until now, Britain had not really contemplated the idea of putting women in any danger. It was considered perfectly acceptable during the early years of the war to use women on the land or in factories, or even in the armed forces, as long as it was not in the face of the enemy, but it was not considered right for women to be used abroad, in any kind of role, in time of war. And so it would require a fundamental change in thinking for the SOE to employ female agents in the field.

The idea of using women as agents had been resisted fiercely but it was now considered the time for SOE to do so. First of all, there was a shortage of suitable male volunteers coming forward and, secondly, those men who were operating in France were generally of the age where they were likely to be rounded up for forced labour and deported to Germany.

Employing female agents in the field would turn out to be a good move, not least because the Germans appeared to be less suspicious of women. Women of all ages were roaming over France and using all forms of transport, especially bicycles and trains, and were often seen carrying bags or luggage, and so they would not attract suspicion, especially if operating as couriers.

Responsibility for the female agents destined for France was given to Vera Atkins. She would take care of everything relating to the agent, including any domestic difficulties in England as well as preparing them for their mission. This would include checking that papers and documents were correct, checking that their clothing and personal items were appropriate for the role and mission they were to undertake, and act as SOE's liaison with her family. Vera would also accompany the agent to the airfield of departure and carry out the final security checks before wishing her good luck and sending her on her way.

It was never going to be easy to find suitable female volunteers. They were generally recruited for their language abilities and so they tended to come from a different pool than the male agents. Not only did they need to have the linguist skills required, they also needed to be able to blend into a crowd and not draw attention to themselves. Age was to be no barrier. Female agents would range in age from young women barely out of their teens to those more mature, in their forties or fifties. But those suitable for selection needed to be clever, quick-witted and brave. They would all be given an officer rank in one of the services in the hope that, if they were captured, they would be treated decently as prisoners of war and in accordance with the Geneva Convention; sadly, that would not prove to be the case.

The first of these female volunteers was Yvonne Rudellat, an extraordinary and attractive Parisienne, a mother and a grandmother at the age of forty-one, and seemingly a most unlikely agent. Yvonne had travelled to England in her teens and later married an Italian, although the marriage ultimately failed. She lived in London for many years, managing an interior decorating business and working for an estate agent in the wealthy parts of the city. Yvonne had come to the attention of the SOE after an agent had noticed her at the hotel where she was also working as a receptionist. Lewis Gielgud, the recruiting officer for F Section, is said to have been aghast when a middle-aged woman walked into his room. But he was so impressed by her bearing and intelligence that he recommended her for training.[1]

Yvonne attended the SOE's first female course with three others: Blanche Charlet, also in her mid-forties; Marie-Thérèse le Chêne, aged fifty-two; and Andrée Borrel, the so-called 'Parisian urchin', who was by far the youngest at just twenty-two. All four were trained under the cover of the FANY and all would go into France during 1942. Yvonne was described by her training officer as a 'little old lady, with chameleon personality, she outshone the others'. And in her book *The Heroines of SOE*, Beryl E. Scott

1. Cookridge, op. cit., p.198.

describes Yvonne Rudellat as 'a vivacious, dainty charmer with dark hair and hazel eyes, whose air of fragility was deceptive'.[2]

Under the alias of Jacqueline Gautier and the codename of 'Suzanne', Yvonne was dropped by felucca (a small sailing boat used extensively in the Mediterranean) on the Riviera at Cap d'Antibes on the night of 29/30 July 1942 with three male agents: Harry Despaigne (Magnolia), who was heading to Peter Churchill to work as his radio operator, Henri Frager (Paul), and Nicholas Bodington (Jean-Paul). Frager was returning from London having discussed with Buckmaster the possibility of CARTE-SOE co-operation, and with him was Bodington, Buckmaster's deputy, who was to check on the state of CARTE for himself, as well as carrying out other tasks for F Section.

Their journey to France had been an eventful one. On the flight to Gibraltar the aircraft in which they had been travelling was attacked by two enemy fighters and ended up landing with only one engine still serviceable and having flown much of the way just a few feet above the sea. Then the felucca which had taken them to the Côte d'Azur was chased part of the way by an Italian vessel.

Having landed in the south of France, Yvonne made her way to Lyons where she met briefly with Virginia Hall, before crossing the demarcation line to make her way to Paris. She had been sent to France as courier for Francis Suttill (Prosper). He was soon to arrive in France to set up his circuit to replace AUTOGIRO, but his arrival had been delayed and so Yvonne made her way to Tours instead to work temporarily as a courier for the MONKEYPUZZLE circuit run by Raymond Flower.

Being the first female sent into France, Yvonne was to have a difficult start to her operational life. Clearly not everyone, including Flower, was onside when it came to having a woman sent from London to be part of the team. When Yvonne arrived in Tours she was left to make her own arrangements for somewhere to stay and ended up in the house of a man who made no secret about his pro-German sympathies. Then, her very existence was put at risk when Flower deposited a number of items including a pistol, a radio transmitter with spare crystals and a list of codes, and a list naming members

---

2. Escott, *The Heroines of SOE*, p.40.

of the circuit, in her digs while she was out, all this to save himself when he thought the Germans were on his tail.

Yvonne immediately informed Pierre Culioli who came to collect everything but it was too late. Her landlord had already ransacked her room and had informed the local police. As Yvonne and Culioli approached the house they saw *gendarmes* waiting and so they quickly made their escape. Yvonne was put on a train to Poitiers where she would spend the next few days hiding but it had been a close call. Her operational life in the field was nearly over before it had even begun.

Culioli confronted Flower about what had happened and threatened to report the incident to London but Flower had seemingly got in first, suggesting to London that neither Culioli nor Yvonne could be trusted as they had apparently gone over to the Germans, such was Flower's dislike of them both. London already had doubts about Flower but they knew nothing of Culioli and it was too early to judge Yvonne. They certainly trusted her but it was not impossible that her inexperience had led to her falling into a trap. And so, for now, London decided to tread carefully with the circuit, although their concerns about Flower's commitment would soon prove to be justified when he failed to prepare a landing ground for the arrival of two agents, despite being given ample warning to do so.

The days of Flower's activities were numbered. In fact, the MONKEYPUZZLE circuit would never really get started, not only because of the incompetence of Flower but also due to the close observation of radio transmissions by the Germans at the time, and it would be wound up the following spring.

Yvonne Rudellat's entry into France was soon followed by that of her SOE course colleague, Blanche Charlet, who was also dropped by felucca on the night of 1 September along the coastline of the Riviera. Blanche was Belgian and had fled to England during the Nazi invasion. She had a number of connections in the art world and when the SOE started recruiting women she was amongst the first to volunteer. Operating under her alias of Sabine Laconte and with the codename 'Christianne', she made her way to Cannes but found that her contact there had been arrested just the day before, and so she made her way to Lyons instead where she met up with Virginia Hall.

Blanche joined the VENTRILOQUIST circuit headed by Philippe de Vomécourt and her first task was to make preparations for a radio operator soon to join her. That was to be Brian Stonehouse, who had been dropped into France at the end of June with the Newton Twins. Stonehouse was, at that time, having to act as the radio operator for both The Twins and Henri Sevenet (Rodolphe), an old family friend of the de Vomécourts, who was preparing a circuit called DETECTIVE to attack the Tours-Poitiers railway line.

While Blanche was content to carry messages between members of the group, she soon became dissatisfied. The network seemed disorganized and Stonehouse, although a very hardworking individual, seemed to spend too long transmitting his messages. Sure enough, while making another prolonged transmission from a house to the south of Lyons during October, his transmission was picked up by direction finders in the area and both he and Blanche were arrested.

The house was searched and the radio and coded papers were discovered. Blanche and Stonehouse were separated and interrogated by the Nazis before they were both imprisoned at Castres. Stonehouse would survive the horrors of the concentration camps at Mauthausen, Natzweiler and Dachau. Blanche, too, would survive. She was held for nearly a year in various French prisons, in extremely harsh conditions, but finally managed to escape with a group of other prisoners. After several attempts to escape France, including two attempts to cross the Pyrenees during the winter, she finally used an escape line through to Brittany where she was picked up by a small boat and eventually arrived back in England. Philippe de Vomécourt had also been arrested by the Vichy police during the round-up. He was imprisoned at the Saint-Paul prison in Lyons, although he, too, would later escape and make his way to England via Spain.

The life of a courier was a busy one and dangerous, even in the unoccupied zone where, in Lyons and Marseilles in particular, the Vichy police watched on closely, knowing the two cities were harbouring members of the Resistance and agents of the SOE. Couriers travelled far and wide, carrying messages, weapons, explosives or equipment. They also got involved with finding suitable landing zones and among the sites identified by Yvonne Rudellat were some used to land agents during the latter months of 1942.

Amongst those to land was another of Yvonne's former course colleagues, Andrée Borrel (Denise), who dropped into France near Paris on the night of 24/25 September to make preparations for the arrival of Francis Suttill. Andrée was a small and stocky young girl but, nonetheless, very athletic. During the early months of the war she had nursed wounded soldiers and had joined the French Resistance and for a while helped with the 'Pat' escape line for downed pilots and prisoners of war. She had then run a safe house near Perpignon but in late 1941, when part of the escape line was betrayed, she became known to the Gestapo and so quickly made her own way out of France and across the Pyrenees to Spain before finally going on to Gibraltar and then England. Having initially offered her services to de Gaulle's Free French, she refused to answer detailed questions about the 'Pat' line and so she turned to F Section instead.[3]

On the same night as Andrée Borrel had parachuted into France, 37-year-old Lise de Baissac (Odile), operating as Irène Brisse, was dropped near Poitiers in west-central France to join up with her younger brother, Claude, in Bordeaux. Andrée and Lise were the first two F Section women to be parachuted into France.

Born of British nationality on the island of Mauritius in the Indian Ocean, Lise was bilingual in French and English. After the fall of France she had made her way to England with Claude. She had initially found work in London but when her brother joined the SOE, Lise also volunteered when she found out that women were being recruited. Lise had attended the second female course during May 1942 and, although small in stature, she had done well, coming across as extremely intelligent and full of confidence. She had trained alongside three other women, all of whom would soon go into France: Mary Herbert, a tall and slim Irishwoman in her late thirties who was fluent in several different languages; 30-year-old Odette Sansom, born in France but married to an Englishman and a mother of three; and Jacqueline Nearne, aged twenty-six who had been born in England but raised and educated in France.

Lise de Baissac had been beaten into France by her brother Claude, once described by Buckmaster as 'the most difficult of all my officers without

---

3. Ibid, p.50.

exception',[4] by just two months. Operating under the codename 'David' he had been dropped blind near Nîmes with his radio operator, Harry Peulevé (Paul), on the night of 30 July to set up a new circuit called SCIENTIST in the area of Bordeaux. Unfortunately, though, both men had suffered injuries during the drop, which appears to have been made too low; de Baissac had broken an ankle while Peulevé suffered multiple fractures of his leg. They did, however, manage to make contact with someone who could get them the medical help they needed, after which de Baissac went his own way to set up SCIENTIST while Peulevé was re-assigned to work on the Riviera, although he would soon get out and make his way back to England by crossing the Pyrenees on a pair of crutches during the winter, after he became concerned by the lack of security within the CARTE circuit to which he had been assigned.

Meanwhile, Francis Suttill finally dropped into France near Vendôme on the night of 1/2 October, accompanied by his assistant, James Amps (Tomas), a tough but cheerful little man and a former racing jockey. Suttill, a 32-year-old army officer, was to set up a new circuit in and around Paris. He had been given a wide range of powers by Buckmaster. The Allies were soon to land in French North Africa and it was vital to have a communications link in Paris under British control. Suttill was, therefore, to establish a network across parts of northern, central and eastern France, by taking forward the work previously carried out by men like Pierre de Vomécourt and Ben Cowburn.

To enable him to move freely around France, Suttill was given the identity of François Desprée, a man working in agricultural produce. Helped by his courier, Andrée Borrel, the Parisian street urchin, she would often have to travel with him, posing as his sister, to do most of the talking.[5] There was a further problem too. Suttill did not have as many, or the range of, contacts as de Vomécourt. Suttill was often left to rely on his contacts from the CARTE circuit in the unoccupied zone, which itself had its problems and often promised more than it could deliver.

---

4. Foot, op. cit., p.179.
5. Escott, op. cit., p.51.

Suttill was soon joined by Gilbert Norman (Archambaud), a 27-year-old radio operator. Norman had been born in Paris, the son of an English father and French mother, and had also served as an army officer before joining the SOE. He dropped by parachute near Boisrenard, to a reception committee arranged by Yvonne Rudellat, with another radio operator, Roger Landes (Aristide), destined for Claude de Baissac's new SCIENTIST circuit in Bordeaux.

Earlier doubts about Pierre Culioli were soon resolved after both Suttill and Norman met with him. Suttill soon sent a signal to Buckmaster informing him that Culioli could be trusted and it had, in fact, been Flower who had been the problem all along. So impressed was Suttill that he would eventually appoint Culioli as a new circuit organizer in the Sologne, called ADOLPHE, with Yvonne Rudellat as his deputy and courier. Also, because of the high workload, a second radio operator, Jack Agazarian (Marcel), a dashing young airman was dropped into the Seine valley to work alongside Norman.

The excellent work of the first women sent into France had convinced London to send more females from F Section into the field. Three more – Mary Herbert, Marie-Thérèse le Chêne and Odette Sansom – arrived on a dark moonless night on the last night of October 1942, landing near the small French commune of Cassis to the east of Marseilles. They had been dropped with three male colleagues: John Young (Gabriel), a fire insurance surveyor in his thirties and now a radio operator with the SOE; Marcus Bloom (Urban), a burly London cinema director in his mid-thirties and also now a radio operator and on his way to Toulouse; and George Starr (Hilaire), who was heading for Lyons to join Duboudin and would later become F Section's chief organizer in Gascony, running WHEELWRIGHT.

Mary Herbert, operating as Marie-Louise Vernier and with the codename 'Claudine', was destined for SCIENTIST in Bordeaux, where she was to join up with Roger Landes. The circuit was already starting to expand and Mary soon found herself travelling far and wide around south-west France. Although she would rarely meet up with Landes, she would see a lot of de Baissac, with whom she got on extremely well. She even accompanied him to Paris as it was safer for him to be seen with a woman rather than to travel alone; they would marry in London before the end of the war.

Meanwhile, Mary-Thérèse le Chêne was due to travel to Lyons to meet up with her husband, Henri (Paul), one of three brothers all working for the SOE, who had arrived in France six months before. She was due to be his courier for the PLANE circuit that he had set up around Clermont-Ferrand but things were about to change. She had been in the unoccupied zone for just a week when the Germans moved south and targeted Lyons where a number of SOE agents were known to be operating. Her role now changed to one of distributing anti-Nazi propaganda leaflets. However, news that Henri's younger brother, Pierre (Gregoire), a radio operator for the nearby SPRUCE circuit, had been captured led to further arrests within PLANE and so the decision was made to wind up its operations. While Henri fled across the Pyrenees, Mary-Thérèse, too old and not well enough to make the same journey during the winter, made her way to Paris instead and was later picked up by a Hudson and returned to England.

After landing near Cassis, Odette Sansom, operating as Odette Meyer and with the codename 'Lise', was to travel north to Auxerre in the occupied zone to establish a safe house for other agents passing through the region. Young, attractive and ebullient, Odette was everything the SOE was always on the lookout for. Although she had endured hardship in her early life in France, including the loss of her father during the First World War and temporary blindness at the age of eight, she had been privately educated at a convent in Amiens. She later married an Englishman and settled in London during the 1930s with the couple's three daughters. After the outbreak of war, her husband joined the army while Odette and her children moved to the safety of rural Somerset.

Although Odette had become an English wife, her heart remained French and after France fell she yearned to do something more active than to just look after her children. She became aware of the SOE after responding to a BBC appeal asking listeners for postcards and photographs of towns and villages along the northern coastline of France. She sent off some photographs from her time in Boulogne and a short letter explaining her background but, inadvertently, she addressed her letter to the War Office rather than the Admiralty. It was a minor administrative error that was to change the course of her war. Her details were passed to the SOE and Odette was invited to attend an interview with Captain Selwyn Jepson, the novelist and now a recruiting officer for F Section. It took no time for Jepson to establish that Odette knew France very well and had an obvious determination and desire to succeed, but there was concern about her suitability to be an agent, given that she was a mother of three. But the fact was that Odette was far too good to let go and, having left her children in the care of a convent school, she joined the SOE. Her training had gone well but an accident during her parachute course had resulted in serious concussion and so she was unable to parachute into France and had been dropped off from the sea instead.

Having stopped at Cannes on her way north, Odette's plans suddenly changed when she met Peter Churchill. Churchill had returned to France to set up SPINDLE in the foothills of the French Alps to replace the work of URCHIN after the betrayal and arrest of Francis Basin, and to support Girard's CARTE network along the Côte d'Azur.

From the outset there was an affinity between Odette and Churchill.[6] He had plenty that needed doing and since she would have to spend a few days in Cannes waiting for more papers to proceed to the occupied zone, she agreed to go to Marseilles for him to carry out an additional task. By the time she returned, Churchill had already arranged with London for her to become his courier. But within days of her returning to Cannes, the Anglo-American landings in French North Africa, called Operation TORCH, led to the Germans moving into the previously unoccupied zone, and the scuttling of what remained of the Vichy French forces ended any semblance of independence in southern France.

The arrival of the Germans in the hitherto unoccupied Vichy south led to mass arrests of resistance leaders, including members of CARTE, although Girard had a lucky escape. All of a sudden, Lyons, Marseilles, Cannes and Nice had become very dangerous places in which to operate but Odette still continued her tasks. She had warmed to Churchill and his radio operator, Adolphe Rabinovitch (Arnaud), and part of her work included finding safe places for him to transmit.

Rabinovitch was an Egyptian Jew in his mid-twenties, a former boxing champion and a giant of a man. He had studied in Paris before settling in the United States before the war, and had first volunteered for the Foreign

---

6. Starns, *Odette*, p.56.

Legion before joining the SOE. He had initially joined CARTE as a stray but was seen by some members of the circuit to be a violent and difficult man with whom to work. But Peter Churchill had been so impressed with him that he sent a signal to London requesting to keep the reliable and dependable Rabinovitch, and his request had been granted.[7]

The relationship between Churchill and Girard remained strained and so they were recalled to London to sort out their differences. But after Odette and one of Girard's men had failed to find a suitable landing ground for Churchill and Girard to be picked up, they simply fell out even more; Girard had accused Odette of being incompetent while Churchill chivalrously defended her.

Girard then refused to go to London. As he put it, he could not trust Churchill to make proper arrangements.[8] There were further problems, too, within CARTE. Girard and his radio operator, Newman, clearly did not get on. Girard seemingly failed to appreciate the difficulty and danger under which his pianist operated and this led to Newman returning to London. There were also quarrels between Girard and his deputy, Henri Frager, about how CARTE should best operate given the arrival of enemy troops in the region. If that was not enough, there was a disastrous breach in security after Girard had offered to help Francis Suttill in Paris. Girard had agreed to send Suttill a list of 200 names from his extensive index of supporters but his courier, André Marsac (End), had fallen asleep during the long train journey from Marseilles. Marsac awoke to find that the briefcase he had been carrying, containing the list of unencrypted names, had been stolen. The briefcase was now in the hands of the *Abwehr* and so the downfall of CARTE was only a matter of time.

Meanwhile, in Lyons, Virginia Hall beat a hasty retreat as the Germans moved in. She was already known to the Gestapo as 'The Limping Lady' and was on their most wanted list. They were soon hot on her heels but she managed to successfully cross the Pyrenees on foot in just a couple of days, a hard enough journey for anyone to endure during the depths of winter. Although she was arrested on the border of neutral Spain and briefly

---

7. Cookridge, op. cit., p.166.
8. Ibid.

imprisoned, Virginia Hall was extricated by the American Consul and was back in London by the turn of the year.[9]

It was no longer possible for ordinary citizens in the former unoccupied zone of southern France to delude themselves into thinking the war was not their direct concern. With so many enemy troops around, it was difficult to conduct any great acts of sabotage with the exception, perhaps, of on the railways, where trains were frequently derailed, and the occasional assassination of senior German officers.

The SOE now decided to boost its presence in France by sending three of its best organizers into the field, all of whom dropped to the south-west of Paris during the November moon. One was Gustave Biéler (Guy), a 28-year-old French-Canadian and a giant of a man who would later be described by Buckmaster as the best student SOE had. Unfortunately for Biéler he landed on rocky ground and severely injured his spine, resulting in him being bedridden for several weeks. But he refused to be evacuated back to England and was taken to Paris where he was looked after by members of another circuit until he was fit to carry on, after which he then set about creating the MUSICIAN circuit in eastern Picardy.

Another organizer inserted into France with Biéler that night was Michael Trotobas who jumped with his radio operator, Arthur Staggs. Trotobas was returning to France for his second mission and on his way to set up FARMER, a sabotage network based in Lille. He had been arrested in 1941 but escaped from Mauzac camp in July 1942 and made his way to London by crossing the Pyrenees. To send a previously arrested man back into France was risky but to send one into Lille more so. It was a tough industrial city in northern France with strong communist links. The resistance groups were mainly controlled by left-wing leaders and, being an area of vital industrial importance to the German war effort, it was an area where Nazi policy towards such groups and their activities was ruthlessly oppressive. The Gestapo was everywhere but the SOE needed a strong man in the area and so Buckmaster had selected Trotobas.

The third organizer to drop into France that month was France Antelme (Renaud), a Mauritian businessman in his early forties on his second mission,

---

9. Escott, op. cit., p.37.

having earlier served in Madagascar. He was dropped near Poitiers on the night after Biéler, Trotobas and Staggs to contact French officials to discuss finance and plans for the protection of supply lines once an Allied landing in Europe had taken place.

Buckmaster was also keen to insert more F Section women into France and so the fourth and final agent of the second female course went into the field. This was Jacqueline Nearne, one of two sisters to work for the SOE, who was dropped blind in the Auvergne on the night of 25 January 1943.

Jacqueline was dropped with her circuit organizer, 29-year-old Maurice Southgate (Hector), to form STATIONER in the Limousin region of central France. Southgate had been born in Paris to English parents and spent his childhood in France. As an RAF officer he had been lucky to escape France while serving with the British Expeditionary Force and then had a further escape when the ship he had been evacuated on, the HMT *Lancastria*, was sunk. Once back in England he was posted to the Air Ministry where his knowledge of the French language brought him to the attention of the SOE.

Southgate and Jacqueline quickly made their way to Clermont-Ferrand and started work almost immediately. Using her own name of Jacqueline as her codename, which, at times, caused confusion, particularly because Yvonne Rudellat was also known by the same name, she had taken on the identity of Josette Norville, a young employee of a chemical company. This meant Jacqueline could move around with relative freedom, which was helped by the fact that her rather small stature and darkish appearance, combined with her shy and sensitive nature, enabled her to easily blend into the background.

With such a large area to cover, and because she was required to work closely with surrounding networks, Jacqueline was constantly on the move with her travels taking her as far as Paris and Toulouse. She and Southgate were quick to establish contacts, from which they were able to establish small and active groups around Vierzon, Châteauroux, Limoges and Tarbes near the foothills of the Pyrenees.

Much of her time was spent liaising with the HEADMASTER circuit run by a young man of Irish descent, Brian Rafferty (Dominique), who had been operating in the Auvergne for several months. The circuit had been set up by Sydney Hudson (Albin) in the autumn of 1942 with his radio operator, George Jones (Isidore), to cover the area to the west of Lyons. But the arrest of Hudson soon after, and a serious injury to Jones, had left only Rafferty to keep the circuit alive.

Being a highland district with mountains, gorges, heavily-wooded slopes and jagged rock formations, much of which was inaccessible for much of the year, the Auvergne was a perfect area in which to conduct guerilla warfare. It was HEADMASTER that carried out one of the biggest sabotage actions of the war by destroying much of the Michelin factory at Clermont-Ferrand. Explosive charges were successfully laid in key areas of the factory and caused a huge fire resulting in the loss of 300 tons of tyres and most of the plant machinery.

George Jones made a sufficient recovery to continue with his mission but he and Rafferty were arrested soon after meeting at a café on the outskirts of Clermont-Ferrand. They had met to organize the escape of a key member of the resistance held in a nearby prison but their conversation had been overheard by a Nazi informer and they were both later arrested. Jones, somehow, managed to escape but Rafferty was taken to Dijon prison and brutally tortured during the months that followed, although the brave Irishman gave nothing away before he was eventually shot at Flossenbürg just days before the end of the war.[10]

Meanwhile, in the central and eastern part of France, PLANE had already been wound up and GREENHEART's short existence had ended with the arrests of the Newton Twins. However, SPRUCE had just about survived after its leader, Robert Boiteux, managed to move its operations out of Lyons into the hills to become a country circuit instead of a city-based one. From their new location, his men were able to sabotage canals and railways in support of nearby PIMENTO, a circuit led by the youngest SOE agent ever sent into the field, 20-year-old Tony Brooks (Alphonse).

While some thought him too young for clandestine operations in the field, Brooks's excellent performance during training had silenced his doubters. After parachuting into the Garonne during July 1942, he had set about establishing a circuit of local saboteurs to disrupt rail traffic heading from Marseilles to Lyons and Toulouse. Posing as a garage worker, Brooks was

10. Grehan & Mace, op. cit., p.146.

able to move around relatively freely under the cover of collecting vehicle parts. Although he had no direct radio link with London, he successfully set up a courier line using trusted railway staff to deliver messages to a communications point in Geneva. With his excellent grasp of the French language, a great knowledge of trade union practices and his extraordinary powers of persuasion for a man so young, Brooks had already built a framework for success but it was after the Allied landings in French North Africa that his circuit had come into prominence.[11]

Amongst his trusted members were André Moch, the son of a socialist minister, Roger Morandat and two police inspectors, Jean-Paul Dorval and Raymond Bizot. Brooks had also taken on Marcus Bloom, who had arrived by the November felucca. But Brooks was worried about Bloom. Not only did his Anglo-Saxon Jewish appearance and imperfect French put him at risk, he also had a rather lax approach to security. Brooks had done so much to protect his own identity, and that of his circuit, and so the last thing he wanted now was for the circuit to be compromised by a man who looked, sounded and even acted English. As Bloom had established contact with another young SOE agent and former training colleague, 21-year-old Maurice Pertschuk (Eugène), the leader of the PRUNUS circuit in Toulouse, Brooks willingly agreed to let Bloom work for Pertschuk instead, although he would still act as a radio outlet for PIMENTO as well.

Now with a radio operator of its own, PRUNUS received a number of air drops. Pertschuk was able to put together a plan to blow up a factory in Toulouse but he would later be betrayed and arrested at the Château d'Equerre near Fonsorbes in the Haute-Garonne where he was staying. Bloom was also at the château at the time. He was arrested, then managed to escape with another member of the group, but was captured again soon after.[12] Within a week the circuit had collapsed. Pertschuk ended up at Buchenwald and was executed just days before the end of the war, six months after Bloom had died at Mauthausen.

There had been many setbacks during the course of 1942. It was, at best, a year of development for F Section. A shortage of air transport had

---

11. Obituary – Anthony Brooks DSO MC – *The Times*, 22 May 2007.
12. Grehan & Mace, op. cit., p.35.

restricted the number of agents parachuted into the field to around fifty, of which about a third were radio operators, although a number more had been inserted by the more cumbersome sea route via Gibraltar to the south of France. But of those who had been sent into the field, several had been caught. Furthermore, the supply of arms and explosives to the resistance groups was, in reality, almost non-existent.

Despite all this, the SOE knew that it had to press on. While still appearing somewhat amateurish at times, the work of F Section and, for that matter, RF, which had in fact outscored F in the number of sabotage activities carried out during the year, looked more promising for the following year. Several circuits had now formed across France, albeit of varying sizes and capabilities, and the introduction of women into the field had proved to those who had earlier doubted their ability that they would have a key role to play in the months ahead.

Chapter 9

Colonel Henri

By early 1943 the CARTE network had descended into chaos, although things could have been far worse. Fortunately for many of its members the Germans had not acted immediately on André Marsac's carelessness a few weeks earlier when he had lost the brief case containing the list of some 200 names. For whatever reason, the Germans chose to wait until the turn of the year before they made their move; it was a delay that allowed some to split from the circuit.

The arrival of Axis troops along the Riviera meant that using small boats to insert agents into the field was more of a risk than previously. Furthermore, the clashes between CARTE and SPINDLE had meant that between them the two circuits had managed just one successful arms supply drop and had seemingly managed to mismanage several tons of arms landed by felucca. Besides, Churchill's SPINDLE was fast becoming too large and cumbersome. Some of its members had become over exuberant to the point of recklessness while security within the many resistance groups was often poor, with some already infiltrated by the Germans and making it difficult for Churchill to fully supervise and control.[1]

If co-ordinated action between SPINDLE and CARTE was to be successful, assuming the latter could survive, it would be more likely through Frager than Girard and so Churchill again made arrangements for both Girard and Frager to travel to London to resolve their differences. Girard, in particular, was still reluctant to go to England and so, in the best interests of the SOE, Churchill sided with Frager, but for one reason or another their return to London kept getting delayed.

The Germans were now raiding resistance hiding places near Cannes and so Churchill decided to take Rabinovitch and Odette to a safer area. He

---

1. Starns, op. cit., pp.56–8.

relocated SPINDLE to the village of Saint-Jorioz in the French Alps, close to the Swiss and Italian borders. Once there, the team split. Churchill and Odette remained at the village and moved into the Hôtel de la Poste with new identities of Monsieur and Madame Pierre Chambrun, while Rabinovitch became Guy Dieudonne and set up his radio post in a tiny village above Faverges, called les Tissots, about fifteen kilometres away.

On the advice of Frager, André Marsac and his wife had also relocated to Saint-Jorioz to act as Churchill's liaison. The Marsacs moved into a small house not far from the hotel and for a while all seemed well. Churchill and Odette settled in by posing as a married couple enjoying a holiday in the mountains, and the owner of the hotel, Jean Cottet, and his wife, Simone, both charming people, proved reliable and trustworthy.[2]

From their new locations the group organized parachute drops and the reception of more agents along the Mediterranean coast. There was no sign whatsoever of what was to unfold over the coming weeks. Indeed, Saint-Jorioz might have become one of the SOE's greatest successes but things were about to take a dramatic turn and it would end up becoming a tragic disaster, brought about because of an unfortunate mistake by one good man and the shrewdness of another.

Having established his group in the Alps, Churchill felt he could finally fly back to London while Odette and Rabinovitch stayed behind. Girard had already been picked up by a Hudson on the night of 20/21 February, and Churchill and Frager were waiting to be notified of a date for their pick-up. They finally received word a few weeks later and so made their way to a field near Estrées-Saint-Denis, near Compiègne, during the evening of 23 March.

It was the last Lysander operation of the March moon and a relatively short trip for the pilot, Squadron Leader Hugh Verity. He was carrying two passengers for the outbound flight from England. One was George Duboudin who was returning to France for his second mission. Duboudin had spent the past five months back in England but his mission would end up with him arrested and then worked into an early grave at Buchenwald after succumbing to malnutrition and pleurisy. The second passenger

2. Cookridge, op. cit., p.170.

was a former school teacher originally from London, Francis Cammaerts (Roger), who was on his way to the Côte d'Azur. Verity's instant thought as Cammaerts had climbed aboard was that he might struggle in France. He was twenty-six-years old, very tall and had a small moustache. He looked more like the English schoolteacher he had once been than a Frenchman that he was supposedly about to become.[3] Cammaerts was, in fact, a former pacifist, stemming from his days at Cambridge where he read English and history.[4] At the outbreak of war his registration as a conscientious objector had been granted, conditional upon him taking up agricultural work, but it had been the death of his younger brother, Pieter, an observer with the RAF, which had changed his views and so, as a fluent French speaker, he had offered his services to the SOE. Cammaerts was going into France to set up DONKEYMAN at Annecy in the upper Rhône valley but he would not be the only former conscientious objector to go into France with the SOE. A former teaching colleague and close friend of his, Harry Rée ('Henri' but also known as 'César'), would soon follow him into France to join the ACROBAT circuit around Montbéliard.

Churchill and Frager arrived at the field in good time. Just before 2.00am they spotted an aircraft approaching the field. Churchill switched on his torch and flashed the coded signal. Verity acknowledged as he passed overhead. As Verity throttled back and circled overhead, the lamps were lit on the ground to mark the line of approach. In a matter of minutes, Verity expertly touched down and brought the Lysander to a halt just yards from where his two new passengers were waiting.

With the Lysander having turned back into wind, Cammaerts and Duboudin quickly climbed out of the aircraft and made their way to a car waiting to take them away while Churchill and Frager climbed up into the rear cockpit. With a thumbs-up from his two new passengers, Verity opened the throttle. The aircraft surged forward and in less than a hundred yards was airborne once more. No one had seen the Lysander come and go. It had been a textbook drop-off and pick-up.

---

3. Verity, op. cit., p.73.
4. Obituary – Francis Cammaerts DSO – *The Times*, 6 July 2006.

Having made their way to London, Frager and Churchill were due to join up with Girard but he refused to meet with them. From that moment on the SOE distanced itself from André Girard, who could not agree with Baker Street's plans, and the Frenchman disappeared from the scene and eventually went into self-imposed exile in the United States.

With Girard out of the picture, Frager was instructed to return to France to pick up the remnants of CARTE, but he was warned to keep clear of a member of the *Abwehr* known to the SOE as Colonel Henri. Unfortunately, though, the warning about Colonel Henri had not reached those in France in time as two men, André Marsac and his associate, Roger Bardet, had already been arrested.

Colonel Henri was, in fact, none other than Hugo Bleicher who had presented himself to the CARTE circuit as a German intelligence officer wanting to defect to the Allies. What appears to have happened was that during one of his many journeys from the mountains, André Marsac had been introduced by a trusted friend to a member of a resistance group called Marette. What the trusted friend did not know, however, was that Marette had earlier been arrested by the Germans and, having been set free under the threat of execution, had turned into a Nazi informer. Marette had then informed on the man she only knew by his codename of 'End', and so a trap was set for the unfortunate Marsac with the intention of also turning him.

The case was given to Bleicher and the trap involved a small and pretty young Irishwoman with auburn hair called Helen James, the mistress of one of the *Abwehr*'s informers. Through Marette, Helen James was introduced to Marsac. She informed Marsac that she knew a number of German officers who seemed to trust her because of her Irish nationality but, in reality, she was an ardent anti-Nazi and that she was prepared to offer him further information. Having then arranged to meet in Paris, at a café in the Champs-Elysées, Marsac was arrested when he arrived; Bleicher was there with two plainclothes *Feldpolizei*.

Marsac was taken to Fresnes prison and for the next few days was questioned by Bleicher. But the Frenchman remained silent. Bleicher decided to try something else and drew on the previous affair of the 'Cat'. Bleicher told Marsac that he was looking to escape to England, stating that he believed the war would soon be lost for Germany, and suggested that he and Marsac should go to England together.

Such were Bleicher's powers of persuasion that he slowly won over Marsac's confidence. Bleicher suggested that Marsac should arrange an aircraft to pick them up so that the two of them could travel to England together. But before Bleicher was able to release Marsac, he told the Frenchman he needed some names and addresses of agents and the location of the group's transmitter so that he could convince his own superiors that Marsac had indeed turned and could, therefore, be released.

Marsac was not that stupid and so for the next few days the situation became stalemate. But after a few days of pondering over what to do, Marsac decided to give Bleicher the address of his wife. He also gave the German two letters addressed to friends explaining the plan, suggesting that Bleicher should go and speak to them. If they all thought it to be a good idea then word could be sent to London.

Now posing as Colonel Henri, and with the cover story of wishing to defect to England, Bleicher met with Marsac's wife, Michelle, in Saint-Jorioz. Being in possession of the two letters, Bleicher soon convinced her that he was a trusted friend of her husband. He then travelled to Annecy and met with Marsac's associate, Bardet, in the railway buffet, who was equally taken in by him and his story.

There are variations in accounts as to how Odette and Bleicher first met. In E. H. Cookridge's book *Inside SOE*, the suggestion is that it was during the meeting between Bleicher and Bardet in Annecy that Odette walked into the buffet having learned of the mystery visitor from Michelle Marsac.[5] However, in a more recent publication titled *Odette* by Penny Starns (published more than forty years after Cookridge's work and taken from Odette's personal file), the author gives a more up to date account.

Odette had first noticed a bespectacled man observing her while she was out and about one day. Her anxiety levels began to rise when the same man was present on the bus back to the hotel. On reaching the hotel, Bleicher, posing as Colonel Henri, approached Odette in the hotel reception, claiming he had important news for her that might be to her advantage. As they sat

---

5. Cookridge, op. cit., p.177.

and had coffee, Bleicher explained he was 'Colonel Henri', a German officer with the *Abwehr* who had become disillusioned with the war and wanted to go to London. He also informed her that Marsac had been arrested that morning and was now languishing in Fresnes prison. He produced Marsac's letter and tried to convince her to go to Paris with him.

Odette declined the invitation. She was not in the least convinced by the story she had just heard but decided to send a courier to Paris with a food parcel for Marsac to establish that he was well. She needed to know he was safe before deciding what to do next, although she did agree to contact London but made it clear to the German that a flight to London would not be possible before 18 April.[6] Bleicher then left the hotel but Odette was suspicious of the man calling himself Colonel Henri, although others had clearly been taken in. She then briefed Rabinovitch, who informed London.

The following day, 'Colonel Henri' and Bardet visited Marsac in his cell. Marsac was now convinced that the German's intent was genuine and instructed Bardet to contact Rabinovitch and arrange a pick-up as soon as possible. Bardet was reluctant to do so but after a few days in Paris he returned to Saint-Jorioz from where he kept Bleicher informed of the developing communications with London.

Back in London, Buckmaster had been kept informed of the goings on in France through the trusted Rabinovitch. Details of Colonel Henri and Bardet's visits to Marsac's prison cell had aroused suspicion. Buckmaster chatted things over with Churchill and Frager, both soon to return to France. At that point they had not connected the fictitious Colonel Henri with their old adversary Hugo Bleicher, but they still decided to send a signal to Saint-Jorioz warning that Colonel Henri was dangerous and to cut any ties with him, and also instructing Odette to wind up the operation in Saint-Jorioz.[7]

Odette went straight to Annecy and warned others to depart. Rabinovitch and Cammaerts both left for new addresses. Odette had done what had been expected of her but, with hindsight, she should also have left at that point. Her decision to remain at Saint-Jorioz now placed her and the hotel owners at risk. But Odette firmly believed that she and the Cottets were safe, for

---

6. Starns, op. cit., pp.79–80.
7. Ibid., p.80.

a few days at least, because she had told the so-called 'Colonel Henri' that no flight to London would be possible before 18 April. Odette, therefore, believed that he would not come searching for her until at least then.

Bleicher, meanwhile, was instructed by his own chain of command to stop playing his game. He was told to immediately arrest Bardet and Marsac's wife, who were still in Paris at the time, and before word could get out of their arrest he was to travel to Saint-Jorioz and arrest anyone else connected with the network that he could find.

On the night of 15/16 April, Churchill boarded an aircraft to be dropped back into France, the same night that Henri Frager landed by Lysander near Tours to continue his work with the remnants of CARTE and to work with Cammaerts and DONKEYMAN. Frager was met by 33-year-old Henri Déricourt (Gilbert), the SOE's air movements officer in France, sent into the field in early 1943 to organize secret landing sites as F Section increased its number of Lysander operations.

Meanwhile, Churchill's drop zone was a rather bleak spot under deep snow on the slopes of a mountain peak high above Saint-Jorioz. It took some time for the reception committee – Odette, Rabinovitch, the Cottets and some local maquisards – to cover the ten kilometres to the DZ and to then mark it out for the drop.

When the aircraft could be heard approaching the drop, the bonfires were lit. Those on the ground could then see a single parachute against the moonlit sky. The drop went as planned. Churchill was then brought up to date on the man calling himself Colonel Henri but, as he was not expected to return to Saint-Jorioz for at least a few days, they all went back to the hotel.

Back at the Hôtel de la Poste they all enjoyed a drink together. With the possibility that Colonel Henri could soon return to Saint-Jorioz, Churchill decided it was no longer safe to hang around and decided they should all soon leave. They should have left at that point. Later that night, Bleicher and the Italian military police arrived at the hotel. As Jean Cottet met the unwelcome visitors in the hallway, he did everything he could to delay the inevitable but his wife was instructed to go to Odette's room to tell her she was wanted downstairs.

While Odette went down to the hotel reception, Churchill remained upstairs as no one was meant to know that he was back in France. Odette was then confronted by the man she recognized as Colonel Henri and a man from the Gestapo. They told her they knew Churchill had returned and was at the hotel, and so asked her to take them to him. Although Odette thought about shouting a warning, she did not want Churchill to be gunned down trying to make his escape, and so she reluctantly agreed. In her testimony later, it is clear that Odette suspected a courier, a man called Chaillan, of betraying her and Churchill.[8]

For Churchill and Odette the war was over. All Odette could do now was to protect the identity and whereabouts of Rabinovitch and others. Fortunately for Rabinovitch, though, he was several kilometres away at the time and avoided capture. However, the destruction of SPINDLE at Saint-Jorioz would have disastrous repercussions. Roger Bardet, whom Bleicher had used as a pawn in his overall game, turned traitor and would eventually lead the *Abwehr* to other SOE circuits and, ultimately, to Henri Frager. In Bleicher's own words many years later, Roger Bardet turned out to be the best assistant he ever had during his time in France.

Bleicher had hoped to take Churchill and Odette straight to Paris but they had been captured in an area under Italian authority, and so they were initially held by the Italians at an army barracks at Annecy. The couple passed themselves off as being married and with Churchill claiming to be a nephew of Britain's prime minister. They hoped that if their story was believed they would be kept alive and were less likely to be shot as spies, and could be used for bargaining at a later date.

At first the couple were treated with a mix of hostility and some respect. Their captors simply did not know whether to believe them or not but, three weeks after they had first been captured, Churchill and Odette were taken to the notorious Fresnes prison in Paris where they were put into solitary confinement.

Churchill remained there for the next ten months before he was taken to Berlin; it appeared that his cover story of being related to Britain's prime minister had been believed. In February 1944 he was told that he was to be exchanged, but no exchange took place. Shortly after arriving in Berlin he was transferred to Sachsenhausen concentration camp at Oranienburg

---

8. Ibid, pp.81–2.

in Germany where he was held in Sonderlager A, an area designated for special prisoners outside the main compound, and for the next ten months he was held in solitary confinement. As the Allies advanced towards Berlin, he was moved again to camps at Flossenbürg and then Dachau where he joined other high profile prisoners, known as *Prominenten*. The plan was to evacuate these special prisoners into Austria but after reaching Innsbruck they came under Wehrmacht jurisdiction, rather than the SS, which probably saved them from execution. On 4 May 1945 the group was liberated by the Americans and Churchill returned to London having testified against his former captors.

Odette, meanwhile, was taken to the Avenue Foch and subjected to lengthy periods of excruciating torture. But Odette remained silent. She then returned to Fresnes but every now and again she would be taken back for more questioning and the inevitable torture. In June she was condemned to death, although no date was ever set for her execution. The combined effects of torture and deprivation soon started to take a toll on her health. She could barely walk, was suffering from internal pains and had developed swellings on her body. Although she was denied any medical help, she was moved to a communal cell. In May 1944, after more than a year of imprisonment, she was taken to Karlsruhe prison in Germany with other women from F Section who had been captured while working with various networks across France.[9] They were then deported to various concentration camps to await their fate. Odette last saw her colleagues in early July when the others all disappeared. She would never see them again; they would all be dead in just a matter of weeks. Odette was instead moved to Frankfurt and then Halle before, on 26 July, she arrived at her final destination, the concentration camp for women at Ravensbrück in northern Germany, about 100 kilometres to the north of Berlin, and a living hell for its inmates. It had been built in 1939 for 7,000 prisoners but by the end of the war the inmate population had risen to more than 100,000, and it is estimated that some 130,000 women passed through the camp during the war; how many survived is not known but estimations average less than one in five.

---

9. The other women were Yolande Beekman, Andrée Borrel, Madeleine Damerment, Vera Leigh, Sonia Olschanezky, Eliane Plewman and Diana Rowden.

Odette spent her first night on the concrete floor of the shower room and was then taken to an underground bunker in a small cell where she was kept in solitary confinement and in complete darkness. From her cell she could hear the regular procession of women being taken for their beating. Punishment invariably involved between twenty-five and fifty strokes to the body, administered by a whip, stick or buckled leather belt with most women beaten until they fell unconscious or died.[10]

Because Odette was believed to be Mrs Churchill, her life in Ravensbrück changed from one day to the next. Sometimes she was given food and exercise while at other times she was starved and beaten. There seemed to be no particular reason for these variations.[11]

Odette remained at Ravensbrück on the edge of death but as the war entered its last months she was deliberately kept alive. She was even moved from the underground bunker and given a cell upstairs to try and improve her health. The camp commandant, Fritz Suhren, believed she would be useful to him when the time came to surrender. But, sadly, there was still time for others to die at Ravensbrück; three more of her SOE colleagues died in January 1945.[12]

In April 1945, Suhren received orders from Himmler that all prisoners were to be executed with immediate effect; this would ensure no witnesses would survive to testify to the horrors of the camp. Fortunately for Odette, Suhren did not comply fully with the order. By the end of the month everything was in complete disarray. Many of the guards made their escape as an eerie silence fell on the camp. Then, as the Soviet Army made its final assault, Suhren took Odette with him in a car and drove to the American lines. He had hoped the Americans would show more leniency than the Russians and that Odette's connection with Churchill, and her charm, would help save him. He was wrong. Odette immediately denounced him and Suhren was hanged after his trial.

---

10. Imperial War Museum, Oral history interview with Odette Hallowes, 1985 and Starns, op. cit., p.96.
11. Starns, op. cit., p.101.
12. Those to die at Ravensbrück on this occasion were Denise Bloch, Lilian Rolfe and Violette Szabo.

Against all the odds Peter Churchill and Odette Sansom had survived. They would marry in 1947 after the death of her first husband, although they would divorce in 1956, after which she married Geoffrey Hallowes who had also served with SOE.

For his four clandestine missions into France, during which he had operated under the names of Raoul, Michel and Pierre Oliver, Peter Churchill was awarded the Distinguished Service Order. His citation concluded:

> Captain Churchill worked tirelessly and unselfishly over a long period in very trying conditions, showing outstanding courage, leadership and organising ability, which earned him the respect and admiration of all who came in contact with him.

Odette returned to England a national heroine. She was the first woman to be awarded the George Cross and the only one of SOE's three female recipients of the award to survive the war. Her long citation concluded: 'During the period of two years in which she was in enemy hands, she displayed courage, endurance and self-sacrifice of the highest possible order.'

Chapter 10

End of PROSPER

Since his arrival in France Francis Suttill had rapidly grown his PROSPER circuit (also known as PHYSICIAN) and it soon covered a large part of northern France. Its saboteurs had already caused considerable disruption in and around Paris. In one month alone, during early 1943, the group had carried out more than sixty separate acts of sabotage, including attacks on the main railway line between Orleans and Paris, and an attack against a power station at Chaingy near Orleans that resulted in cutting power over a wide area.

Suttill's PROSPER would peak with nearly sixty supporting *réseaux* and groups stretching from Saint-Quentin in the north-east of the country to Angers in the west and as far south as Bourges. Amongst the sub-circuits he set up was BUTLER, led by a left-wing former journalist, Jean Bouguennec, operating as François Garel (Max). Bouguennec had been one of F Section's earliest contacts in the Vichy south. Having made his way to England via Spain, he dropped into France at the end of March 1943 with Marcel Rousset (Leopold) and Marcel Fox (Ernest). He built up two important groups, one based at Château du Loire and the other at Sablé-sur-Sarthe and, having received a number of successful air drops, his groups carried out several attacks on the railway network in the region.

BUTLER overlapped territorially in the Sarthe with SATIRIST, a group run by Octave Simon (Badois), a 29-year-old notable sculptor and former associate of Philippe de Vomécourt, and to its south was PRIVET, centred on Angers in the Maine-et-Loire and run by Edward Wilkinson. After his earlier arrest, Wilkinson had escaped from a prisoner-of-war camp at Chambaran and had then made his way to Angers and set up the circuit with a small group of his friends. Unfortunately for Wilkinson, though, he would be arrested for a second time in June 1943 after walking into a Gestapo trap in Paris. This time there would be no escape and Edward Wilkinson, the man Buckmaster later described as being 'as hard as they come',[1] was executed at Mauthausen in September 1944.

Running parallel with Suttill's circuit was the much smaller BRICKLAYER, led by France Antelme, now back in France for his second mission. There would soon be more circuits overlapping PROSPER to the west and operating in eastern Brittany and the Vendée, including PARSON, one of two Breton circuits centred on Rennes and run by François Vallée (Oscar). Vallée had been joined by his long-term Belgian colleague, 47-year-old Henri Gaillot (Ignace), known in Baker Street as *'grandpere'* because of his age, and a radio operator, George Clement (Edouard). When the time came their task would be to isolate Brittany through sabotage of the rail network, factories, fuel dumps and power stations and within just a few weeks they had set up a number of small groups within the triangle Saint-Brieuc-Rennes-Nantes.[2] They were so successful in recruiting local volunteers that one of their men, André Hué, set up another circuit, HILLBILLY, all on his own. And there was also SACRISTAN, led by Ernest Floege (Alfred), an American in his mid-forties, with its nucleus at Angers, where he had run a large haulage business for the previous twenty years, who was soon joined by a brave young pianist, 23-year-old André Bouchardon (Narcisse).

But while PROSPER had initially been built up in a climate of security, it was rapidly becoming the biggest and most powerful circuit in France. It was already starting to become unwieldy and during April and May 1943 a number of rather puzzling arrests occurred amongst its members. The first were those of the Tambour sisters, Germaine (Annette) and Madeleine. These two middle-aged women had been in the fight against the Nazi occupation from its very early days, initially working closely with the French Resistance and then CARTE but more recently they had given valuable support to PROSPER. Germaine had been amongst Suttill's first connections when he arrived in Paris some six months before and had introduced him to many reliable and trustworthy people. Her arrest had been one of many that had seemingly cascaded from the debacle at Saint-Jorioz.

---

1. Grehan & Mace, op. cit., p.196.
2. Foot, op. cit., pp.223–4.

The arrests of the Tambour sisters had perturbed Suttill. He even went as far as trying to secure their release by offering to bribe a couple of German officers. At that time he was unaware of the circumstances behind Marsac's arrest, or that Roger Bardet had turned double agent, but the fact that his circuit had spread so far and so quickly now meant that too many people knew about it.

It had become all but impossible for Suttill to maintain any form of security and so he was recalled to London to discuss the recent run of arrests. Suttill was picked up from a field at Azay-sur-Cher, near Tours, on the night of 14/15 May by a Lysander organized by Henri Déricourt.

With four agents being taken across to France, the drop involved two Lysanders, known as a Double Lysander, both from 161 Squadron, the second of the Special Duties squadrons to have been formed. For this operation they were flown by Squadron Leader Hugh Verity and Flying Officer Bunny Rymills. Three of the four agents inserted that night were to revive one of Suttill's sub-circuits called INVENTOR. The circuit had been active in late 1942 and responsible for the destruction of a number of goods trains shortly after the German occupation of the Vichy south, but being too far south to be re-supplied by air, it had ceased operations during the winter months. Its organizer, Sidney Jones (Elie), had returned briefly to London on one of the February Hudsons and was now returning to relight the fire. Travelling with him was his radio operator, Marcel Clech, also on his way back into the field after travelling to London the month before, and their courier, Vera Leigh (Simone), a 40-year-old woman of great charm and intelligence. The fourth agent inserted that night was another female, Julienne Aisner (Claire), a resident of Paris who was returning to France having been across the Channel for SOE training. She was to work as an assistant for Henri Déricourt in a small but separate circuit called FARRIER, an organization forming part of an escape line back to England.

Suttill's stay in London was only brief but he conferred with SOE's chiefs and left them in no doubt that he had reasons to believe that his circuit had been infiltrated by the Germans, giving details of the many arrests during April and May. Suttill was concerned he might have a double agent in the camp.

Whether the higher echelons of Baker Street knew of any such double agent operating in France at the time is not known but, having urged his chiefs to send him reinforcements, so that he could shuffle his pack, Suttill returned to France by parachute on the night of 12/13 June.[3]

One of Suttill's key sub-circuits was ADOLPHE in the Sologne where Pierre Culioli and Yvonne Rudellat had turned one of the most beautiful parts of central France into their hunting ground. Several air drops had been made and, from the small towns and communities, the saboteurs could emerge to strike out at factories and important installations. Many of these raids were led by Yvonne, now operating with a sense of freedom after her earlier experience of working with Flower. She would often cycle round the countryside on her bike filled with plastic explosives. One raid was against a power station while another was blowing up a factory at Blois where aircraft parts were being manufactured for the Luftwaffe. She was also responsible for blowing up hundreds of high-tension electricity pylons, many locomotive sheds and she derailed at least a dozen or more German troop trains. During one month alone, the railway lines linking Orleans, Tours and Vierzon were put out of action six times, killing an estimated 200 or more German soldiers.[4]

These losses convinced the Germans to send in a number of SS units to seek out the saboteurs who were described by one SS colonel to be 'the most dangerous and difficult in the whole of France.'[5] From their headquarters at Blois the Germans made every effort to discover the saboteurs and their hides but all that they managed to find out was that the resisters were led by a woman, although they never found out who she was.

Eventually though, Yvonne's luck was to run out; so, too was Culioli's. The build-up to the disaster that was to unfold in the Sologne, and one that would spread far beyond central France, began on the night of 12 June 1943 when a couple of containers dropped from an aircraft caught fire and exploded on impact with the ground. The reception committee, which included Culioli and Yvonne, salvaged what they could before making a

3. Cookridge, op. cit., p.225.
4. Ibid, p.204.
5. Ibid, pp.204–5. (Words of SS Colonel Mersch).

hasty retreat before the Germans could arrive, but the following morning the wrecks of the containers, plus two more intact, were discovered by the farmer.

Aware that there would be repercussions for him and his family if the matter was not reported, the farmer went to the *feldgendarmerie* at Bracieux. The Germans responded in force. After months of being harassed by Culioli's saboteurs, their patience ran out. Within twenty-four hours the area had been reinforced by an estimated 2,000 German troops with dozens of raids mounted in the local towns and villages and many arrests made. Culioli immediately sent a message to Henri Déricourt instructing him to warn London to cancel all planned air drops in the area with immediate effect.

As things would turn out, Déricourt's actions would later come under close scrutiny, which would continue long after the war had ended. Whether he had turned double agent or whether some of the decisions he made in France were merely operating under British orders is unclear, but, for the following week, during what would turn out to be the most crucial week for PROSPER, all air drops from England continued as normal. Culioli had received no acknowledgement from London to his request to cancel all air drops and so all he could do was to prepare as best as he could for the reception of agents about to be dropped into France.

On the night of 15/16 June two agents, Frank Pickersgill (Bertrand) and John Macalister (Valentin), both Canadians, were dropped in the Cher valley north of Valençay to set up a new circuit called ARCHDEACON in the Ardennes. They were first to go to Paris and so, a few days later, on the morning of 21 June, they were travelling in a car with Culioli and Yvonne when it was stopped at the village of Dhuizon at one of many checkpoints in the area.

Unknown to any of them, the Germans were looking for someone arriving from England but how they knew of the parachute drop is not known. Although they successfully passed through the first checkpoint, they were stopped again at a second. This time the two Canadians aroused suspicion and were asked to get out of the vehicle. Two SS soldiers then got into the car and ordered Culioli to drive to the town hall where their papers could be checked while the two Canadians, escorted by two more Germans, were left to follow on foot.

Once at the town hall they were questioned but Yvonne's and Culioli's papers seemed in order and so they were allowed back to their car. While waiting for the two Canadians to come out of the town hall, an SS officer suddenly appeared and asked them to get out of the car once again. At that point Culioli knew they were in trouble and sped off. The car was fired upon but neither of them was hit; however they were soon pursued by three cars, all far faster than the little old car they were travelling in. Having closed to within range the Germans fired on them again. This time bullets ripped into the car. Yvonne was hit twice. As she slumped across Culioli he could see that she had been hit in the head. One of the chasing cars then overtook and forced him to drive into a wall. Culioli then tried to make a break but was soon overpowered.

The car, containing new radio crystals and all the information carried by the Canadians, as well as information about their own circuit, was impounded. And so began a series of arrests. Culioli and Yvonne were taken to Blois where they were separated. He was taken first to a military hospital and then to the Avenue Foch for interrogation, and would later end up at Buchenwald but somehow survived the war. Yvonne Rudellat, meanwhile, was taken to hospital where she lay gravely wounded for several weeks, a bullet lodged in her skull. She was later taken to Fresnes prison and then to Ravensbrück before she finally ended up at the Bergen-Belsen concentration camp, where conditions were worst of all with typhus and dysentery rife. By the time the war was entering its final phase, Yvonne had become dangerously ill. Although she was still clinging to life when the camp was finally liberated during the last weeks of the war, Yvonne Rudellat died just days before the end of hostilities.

Meanwhile in Paris, Suttill, Andrée Borrel and Gilbert Norman had been waiting for the arrival of Pickersgill and Macalister. When they failed to show, Suttill became increasingly concerned. Unaware of what had happened down in the Sologne, he decided to take no chances and quickly moved out of his accommodation. Andrée and Norman changed addresses as well but they were both arrested at Norman's new safe house a couple of nights later, just as they were preparing a new radio transmission.

This unfortunate episode triggered a series of hundreds of arrests over the next few weeks, including the prize catch of Francis Suttill the following day; he was arrested after returning to his new address, a hotel in Paris, only to find a number of men waiting for him in his room. Just how Suttill's whereabouts had become known to the Germans remains a mystery. He had only been at the hotel for one day and had never used the address before but he must have been betrayed.

In what seemed like no time at all, the once mighty PROSPER was dead. It had been destroyed in a matter of just a few weeks, and very few of its leaders would survive. Francis Suttill was eventually taken to the concentration camp at Sachsenhausen near Berlin where he was held in solitary confinement until he was hanged just weeks before the end of the war. Gilbert Norman ended up at Mauthausen where he was shot. Andrée Borrel spent time in Fresnes prison and was interrogated at the Avenue Foch. A year later she was transferred to the women's prison at Karlsruhe and then to the Natzweiler concentration camp where, on the night of 6 July 1944, she was injected with phenol. And so ended the life of a very brave young woman, aged just twenty-four at the time of her death.

Chapter 11

The Disastrous Double Lysander

With Peter Churchill in the hands of the Germans, it was left to Francis Cammaerts, the man known only as Roger, to reorganize what remained of the debilitated resistance groups on the Côte d'Azur. Cammaerts had been quick to escape the debacle at Saint-Jorioz and, to a certain extent, had seen things coming. He had liked, and trusted, Odette and Rabinovitch but had always distrusted Bardet.

After leaving the mountains, Cammaerts moved to Cannes where he kept a low profile for the next month at an address provided to him by Rabinovitch. Such was his concern with safety and security, this would be the only time Cammaerts would spend more than a handful of days at the same address.

Cammaerts had only been in France for a short time and so it would take him a while to build up his confidence and trust in others but he soon set about creating his own circuit, known as JOCKEY, with the help of a handful of men. The most notable was his radio operator, Auguste Floiras (Albert), who would become one of the most successful pianists. He made hundreds of transmissions during his time in the field as JOCKEY stretched across a vast area of south-eastern France, from the Isère and Ardèche to the Maritime Alps.

In June 1943 Buckmaster sent Cammaerts two assistants: Pierre Raynaud (Alain), a sabotage instructor, and a courier, Cecily Lefort (Alice). Cecily was inserted by a Lysander arranged by Henri Déricourt to the north-east of Angers on the night of 16/17 June. She arrived with three others: Charles Skepper (Bernard) and two other women, Diana Rowden (Paulette) and Noor Inayat Khan (Madeleine).

With four agents to be dropped off it required a Double Lysander, flown by Flying Officers Bunny Rymills and Jimmy McCairns. It was a particularly fine moonlit night in the Loire and the flight outbound passed without incident. Rymills had with him Cecily and Noor while McCairns carried Diana and Skepper.

Having dropped off the four agents, Rymills and McCairns picked up five more agents for the return trip to England, including Jack Agazarian, one of Suttill's radio operators who had also been working with other circuits because of the shortage of pianists at the time. The Gestapo had known that Agazarian had been transmitting and were constantly on his tail. On several occasions he had narrowly escaped arrest and so it was now time for him to leave France. Travelling with him was his wife, Francine (Marguerite). She had been in France for three months, having been sent in by Lysander to work as her husband's courier, but she had spent most of her time working directly for Suttill. The timing of their departure from France was to prove a stroke of fortune as the break-up of PROSPER, and the mass arrests that followed, were literally just hours away.

Having been dropped off, the four new arrivals went their own way. Cecily was to join up with Cammaerts while Skepper, a former antiques dealer in his late thirties, went off to organize a new circuit called MONK at Marseilles. Meanwhile, Diana headed towards Dijon as she was destined for the Franche Comté, a beautiful and sub-alpine region of eastern France, to be courier for the ACROBAT circuit led by John Starr (Bob), and Noor headed off to the railway station at Angers. She was to catch a train to Paris, the most dangerous place of all, to provide much needed radio support for one of Francis Suttill's small sub-circuits in the Chartres-Étampes district to the south of the city, run by Emile-Henri Garry and known as both CINEMA and PHONO because of Garry's apparent likeness to the American film actor Gary Cooper.

Sadly, all four new arrivals were heading for disaster. Of the four, Charles Skepper lasted longest in the field. He did succeed in setting up MONK with his young radio operator, Arthur Steele (Laurent), a London music student in his early twenties, and a young and attractive female agent, 25-year-old Eliane Plewman (Gaby), who parachuted into the Jura during August. They recovered those remnants of CARTE considered worth salvaging and set up a small but effective circuit centred on Marseilles, an area heavily reinforced by German troops given the expected landing by Allied troops along the southern coastline of France. For the next few months MONK became one of the main centres of clandestine traffic operating between Algiers and occupied France and carried out numerous acts of sabotage. During one month alone, the small circuit succeeded in disrupting a major rail route to Toulon, putting it out of action for several days, and destroying up to thirty trains. But because of its location and importance, the Gestapo put every effort into destroying the circuit and Skepper's luck would eventually run out in March 1944 when his circuit was infiltrated by a collaborator and betrayed to the Gestapo. Skepper was arrested at his flat and died at the hands of the Germans the following month.

As for the three women dropped on the night of the Double Lysander of 16/17 June 1943, Cecily Lefort assumed the identity of Cécile Legrand and made her way to Montélimar to meet up with Cammaerts as planned. Aged forty-three, she was on her first mission and reminded some more of a vicar's wife than an SOE agent. Like other couriers, Cecily would have to do much travelling but JOCKEY covered a vast area across south-eastern France and she was also required to travel up to Lyons and as far west as Toulouse. She seemed to spend her whole life on trains or cycling between the different members of the circuit.

Being one of the farthest circuits from the RAF airfields in southern England, JOCKEY was at the end of a long supply chain and, therefore, did not always get the attention needed when it came to arms and supplies dropped from the air. But that changed after the Allies landed in Sicily and began the long advance northwards through Italy. The work for JOCKEY increased as preparations were made to receive Allied forces. Arms and ammunition were dropped and so began a new and intense period of sabotage against the enemy. The targets were power stations and other industrial targets, as well as the railways. Raynaud was at the heart of everything that was destroyed and Cecily was only too glad to help as much as she could.

This increase in sabotage activity resulted in the Germans raising their anti-terrorist presence in the south-east of France in a desperate attempt to find the perpetrators. Then, in September 1943, despite the warnings and the risks of carrying on what they were doing, Raynaud and Cecily were surrounded while calling at a house of one of the local resistance leaders. The Germans had been tipped off. Raynaud and the resistance leader somehow managed to escape but Cecily was arrested and taken to the Gestapo prison at Lyons, from where she was taken to the Avenue Foch. She refused to disclose anything to her captors so that other members of her circuit could survive. However, for the courageous Cecily, it was to be the usual grim ending. Like so many SOE operatives, she was to die in a concentration camp before the end of the war. In her case it was Ravensbrück, although the exact circumstances of her death are unclear.[1]

Despite Cecily's arrest, JOCKEY survived intact. Cammaerts and Raynaud headed off to Seyne-les-Alpes where they regrouped with several small and semi-autonomous groups extending down the left bank of the Rhône, between Vienne and Arles, and eastwards to the Isère valley. Cammaerts had always maintained his circuit should be centred on reliable and trusted individuals, who understood what it took to maintain security. He always kept his circuit relatively small and manageable in numbers with his members briefed to keep as low a profile as possible and always have good cover stories behind what they were doing in case they were ever stopped and questioned. Together with members of the local resistance groups, JOCKEY set up numerous drop zones across the region and carried out several successful sabotage missions.

Another of the females from the Double Lysander destined not to last long in the field was 28-year-old Diana Rowden. Operating as Juliette Fondeau, Diana was the courier for ACROBAT but, when she arrived in eastern France, her circuit organizer, John Starr, was concerned that she was not French enough. Indeed, Diana was not French. She had been born into a wealthy English family but had spent much of her childhood in the south of France. After leaving school she returned to France to become a journalist but following the outbreak of war she made her way to England and joined the Women's Auxiliary Air Force (WAAF). Her knowledge of the French language soon brought her to the attention of the SOE and so she was recruited by F Section.

Diana was accommodated in a beautiful château in Saint-Armour with John Young, the circuit's radio operator from the north-east of England.[2] With neither appearing to be convincingly French, Starr had made sure his two operators were out of the way, although both were able to carry on with

---

1. In *Unearthing Churchill's Secret Army*, p.105, Grehan and Mace offer two views as to how Cecily Lefort died at Ravensbrück. One is that she died of an overdose and the other is that she was gassed.
2. Escott, op. cit., p.108.

their work from the château. From there, Diana made frequent journeys as far as Paris and as far south as Marseilles but her whole time in France was fraught with danger and narrow escapes.

John Starr was arrested in Dijon during July and taken to the Avenue Foch. Although he underwent long interrogations, he kept quiet about activity in the Jura but his arrest had put the whole circuit in imminent peril and it seems to have triggered a chain of rather unfortunate events that would ultimately lead to the arrest of Diana and John Young. Harry Rée, who had returned to the Jura in September to resume some of his old contacts, was convinced there was a double agent in the camp. He believed that person to be a man called Pierre Martin, and so he arranged to have both Diana and Young warned. Diana Rowden and John Young somehow managed to keep one step ahead of their pursuers and after Starr's arrest they moved to a sawmill at Clairvaux from where they were able to continue their work. But eventually, in November, their luck ran out.

The Germans had become increasingly confident in impersonating SOE agents in the field and so, at the Avenue Foch, Hans Josef Kieffer decided to use a similar method to bring down the network in the Jura. A number of signals were exchanged with London using captured wireless sets and codes, and so the Germans knew all about the arrival of a Hudson, with more agents on board, which was due to land near Angers on the night of 15/16 November.

The Hudson was flown by Wing Commander Lewis 'Bob' Hodges, the commanding officer of 161 Squadron, and, as usual, had been organized by Henri Déricourt. Unknown to the Hudson crew, or the five agents on board, their arrival was being watched closely by the Germans. So important was it for the five inbound agents to arrive safely, and without suspecting that anything was untoward, that Kieffer was prepared to let the outbound agents depart unscathed. Quite remarkably, these included Francis Cammaerts. Although he would let a prize catch get away, Kieffer was ready to make this sacrifice for the sake of later capturing the five new agents and using them in a game of deception that he was planning to play.

The five dropped off that night were: Victor Gerson, on his third mission as the organizer of the Vic escape line; Edward Levine, on his second mission and on his way to join DONKEYMAN; Jean Menesson, a young French schoolmaster who had already been working with the SOE in Lyons; Paul Pardie, on his way to join Claude de Baissac; and, most crucially, the new organizer in the Jura – André Maugenet (Benoit).[3]

The new arrivals were allowed to disappear into the night as they would expect but each was trailed by Germans and French collaborators. Gerson, being the experienced and cunning operator that he was, managed to give his follower the slip and disappeared. So did Levine initially, although he was later picked up. The three others, however, were all taken in at the Gare de Montparnasse in Paris when they stepped off the train from Angers. It appears that neither Menesson nor Pardie talked before their lives ended but it was André Maugenet that Kieffer was specifically interested in. Kieffer believed that he was carrying a letter for John Young from his wife.

The fact that his captors seemed to know everything about him and his mission must have come as a big shock to the unsuspecting Maugenet so soon after his arrival in France. In reality there was nothing he could have done but how much he revealed, or how co-operative he might have been with the Germans, can only be speculated. Maugenet's orders were to join Young and Diana Rowden, neither of whom had ever met him, and so it occurred to Kieffer that it would be reasonably easy for someone to impersonate Maugenet, particularly as he would be carrying a genuine letter from Young's wife, when he arrived at his destination in Lons-le-Saunier.

Whether it was the real André Maugenet that Young and Diana met at the sawmill in Clairvaux, or whether it was an English-speaking impersonator who could have been either a French collaborator or a German, is not known. There has been post-war speculation about both of these possibilities but, either way, it made no difference. Young and Diana were arrested.

Although the Germans had succeeded in capturing Rée's colleagues in the Jura, they had not caught Rée. After the capture of Young and Diana at Clairvaux, more arrests followed through the Franche Comté with some seventy members of the French Resistance rounded up. Rée vowed to avenge his comrades whom, he believed, Pierre Martin had betrayed and, soon enough, Martin was assassinated at a hotel in Besançon, not by Rée but by someone else.

---

3. Cookridge, op. cit., p.283.

What happened to Young immediately after his arrest is not known, as he seems to have been moved around several times while in captivity, but he was eventually executed at Mauthausen the following year. Diana was taken to the Avenue Foch where she was shocked to see her former circuit organizer, John Starr. Whether Starr had been 'turned' by the Gestapo is unclear but he survived the war when others did not; again, there has been postwar speculation. As for Diana, she gave nothing away. She was eventually taken to Karlsruhe and then to the concentration camp at Natzweiler, where she died in July 1944 having been injected with phenol.[4]

And so, the fate of three of the four agents dropped in the disastrous Double Lysander has been covered, which leaves just one – the story of what happened to Noor Inayat Khan.

---

4. After the war, in 1946, the camp doctor at Natzweiler, who had supervised the murders of SOE women and, in several cases, had administered the poison, and several SS jailers, were sentenced to death and executed.

Chapter 12

Madeleine

With the outcome of three of the four agents dropped into the field from the Double Lysander on the night of 16/17 June 1943 known, it is the story of the fourth, Noor Inayat Khan, which, perhaps, is worth looking at in a bit more detail as it provides a valuable insight into a female radio operator going into the field. It is also a story that would later capture the imagination of the British public and would see the gallant young Noor recognized for her extraordinary courage by the posthumous award of the George Cross, Britain's highest gallantry award in such circumstances.

Noor was aged twenty-nine when she went into the field. Born of Indian origin in pre-revolutionary Russia, but raised in England and France, she had escaped to Britain following the Nazi occupation and trained as a radio operator in the WAAF. At first glance she was a most unlikely looking agent. Reportedly a loner and timid, gentle and unwieldy, she was terrified of loud noises and heights. Furthermore, her brown hair and skin, with hazel eyes and foreign accent, would probably make her noticeable, even in a crowd.[1]

Yet, Noor was determined to do her bit for France and, as a trained radio operator, she joined the SOE. At the end of her preliminary training at Wanborough Manor in March 1943, her instructor summarized her overall performance: 'Lacked confidence to begin with but has come on very well and shown considerable promise. Active, plenty of spirit and could be relied on to come up to scratch when the occasion arose.'

To which the commanding officer, Major Roger de Wesselow, added:

Hadn't the foggiest idea what the training was going to be about. From a shaky start has developed a certain amount of confidence. Energetic.

---

1. Escott, op. cit., p.97.

Experienced W/T operator though she dislikes the work: extremely earnest in her intentions and despite a timid manner would probably rise to an emergency.[2]

Noor moved on to the next phase of her training at Thame Park in Oxfordshire where she was given wireless and security training. She worked hard week after week, doing nothing but Morse training and learning about her wireless set and radio procedures, and was soon up to a speed of transmitting at sixteen words per minute and receiving at nineteen. A report written on her during April sums up Noor's motivation for joining the SOE and how she was seen by her instructors at that time:

This student has thrown herself heart and soul into the life of the school. She has any amount of energy and spends a lot of it on voluntary P.T. [physical training] with the object of overcoming as far as possible feminine disabilities in the physical sense. She is, also, very feminine in character, very eager to please, very ready to adapt herself to the mood of the company, or the tone of the conversation, interested in personalities, capable of strong attachments, kind-hearted, emotional and imaginative. She is very fond of her family (mother, brother in the Fleet Air Arm and sister), and was engaged for about five years, but broke it off. The motive for her accepting the present task is, apparently, idealism. She felt that she had come to a dead end as a WAAF and was longing to do something more active in the prosecution of the war, something which would make more call on her capabilities and, perhaps, demand more sacrifice. This appears to be the only motive; the broken-off engagement is old history, nor does she appear to have any romantic ideas of the Mata-Hari variety. In fact, she confesses that she would not like to have to do anything 'two-faced', by which she means deliberately cultivating friendly relations with malice aforethought. The fact that she has already given some thought to preparing her mother for the inevitable separation and cessation of correspondence shows

2. NA HS 9/836/5, Personnel File, Noor Inayat Khan (Preliminary Report dated 10 March 1943).

that she has faced some, at any rate, of the implications of the job. It is the emotional side of her character, coupled with a vivid imagination, which will most test her steadfastness of purpose in the later stages of her training.[3]

Her speed of transmitting and receiving continued to rise but, in May, concerns were raised about her going into the field following her performance at SOE's Finishing School at Beaulieu. Her report includes:

Not over-burdened with brains but has worked hard and shown keenness, apart from some dislike of the security side of the course. She has an unstable and temperamental personality and it is very doubtful whether she is really suited to work in the field.[4]

Interestingly, the opening sentence of the report has been underlined with a handwritten comment scrawled next to it, presumably by Buckmaster that reads 'We don't want them overburdened with brains'. And where Noor is described as having 'an unstable and temperamental personality', he has simply written 'Nonsense', and at the bottom of the report is written 'Makes me cross – F'.

Noor was desperately needed in France and so her training was brought to an end before the point of normal completion of the course. By the time her final report was written on 30 June 1943, Noor was already in France but for the record it reads:

This student was withdrawn during the month at the request of her Country Section. While she cannot be considered a fully trained operator because of her shortened course, she is quite capable of handling her set, and of passing messages. She should, however, gain more confidence in time. While at this school she showed signs of being easily flustered when difficulties cropped up, especially if they were

---

3. Ibid. (Report on Officer Student dated 19 April 1943).
4. NA HS 9/836/5, Personnel File, Noor Inayat Khan (Finishing Report dated 21 May 1943).

of a technical nature, and it is doubtful if she will ever be able to fully overcome this.[5]

With an honorary commission in the WAAF and rank of assistant section officer, made effective from 16 June 1943, the date she went into France, Noor became F Section's first female radio operator sent into the field. She was to operate under the name of 'Jeanne-Marie Renier' and would soon find herself in one of the principal and most dangerous posts in France.

Noor had received her brief about Jeanne-Marie and details of her mission a week before she flew out to France. Agents were quizzed at length about their new identity to see if they could remember the details and to test the profile for any flaws. Where possible, elements of the agent's real life were used to make it easier to remember. Jeanne-Marie Renier had been born in Blois on 25 April 1918. Her father, Auguste, was a professor of philosophy but had been killed during the Great War, and her mother was American by birth but French by marriage. Jeanne had gone to school in Saint-Cloud, after which she had gone to the Sorbonne in 1935 where she studied until 1938, specializing in child psychology (Noor had studied child psychology before the war). She then looked after children in various families but was now working as a nurse in Paris. And so it went on.

With the codename 'Madeleine', Noor's mission was (quoted from her brief) 'to work as the wireless operator for a locally recruited organizer, who is established in the region of le Mans.' Her mission brief then included details of how she was to go into the field, how to approach her circuit organizer, including the address where she should go to make contact with him and the password she should use with the reply she should get back, and the method she was to use in order to meet her aim. There followed details about finance and communications with her mission brief concluding:

You have had our general training, our W/T training and been given our general briefing. You have also read the foregoing (referring to the profile of Jeanne-Marie Renier), have had an opportunity of raising any questions on matters that have not been clear and have had a trial viva

5. Ibid. (Monthly Progress Report for Noor Inayat Khan dated 30 June 1943).

voce of the methods outlined. You understand that you are to receive your instructions from Cinema and that you are to carry them out to the best of your ability. If, through any unforeseen circumstances, Cinema should disappear, you will advise us and receive further instructions direct from us.

Fully briefed, Noor landed with the others on the night of 16/17 June and went to Paris, as planned, where she was able to make contact with her circuit organizer, Emile-Henri Garry. She also met with France Antelme who gave her a tour of Paris so that she could settle down and familiarize herself with the area in which she was to work.

At that stage Noor's wireless set had not arrived – in fact she would not receive her own set until a couple of weeks later – and so she met with Gilbert Norman. His radio set was concealed in the Agricultural Institute at Grignon in the western suburbs of Paris and, by using Norman's wireless, Noor was able to make her first transmission. It was just three days after her insertion and was the quickest response from a radio operator after arriving in the field.[6]

Then, just days later, came the arrests of Francis Suttill, Gilbert Norman and Andrée Borrel. Noor immediately went into hiding although she was able to inform London of the disaster that was unfolding with PROSPER. Baker Street wanted to recall her immediately but Noor was determined to carry on and so for the time being she continued helping other agents and circuits, constantly moving around and keeping her transmissions short to avoid being intercepted by the many radio detection vans operating in the area.

Noor had made her case to stay on the grounds that she was now the only radio operator in Paris and so she could keep London informed of what was going on at that most crucial time. Buckmaster was in a horrible dilemma. On one hand he knew the perilous position Noor was in, and that it was only a matter of time before she was arrested, but he also knew she was the last link with Paris and that she now had the most crucial role of all. While Noor

---

6. Basu, *Spy Princess*, p.147.

could have got out, she was allowed to stay but on the understanding that she kept her head down for a while and only transmitted in short bursts.

And so Noor was virtually alone. Meanwhile, back in London Jack Agazarian had wasted no time in voicing his concerns about what was going on in France and, in particular, questioning Henri Déricourt's loyalty. But Buckmaster remained unconvinced and so in July, just a month after Suttill's arrest, he sent his deputy, Nicholas Bodington, to Paris to find out what was going on. It was Bodington's second mission and he took Agazarian with him. For Agazarian, it was going to be a huge risk going back to France so soon. He had only left a month before and knew the Germans would still be on the lookout for him.

Bodington and Agazarian parachuted into France on the night of 22/23 July. All they knew at that stage was that transmissions were being made from Gilbert Norman's radio set but they were not sure whether he was transmitting under duress or even if it was Norman transmitting at all. When they arrived in Paris a meeting was arranged near the Gare St Lazare with the man they had been led to believe was Gilbert Norman. But rather than putting both Bodington and Agazarian at risk, they decided that only Agazarian should go.

The Gestapo were already aware that Bodington was in Paris and there had been discussions between Hans Josef Kieffer and Hugo Bleicher as to how they were to try to have him arrested. And so the decision to send only Agazarian to the meeting point meant that, for Bodington, it was a lucky escape.

The location for the rendezvous was under German surveillance and so when Agazarian turned up he was promptly arrested. Although Bodington had been the prime target, it was still a massive coup for the Gestapo. Jack Agazarian was a wanted man and knew so much, but he would give nothing away. After being taken to Fresnes prison and the Avenue Foch, where he was tortured for the next six months, he was eventually taken to the concentration camp at Flossenbürg where he was executed just weeks before the end of the war.

After Agazarian had failed to return from the supposed meeting with Gilbert Norman, Bodington's doubts and suspicions had been confirmed.

He immediately moved to a new location for his own safety and, thereafter, moved address every few days.

Days later, Vera Leigh, now settled in Paris and an important SOE foothold in northern France, requested a meeting with Bodington and Julienne Aisner. Vera's work with INVENTOR had taken her farther afield as her circuit's activities stretched far and wide and were now merging further south with those of DONKEYMAN.

During the meeting, Vera made the point that Henri Frager, the organizer of DONKEYMAN, had accused Henri Déricourt of being a traitor. Bodington, in turn, asked to see Frager and the two men met during the second week of August at Robert Benoist's home in the suburb of Auffargis. The result of that meeting was that Bodington now wondered whether it was Frager who was, in fact, a double agent![7] It had also become obvious to Bodington that Lise de Baissac's position in the Poitiers area had become precarious and so decided that he would take her back to England with him.

Déricourt was informed of the accusations made against him but nothing was resolved, or decided, by the time Bodington left for England on the night of 15/16 August. During his time in Paris, he had seen for himself the importance of Noor as he relied on her to keep in touch with London. Through her he also found out that all was not lost as there were elements and sub-circuits of the huge PROSPER network still intact.

And so, for now, things carried on as normal but Vera would meet again with Julienne later in the year to warn her that she was also in danger by working so closely with Déricourt. Vera had been warned by others that she, too, was in danger and should leave Paris. But in the same way that Julienne dismissed the warning from Vera, not believing the allegation about Déricourt, Vera also dismissed the warning about herself and decided to stay.

As things were to turn out, Frager would soon leave France on an October Hudson and would not return until early the following year, leaving Roger Bardet, who had rejoined him after the SPINDLE debacle, to run DONKEYMAN. But Bardet was still very much in touch with the *Abwehr* and, at the end of October, Vera was arrested after being lured to a

---

7. Escott, op. cit., p.94.

rendezvous at a café near the Place des Ternes in Paris, a trap that had been laid with Bardet's help.

Just days later, Vera's circuit organizer, Sidney Jones, was also arrested. Hugo Bleicher would later remark on Jones' bravery by taking his arrest so calmly and saying 'It's a pity, it's such a nice day today'.[8] Next behind bars was the pianist, Marcel Clech, although he had first managed to send word to London of the arrest of the others.

The axe had fallen on INVENTOR and none of its key agents would survive. Vera was taken to the Avenue Foch and from there, sadly, the end was predictable. First she was taken to Fresnes prison, then to Karlsruhe and finally to Natzweiler where, in July 1944, her life ended after an injection of phenol. Around the same time, Sidney Jones was executed at Mauthausen, four months after Marcel Clech's death at the same camp.

All these arrests had led Buckmaster to conclude that it was safer to keep Frager in London, for the time being at least, and to impose a deliberate lull upon activities of SOE groups in Paris and northern France until the new year.

Although she had been instructed to lie low, Noor continued to transmit. She was also working with French Resistance groups in the area and transmitting for many others, including, of all people, Henri Déricourt. During the period August to October 1943 she made twenty important transmissions in extremely difficult circumstances. She even helped in the escape of thirty Allied airmen who had been shot down over France, as well as organizing drops of arms and money to the Maquis. It was extremely dangerous work. Not only were there the transmissions to make, Noor had to carry her wireless set round with her most of the time. She had already had one lucky escape, during a meeting with Octave Simon in August, and so she had to be continuously on the move in search of new locations from where she could transmit.

But the Germans were now on to the lady they only knew as Madeleine, and Noor had become top of their most wanted list. Finally, in October 1943, she was betrayed. Who betrayed her has, like so many other things involving the SOE, been the subject of post-war speculation. It might have

---

8. Grehan & Mace, op. cit., p.89. (Quote by Hugo Bleicher).

aurice Buckmaster, the head of F Section. He
d joined the section as the Information Officer
ring the spring of 1941 before taking over the helm
September. As a former reporter with a French
wspaper and a senior manager with the French
anch of the Ford Motor Company, he had useful
d extensive contacts in France, and knew the
untry well. (*Imperial War Museum*)

Major General Colin Gubbins, the head
of SOE and the power behind its success
during its key years of the Second World
War. (*Imperial War Museum*)

The SOE initially made use of offices at a
requisitioned hotel in Caxton Street but when
accommodation became too cramped it set up its
main headquarters here, in a greyish five-storey
building at 64 Baker Street. For a long time its
very existence remained unknown, even to high-
ranking Service officers. (*Author*)

A plaque marks the significance of this historic
building that was once the main headquarters of
the SOE. (*Author*)

George Bégué, a radio operator and acknowledged to be the first F Section agent sent into France. He parachuted into central France on the night of 5/6 May 1941. (*The National Archives*)

Virginia Hall was the first resident woman to go into France in 1941, under the cover of being a correspondent for the *New York Post*. With her American passport she enjoyed relative freedom to move around, although that changed once the United States entered the war. A talented linguist and incredibly brave woman, Virginia became the focal point for all activity in east-central France, becoming known as 'Marie of Lyons'. (*The National Archives*)

Pierre de Vomécourt was one of three brothers to work for the SOE. The eldest, Jean, set up an escape route into Switzerland from his estate near the border while Philippe, the youngest, remained at his estate near Limoges to run the VENTRILOQUIST circuit. Pierre, meanwhile, based himself at his house in Paris and set up AUTOGIRO. These two circuits were F Section's first two major activities in France. (*The National Archives*)

Many training schools were set up across southern England in so wonderful locations for agents to be taught the many skills they wo need to survive in the field. Here, at Milton Hall near Peterborough, ancestral home of the Fitzwilliam family since the sixteenth centu the walled garden became a pistol range. (*Courtesy of Milton Hall*)

SOE training included a course at the Parachute Training School at RAF Ringway in Manchester, during which up to a handful of jumps were made from a tethered balloon from a height of 700 feet followed by a jump from an aircraft. (*Courtesy of the Dallow family*)

nce in the field, agents often und it difficult to move around, articularly when crossing the emarcation line between the ichy south and the Nazi-cupied north before the ermans occupied all of France wards the end of 1942. Even en, moving around was never sy with so many checkpoints ound the country. (*Author's llection*)

The preferred method of insertion into the field for many agents was by parachute. It avoided a long journey via Gibraltar and then a sea passage to the French Riviera, which itself proved hazardous once the Germans had moved into the south of France. Agents could be dropped to a reception committee or blind, where no one was there to meet them, depending on the resources available. (*Author's collection*)

In September 1941 the Lysander was introduced for dropping and picking up agents as it was the most accurate method of insertion. The Lysander's short take-off and landing ability, combined with its robustness, made it ideal for this role as it meant operating from unprepared fields. But it was also extremely hazardous for the pilots and not all landings were perfect, although the vast majority were. (*Air Historical Branch*)

Ben Cowburn parachuted into France for the first of his four missions in September 1941, one of six agents dropped that night and the largest insertion at the time. With a great knowledge of the oil industry and fluent in French, he was a great addition to the SOE and was awarded the Military Cross and Bar. (*Special Forces Club*)

The vast rail network across France was a vital communications link for the occupying German forces but it was also an obvious target for sabotage. (*The National Archives*)

Organizing air drops to help arm the French Resistance was one of the agent's main responsibilities in the field. (*Author's collection*)

The French collaborationist police, the *Milice*, effectively a French Gestapo, were set up by the Vichy French to assist the Germans in their campaign against the French Resistance and SOE agents known to be operating across France. Stops and checks were frequent occurrences. (*Author's collection*)

Those who proved troublesome in the Vichy south were rounded up by the *Milice* and faced an uncertain future. Fortunately, some would survive after being given the 'opportunity to escape' by sympathetic Vichy French camp commanders as the Germans moved south to occupy all of France rather than turn their own countrymen over to the Nazis. (*Author's collection*)

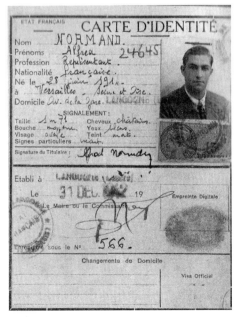

Newton, one of two ers known as 'The '. They were living heir families in France time of the German ation but when their family, including l's three young children, wiped out by a German t as they sailed for nd on board a mercy he two brothers were med with a passion for ge against the Nazis. g made their way to nd, they joined the SOE 2. (*Author's collection*)

Henry Newton, the second 'Twin', although he was in fact ten years older than Alfred. (*Author's collection*)

Alfred Newton's fake identity card, showing his cover name of Alfred Normand. (*Author's collection*)

The Newton 'Twins', Henry (left) and Alfred (right), pictured with Maurice Southgate at the end of the war on their return from Buchenwald. (*Author's collection*)

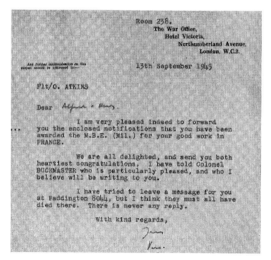

Congratulatory letter sent to the Twins from Vera Atkins after both had been notified of their appointment as Members of the Order of the British Empire for their mission in France and courage after capture. (*Author's collection*)

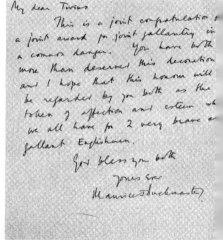

Letter from Maurice Buckmaster congratulating the Twins on their awards. (*Author's collection*)

y Brooks was the youngest
uit organizer sent into the field
·n he parachuted into France in
· 1942 shortly after his twentieth
·hday. Some doubted his ability to
·nto the field but Brooks superbly
·PIMENTO in the Lyonnais and
·d up as the longest serving F
·ion organizer in the field, ending
·war with the rank of major and
·stinguished Service Order and
·tary Cross at the age of twenty-
e. (*Special Forces Club*)

Peter Churchill, an intelligence
officer, joined F Section in 1941 and
became a pioneer of inserting agents
into France. He first went into the
field in early 1942, having been
landed by submarine on the French
Riviera, and then set up SPINDLE
in the foothills of the Alps. He would
later be captured but survived the
war having convinced his captors
that he was related to Britain's
Prime Minister, Winston Churchill.
(*The National Archives*)

Lise de Baissac, codenamed
Odile, was dropped with
Andrée Borrel in west-central
France on the night of 24/25
September 1942, the first two
F Section women parachuted
into France. Lise successfully
completed two missions
and worked closely with her
younger brother, Claude,
with the SCIENTIST
circuit. (*Special Forces Club*)

·ette Sansom, codename
·e, was one of three female
·nts inserted near Cassis late
·1942. She was later captured
·ngside Peter Churchill as
·t of the 'Colonel Henri'
·acle but she survived the
·· having convinced her
·tors that she was married to
·urchill, a relative of Britain's
·ne Minister, and was later
·rded the George Cross for
· outstanding courage after
·ture. (*The National Archives*)

Hugo Bleicher of the Abwehr
(German intelligence) proved a thorn
in F Section's side during the 'Cat'
affair and then again while posing as
'Colonel Henri' when he managed
to convince certain circuit members
he was a German intelligence officer
wishing to defect to England. It
was a trap that led to the arrests of
Peter Churchill and Odette Sansom
in April 1943 and the subsequent
demise of SPINDLE with disastrous
repercussions. (*Imperial War Museum*)

Francis Suttill parachuted
into France in October 1942
to set up a new circuit in and
around Paris to replace the
earlier work of AUTOGIRO.
Suttill's own PROSPER
would expand rapidly and
spread far and wide across
northern France but an
unfortunate chain of events
in June 1943 triggered the
arrests of hundreds, including
Suttill. He was hanged at
Sachsenhausen just weeks
before the end of the war.
(*The National Archives*)

The brave young 'Parisian Street Urchin', Andrée Borrel. She worked tirelessly for Francis Suttill, travelling with him and posing as his sister, but like so many others she got caught up in the PROSPER web and was later executed at Natzweiler at the age of twenty-four. (*The National Archives*)

Frank Pickersgill, the unfortunate Canadian whose arrest with John Macalister led to the downfall of PROSPER. The Germans later tried to use Pickersgill as part of their deception game but the gallant Canadian refused to co-operate and was executed at Buchenwald in September 1944 alongside Macalister. (*Special Forces Club*)

John Macalister was sent into France with his Canadian colleague, Frank Pickersgill, to set up ARCHDEACON in the Ardennes but it was their arrests on 21 June 1943 that triggered the sequence of events leading to the downfall of the mighty PROSPER network. Macalister's life ended at Buchenwald. (*The National Archives*)

Agents and the Maquis used a range of methods for transporting arms and supplies around France making all vehicles subject to regular checks. (*Author's collection*)

Gilbert Norman was the radio operator for
Francis Suttill's PROSPER, concealing his radio
set in the Agricultural Institute at Grignon in
the western suburbs of Paris until his arrest.
Norman's radio was then used by the Germans
to impersonate him and so started the radio
games, deceptions and lies that continued into
1944. Gilbert Norman ended up at Mauthausen
where he was shot. (*The National Archives*)

The increased number of agents sent into France
merely increased the number of checks by the
Germans on anyone suspected of being involved
with the SOE or French Resistance. The cities
were particularly dangerous places for the agents
to operate. (*Author's collection*)

Francis Cammaerts, a former
pacifist stemming from his
pre-war university days, joined
the SOE after the death of
his brother serving with the
RAF. He went into France
in March 1943 to set up
DONKEYMAN in the upper
Rhône valley and then led
JOCKEY in south-east France.
For a former conscientious
objector, Cammaerts proved to
be an outstanding leader and
was awarded the Distinguished
Service Order at the end of the
war. (*The National Archives*)

Harry Rée, a former
teaching colleague of Francis
Cammaerts, was another former
conscientious objector to join
the SOE. Rée parachuted
into France in April 1943
to join ACROBAT around
Montbéliard and later set up
STOCKBROKER on the
Swiss border, for which he was
awarded the Distinguished
Service Order. (*The National
Archives*)

Charles Skepper was one of four
agents inserted by a Double
Lysander on the night of 16/17
June 1943. A former antiques
dealer in his late thirties, he would
last longer in the field than his
three female companions that
night. But after setting up MONK
in Marseilles, he was captured
in March 1944 after his circuit
was infiltrated and betrayed to
the Gestapo; Skepper died the
following month. (*The National
Archives*)

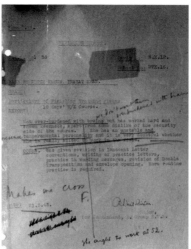

Also inserted on the Double Lysander in June 1943 was Noor Inayat Khan, the first F Section female radio operator sent into France. She soon became the last radio operator left in Paris and was given the chance to get out, but chose to stay. She was later betrayed and executed at Dachau in September 1944. Despite the interrogations, Noor gave nothing away and was later awarded a posthumous George Cross for her extreme courage after capture. (*The National Archives*)

Noor Inayat Khan's report from SOE's Finishing School at Beaulieu dated 21 May 1943. The report has been underlined and scrawled over with comments such as 'Nonsense' and 'We don't want them overburdened with brains' and 'Makes me cross'. These, presumably, are the comments of Maurice Buckmaster as he uses the initial 'F'. (*The National Archives*)

Michael Trotobas parachuted France in November 1942 to s up FARMER, a sabotage netw based in Lille. In June 1943 he his saboteurs in a daring raid c the locomotive works at Fives the eastern suburbs, leaving th railway yard in a mass of twist steel and burning rubble. But, November, the Gestapo caugh up with him and he eventually fell dead at his door after the l rounds of his revolver had gor (*Author's collection*)

With more drops of explosives and with greater expertise, the level of sabotage increased. This viaduct the Corrèze carried a vital rail link until the Maquis got to work. (*Author's collection*)

ustave Biéler, a French-
anadian, was described by
Maurice Buckmaster as the best
udent the SOE had. Although
verely injuring his spine
ter landing on rocky ground
hile parachuting into France,
e refused to be evacuated
ack to England and set up
e successful MUSICIAN
rcuit in eastern Picardy. Biéler
as betrayed early in 1944
d executed by firing squad
Flossenbürg concentration
mp in Bavaria. (*The National
rchives*)

George Starr, codenamed
Hilaire, went into
France in late 1942
and led the successful
WHEELWRIGHT
circuit in south-west
France, bordering the
Pyrenees, for which
he was awarded the
Distinguished Service
Order and Military Cross.
(*Special Forces Club*)

Tommy Yeo-Thomas, the 'White
Rabbit', first parachuted into France in
1943 at the age of forty-one. During the
next year he twice more went back into
the field but was eventually betrayed and
ended up at Buchenwald. He survived
the war by changing identity, having
hatched a daring and collaborative plan
with one of the camp doctors. Yeo-
Thomas was later awarded the George
Cross to add to his Military Cross and
Bar. (*Imperial War Museum*)

No matter where the
Germans set off from
to make their way to
Normandy to resist
the Allied landings,
there were circuits
and saboteurs just
waiting to hamper
every move. The rail
network remained an
obvious target until the
liberation of France.
(*Author's collection*)

Not all parts of France were ideal for air drops, particularly in the foothills of the Alps. (*Author's collection*)

During 1944 the number of air sorties flown by the RAF in support of the SOE circuits and French Resistance reached an all-time high with over 4,500 sorties flown during the year. (*Author's collection*)

The SOE monument on Albert Embankment in London with the fitting design of Violette Szabo on a plinth to represent all agents of the SOE and those who did not survive. (*Author*)

Violette Szabo became the symbol of courage after being posthumously awarded the George Cross. Young and attractive, she joined the SOE after her husband had been killed in North Africa. She was captured soon after D-Day after bravely holding off German soldiers so that a colleague could escape. After suffering at the hands of her captors, Violette was executed at Ravensbrück in early 1945; she was just twenty-three. (*The National Archives*)

olin Ogden-Smith, a commando before
ining the SOE in 1942, led the Jedburgh
:am Francis behind enemy lines in
:ittany during July 1944. The Jeds were
:rachuted into France after D-Day to
ık up with the French Resistance and to
;anize air drops of weapons, ammunition
.d explosives. It was extremely dangerous
ork and cost Ogden-Smith his life; he was
.led on 29 July 1944 fighting alongside
ench colleagues. (*Author's collection*)

Arthur Dallow, the radio operator of
Jedburgh Team Francis. Dallow was just
nineteen years old when he parachuted into
France and later served with Force 136 in
Burma; he was awarded the Military Medal
for his courage while serving with the SOE.
(*Courtesy of the Dallow family*)

As parts of France were
liberated by the Allies,
resistance groups across
the country could pose
for victory photographs.
(*Author's collection*)

A scene typical of any French city or town during the liberation of France. (*Author's collection*)

After the war it was left to men such as Captain Bill Durndell (left) of the War Crimes Investigati[on] Unit to carry out the unpleasant task of visiting concentration camps and interviewing Germans cited [as] responsible for committing horrific war crimes during the Nazi occupation of France. (*Courtesy of P[.] Peacock and the Durndell family*)

he Tempsford memorial was unveiled in 2013 to honour the women of the SOE who flew from the airfield to occupied Europe during the Second World War. (*Author*)

he SOE monument has stood on the Albert Embankment since 2009 and poignantly looks across the ver Thames to the Houses of Parliament where the most difficult of decisions are made to send the nation war. (*Author*)

Ensuring the work of the SOE will never be forgotten. A gathering of local villagers and histori enthusiasts meet at the Stuart Memorial Village Hall in Tempsford during November 2014 to listen Francis J. Suttill talk about the release of his book about his father who led the PROSPER circuit. (*Auth*

For many who served with the SOE there is no grave but one to have remained buried in France is Maj Colin Ogden-Smith who lies in a vault at Guiscriff Communal Cemetery in Brittany alongside his tv French colleagues; they were all killed in action just days before the Allies liberated this part of Fran (*Author's collection*)

been Henri Déricourt or it could have been Renée Garry, the sister of her circuit organizer, Emile-Henri Garry, but although she was tried after the war by a French military court on charges of betrayal, Renée Garry was acquitted.[9] But whoever it was, Noor had been caught in a trap and although she put up a considerable fight, she was arrested and taken to the dreaded Avenue Foch.

The following day, Emile-Henri Garry and his wife, Marguerite, were also arrested. They had been due to go to London in the following few days but had stayed overnight at an apartment being watched by the Germans and were then tricked by a man claiming to be a courier working for the SOE. It appears the Gestapo did not realize the importance of Garry as he was treated as a member of the French Resistance, rather than an agent of the SOE, but the outcome was just the same. He was sent to Buchenwald and hanged the following year, although his wife would survive the horror of Ravensbrück.

Sadly, there were more losses before London realized the extent of what was happening, even though a young and locally recruited agent, 20-year-old Sonia Olschanezky, had sent word of Noor's arrest. Unfortunately, though, Sonia's warning seems to have been ignored. She had not been trained by the SOE and, therefore, was unknown to London, and so her warning had been treated as unreliable.

Using the captured radios, the Germans continued the false radio transmissions from Paris. There were further arrests and, ultimately, more deaths, including Sonia Olschanezky. Unknown to London, she had worked tirelessly for the SOE, particularly with JUGGLER, one of Suttill's sub-circuits responsible for several acts of sabotage in and around the suburbs of Paris. She had even tried to hold the circuit together following the arrest of its leader, Jean Worms (Robin), in the aftermath of the PROSPER disaster. Sonia had managed to escape arrest then, along with the circuit's deputy, Jacques Weil, and the pianist Gaston Cohen (Justin), but her luck eventually ran out and she would later die in Natzweiler alongside Andrée Borrel.

These were tragic consequences of Noor's capture but she gave nothing away. An extract of a deposition on oath of Hans Josef Kieffer, commandant

---

9. Basu, op. cit., p.231.

of the Paris Gestapo, sworn before a war crimes' investigation unit in January 1947 states:

> I remember the English W/T operator, Madeleine (Noor Inayat Khan's code name), and recognize her on the photograph shown to me. We were pursuing her for months and as we had a personal description of her we arranged for all stations to be watched. She had several addresses and worked very carefully. Madeleine, after her capture, showed great courage and we got no information whatsoever out of her.

Noor even tried to escape one night when, using a smuggled screwdriver, she managed to get out of the skylight above her cell and onto the roof only to be recaptured in an adjoining house during an air raid.[10] Noor was then transferred to Germany and during the transit she even tried to escape again. She was imprisoned at Pforzheim and placed in solitary confinement. In his deposition during the war crimes' investigation, dated November 1946, Wilhelm Krauss, the governor of Pforzheim prison, states:

> I remember that in November 1943 an English woman was delivered into Pforzheim prison. I was told that she was to be treated in accordance with regulations for 'Nacht und Nebel' ['night and fog'] prisoners. It was the expression used for people who 'disappeared' and once in custody were kept on the lowest rations, in solitary confinement and, moreover, that she was to be chained hand and foot. This order was carried through.

Then, in September 1944, Noor was taken to Karlsruhe, where she was imprisoned with three other SOE women, before she was finally taken to the concentration camp at Dachau. It seems that the three other female prisoners were abused and then shot but the exceedingly brave Noor was to suffer further at the hands of her captors before she was finally finished off by a bullet to the head, probably on 13 September.

---

10. Foot, op. cit., p.295 and Fuller, *The Starr Affair*, pp.68–84.

Noor's SOE Battle Casualty form records her death as 'possibly October 1943' but in October 1944 her mother received the dreaded of all letters, which includes:

Dear Mrs Baker-Inayat, I am extremely sorry to have to inform you that we have recently been out of touch with your daughter. Due to the confused state of affairs in France we were not unduly worried, but I am afraid now your daughter must be considered as missing although there is every reason to believe that she will eventually be notified as a prisoner of war.[11]

But the reality was poor Noor was already dead. As the full story of her time in France became clear, Noor was ultimately recommended for the George Cross, the highest gallantry award the nation can give for such circumstances. The full recommendation reads:

Assistant Section Officer Nora (sic) INAYAT-KHAN was the first woman operator to be infiltrated into enemy occupied France, and was landed by Lysander aircraft on 16th June, 1943. During the weeks immediately following her arrival, the Gestapo made mass arrests in the Paris Resistance groups to which she had been detailed. She refused however to abandon what had become the principal and most dangerous post in France, although given the opportunity to return to England, because she did not wish to leave her French comrades without communications and she hoped also to rebuild her group. She remained at her post therefore and did the excellent work which has earned her a posthumous Mention in Despatches.

The Gestapo had a full description of her, but knew only her code name 'Madeleine'. They deployed considerable forces in their effort to catch her and so break the last remaining link with London. After 3 ½ months, she was betrayed to the Gestapo and taken to their HQ in the Avenue Foch. The Gestapo had found her codes and messages and

11. NA HS 9/836/5, Personnel File, Noor Inayat Khan (Letter from Major I K MacKenzie to Mrs O R Baker-Inayat dated 15 October 1944).

were now in a position to work back to London. They asked her to co-operate, but she refused and gave them no information of any kind. She was imprisoned in one of the cells on the 5th floor of the Gestapo HQ and remained there for several weeks during which time she made two unsuccessful attempts to escape, but both failed. She was asked to sign a declaration that she would make no further attempts at escapes. She refused and the Chief of the Gestapo obtained permission from Berlin to send [her] to Germany for 'safe custody'. She was the first agent to be sent to Germany.

Assistant Section Officer INAYAT-KHAN was sent to Karlsruhe in November 1943, and then to Pforzheim where her cell was apart from the main prison. She was considered a particularly dangerous and uncooperative prisoner, and on orders from Berlin she was put into chains and kept on the lowest rations. After some months the Prison Director asked for permission to remove her chains, but this request was refused. Later, a fellow prisoner, a Frenchwoman, Madame Yolande LAGRAVE managed to make secret contact with her and has since supplied us with details of the brutal conditions under which ASO INAYAT-KHAN was held. The Director of the prison, Wilhelm KRAUSS, has also been interrogated and has confirmed that ASO INAYAT-KHAN, was kept in solitary confinement, in chains, and on the lowest rations scale for ten months, and that when interrogated by the Karlsruhe Gestapo she refused to give any information whatsoever, either as to her work or her colleagues.

She was taken with three others to Dachau Camp on the 12th September 1944. On arrival, she was taken to the crematorium, made to kneel against a mound of earth, and shot through the back of the head.

It is recommended that in recognition of her outstanding courage, both moral and physical, she be awarded posthumously the George Cross.[12]

The recommendation was signed by Colin Gubbins with the statements of three independent witnesses attached. Then, on 5 April 1949, came

---

12. Ibid. (Recommendation for the George Cross – Noor Inayat Khan).

the announcement in the *London Gazette* of the posthumous award of the George Cross to Noor Inayat Khan to add to the French Croix de Guerre announced three years earlier. The agent who had once caused concerns during her training as to whether she should go into the field had become a national heroine.

Today there are plaques commemorating Noor at various locations and, in November 2012, a bronze bust of her was unveiled by HRH The Princess Royal in Gordon Square Gardens, close to where Noor had lived. Thankfully she will never be forgotten but the story of Noor Inayat Khan, the agent known as 'Madeleine', is, perhaps, one of the saddest stories of all.

Chapter 13

The Man Called Gilbert – Agent, Double-Agent or Triple-Agent?

It is debatable whether the deaths of all four agents from the Double Lysander insertion of 16/17 June 1943, all of whom were caught within a short period of time after going into the field, is an unfortunate coincidence. Maybe it was because of betrayal, which Henri Déricourt, the man called 'Gilbert', may have been responsible for or, at least, have known something about. Or maybe it was simply bad luck. Who knows? Either way, four courageous agents were dead and many others died as a consequence. Post-war suggestions are that all four agents were doomed from the start of their missions, possibly as a result of the Henri Déricourt affair. For the three unsuspecting and desperately unlucky women, it could well be that they were all followed to their destinations in the hope that they would eventually lead the Gestapo to their circuit organizers, as it was they who were the most wanted.

So what can be made of Henri Déricourt? Was he a French agent working for the SOE as people had initially thought, or had he been turned into a double agent working for the *Sicherheitsdienst* instead? Or, as has also been suggested, had he become a triple agent who the Germans thought were working for them but was really working on instructions from London? In which case, if this were to be true, was he acting on instructions from the SOE or, as has also been suggested, from Britain's Secret Intelligence Service, the SIS, and his work for the SOE was just a cover to get him close to the Germans?

The number of arrests of SOE agents and members of the French Resistance during 1943 had certainly led to many pointing the finger at Déricourt. He was, according to some, in regular contact with senior officers of the SD. However, those at the top in London, including Maurice Buckmaster, clearly refused to believe the allegations and so Déricourt would be left to continue in France until February 1944 when he was finally recalled to England, and only then because of uncertainties following more accusations of betrayal.

The fact that Buckmaster had finally decided to terminate Déricourt's time in France does not mean he had concluded that Déricourt had become a traitor. The first attempt to bring him home was made on the night of 4/5 February when the first Hudson of the year, with Gerry Morel on board, landed on one of Déricourt's fields just outside Angers. Although Déricourt would not return that night, because he claimed he had some important business to attend to, he was picked up by a Lysander four nights later, taking his wife with him to England.

The FARRIER circuit was wound up just a few weeks later but, to balance the accusations made against him, Déricourt had, by then, conducted seventeen operations involving twenty-one aircraft in just over a year of clandestine activity; during that time forty-three agents had been successfully inserted into the field and sixty-seven had left France under his organization.[1]

Although doubts about Déricourt's possible, likely even, duplicity had been raised many months before, when there had been widespread belief amongst many in France that he might be a traitor, it took until Déricourt was recalled to England for the matter to come under closer investigation. Tasked with looking into the case was the SOE's Director of Security, Intelligence and Personnel, Air Commodore Archibald Boyle, and Harry Sporborg, the Principal Deputy to Colin Gubbins.

At first glance, Sporborg favoured the side of Déricourt; his legal experience led him to conclude there was a lack of direct proof of any guilt and how flimsy much of the circumstantial evidence was. However, the security service felt otherwise and stated that if the decision were theirs then the case was regarded as serious enough to prevent Déricourt from undertaking any further work outside Britain. In face of this, Sporborg decided that Déricourt should not be allowed to go back to France.[2]

---

1. Foot, op. cit., p.265.
2. Ibid, p.268.

It is clear that, at some stage, Déricourt was in contact with the Gestapo and it may well be that he had been in contact with the SD from the moment the SOE had first sent him into France. The matter again came to the fore after the war when, in 1946, Déricourt provided a different account of his story to the French than he had given to the British during the investigation of 1944. Now there were ample grounds for suspicion, though few of proof. Nonetheless, when war crimes investigators looked into the case, they managed to reveal from German sources that Déricourt had been working as one of their agents and that information from him had led to the arrest and subsequent execution of many SOE agents.

French authorities arrested Déricourt but, during his trial in June 1948, when he faced a string of charges, his testimony was somewhat ambiguous and so the charges were gradually whittled away. Furthermore, a number of witnesses required by the prosecution were unavailable for the trial and the prosecution collapsed when Nicholas Bodington, Buckmaster's deputy and Déricourt's main supporter during the trial, testified that he had authorized Déricourt to make and maintain contacts with the Germans. Bodington was also asked by the judge whether he would again trust his life to an operation by Déricourt, to which he replied 'Certainly, without hesitation'.[3] And so Déricourt was acquitted, claiming himself that SOE agents were deliberately sacrificed to distract the Germans from the Allied landings.

Bodington's testimony came as a shock to former SOE agents who had been fortunate to survive the war. They felt that if Bodington had authorized Déricourt to make and maintain contacts with the Germans then this was well beyond his authority, or Buckmaster's for that matter. And so questions were then raised about Bodington and whether someone from higher up had authorized him to give such evidence. Had he really been the person to authorize Déricourt to make contact with the Germans and, if so, why? Or had it been someone more senior, with Bodington taking the rap at the investigation?

Since his trial, the question of which side Henri Déricourt was really on has been disputed in a number of books and in the French press where

---

3. Ibid., p.271. (Also based on private information).

l'affaire Déricourt provided a major sensation. In his book *SOE in France*, the SOE historian M. R. D. Foot summarizes his belief about Déricourt with:

> The truth is that his only unswerving loyalty was to himself; he was trapped by circumstances between the upper millstone of loyalty to workmates in SOE and the nether millstone of inextricable entanglements with the Gestapo, and did what he could to serve both sides at once.[4]

Henri Déricourt is believed to have died in an aircraft accident in 1962, and with his life went the truth. His time with the SOE in France remains a subject of much post-war speculation but the fact remains a lot of good agents died in horrific circumstances. Perhaps they were pawns in a game being played where each side was trying to outscore the other. Whatever the truth, those agents who went into France, and who seemingly knew and accepted the risks they were taking, should at least have been able to go into the field trusting those who had sent them as well as those who received them.

---

4. Ibid, p.259.

Chapter 14

Bad Salesmen, Troublesome Farmers, Dangerous Musicians and Tinkers

While PROSPER and its many sub-circuits had taken care of much of northern France during their existence, another circuit, operating in the area between Rouen and le Havre, had continued to work independently of Suttill and, therefore, had survived intact. This was SALESMAN led by Philippe Liewer, a 32-year-old former Paris journalist.

Liewer was an old hand when it came to the SOE. He had been arrested in 1941 for carrying out various intelligence-gathering and propaganda activities but the following year had been one of a number of prisoners to escape from the Mauzac internment camp, after which he had flown to England. He had then gone back into France in April 1943 with his radio operator, J. C. G. Chartrand (Dieudonné), and the two men spent the next few weeks establishing themselves in Rouen before Chartrand was allocated to Bouguennec's BUTLER circuit instead.

Liewer then had to wait until July before a replacement pianist, Isidore Newman, back in France on his second mission, arrived and the following month they were both joined by a 20-year-old sabotage instructor, Bob Maloubier (also known as Robert Mortier). Liewer was keen to keep his numbers small and very soon SALESMAN was an extremely well organized, well trained, competent and efficient circuit. With the benefit of being amongst the closest of circuits to RAF airfields in southern England, a number of arms drops were made during the autumn months, enough to equip his 350 men.

Because of the risks faced by the circuit radio operators, Liewer was keen to protect Newman; only he and his second-in-command, his half-brother Claude Malraux (Cicero), knew how to contact him. Compared to many other circuits, the security of SALESMAN was very good, largely due to the restricted numbers and measures put in place by Liewer. Because of this, the circuit was able to conduct sabotage missions relatively freely and with a good deal of success.[1] One example was during early October 1943 when Claude Malraux led a group of eight saboteurs in an attack on a factory making aluminium aircraft parts for the Luftwaffe, an attack that reduced output from the factory to just 10 per cent for four months. This was followed up at the end of the month with an attack against the Dieppedalle electric sub-station near Rouen, when saboteurs used just a small amount of plastic explosive, but it had been so well placed that it brought the sub-station to a standstill for six months.

While the results of these raids are impressive, the circuit's attack against a small enemy warship the month before was even more remarkable. The ship, an enemy minesweeper of around 900 tons, had been undergoing repairs at the shipping yard at Ateliers-et-Chantiers-de-Normandie, near Rouen, after suffering damage during an air attack. With the repairs complete, the minesweeper was ready to undergo sea trials before returning to operational service. The sea trials went well, after which the ship was loaded with ammunition and stores ready to go back into operational service the following morning. But, unknown to the Germans, a saboteur from SALESMAN managed to get on board the ship and plant plastic explosives inside the hull. Although it was only a small amount, the saboteur had expertly placed the charge with six-hour time pencils so that it would blow a sizeable hole in the ship.

Later that night the charge exploded and the ship sank in minutes. When workers arrived at the shipyard the following morning all they could see was the funnel showing above the water. It did not take long for the Gestapo to realize the ship had been sabotaged from the inside. Only thirteen men had been granted access to the ship and so each one was taken aside, and threatened with being shot unless he revealed who had set the charge. But fortunately for them, the *Kriegsmarine*, who seemingly had no time for the Gestapo, brought in its own team of divers and specialists and determined that the charge could have only been placed externally, and so the thirteen Frenchmen were spared.[2]

---

1. Foot, op. cit., p.234.
2. Ibid, pp.235–6.

There were other attacks too, against factories and the railways, including an attack on rolling stock at the *Compagnie Industrielle de Matériel de Transport* at Mantes, which brought production to a halt for a couple of days. Liewer had also established reliable contacts in the Rouen *gendarmerie* who provided him with timely warnings of likely raids or round-ups. But inevitably the circuit's luck could not last and it would only be a matter of time before someone was betrayed. London had become anxious and did not want Liewer to push his luck any further and so on the night of 4/5 February 1944 Liewer and Maloubier were picked up near Soucelles by the last Hudson organized by Henri Déricourt.

To the east of SALESMAN, other circuits had also done valuable work. Two of them, FARMER and MUSICIAN, covered the area from the Belgian border – including the vital ports of Dunkirk, Calais and Boulogne – and stretching southwards to Reims and across to the north of Paris. It was a vast and important area, particularly because the Germans felt that any Allied landings would take place in the Pas de Calais, and so the two circuits focused their efforts on destroying and disrupting German rail movements to the area.

The FARMER circuit in Lille had been set up with sabotage in mind. Since arriving back in France, Michael Trotobas had wasted no time in getting to work. The first successful derailment, when forty railway trucks were destroyed and a main line between Lens and Bethune was closed for two days, occurred during the early weeks of 1943. Then, in June, came the request to destroy the locomotive works at Fives in the eastern suburbs of Lille, the second largest of its kind in France. Air raids against the railway sheds had failed to achieve any success and had, in fact, caused considerable collateral damage in the surrounding residential districts, resulting in a number of civilian casualties, and so Trotobas agreed to carry out a raid.

On the evening of 27 June, Trotobas and a dozen saboteurs entered the railway yard. They had been helped by a foreman and were wearing borrowed uniforms, and so they were able to pass through the German security checks disguised as *gendarmes*. The raiders then made their way into the works alongside the normal night shift of workers.

For the next few hours they worked feverishly, placing eighteen large explosive charges in carefully selected positions, including the transformer room and the telephone exchange. Around 2.00am they made their escape with the foreman having already warned the workforce that it would be advisable not to be at their work positions after this time. A series of huge explosions then rocked the whole city and within minutes the railway sheds were a blazing inferno.

Significant damage was caused to more than twenty transformers with the blaze being fuelled by some 4 million litres of oil. While the Germans set about dragging French hostages out of their homes and threatening to kill one in ten of the yard's workforce in retaliation, the fires continued burning into the following afternoon. A reward of a million francs was also offered for information leading to the arrests of those involved.

By the time the fires had gone out, the railway yard was left in a mass of twisted steel and smouldering rubble. Word had been sent to London that the raid had been completed but, quite remarkably, a reply later came back asking for photographs as proof of the damage. What is even more remarkable, though, was that Trotobas set about getting some. While most circuit organizers might have considered sending a rather abrupt response to those armchair senior officers making the request, Trotobas put together a cunning and quite audacious plan to get back into the yards and to get the photographs required. Posing as an industrial company official, and with well-forged documentation as proof, Trotobas returned to the yards. He then persuaded the German SS officers in command that his company would be required to pay out millions of francs in compensation and so he needed photographs to assess the damage. It worked and the photographs were duly sent to London with a small card – 'with the compliments of the Resistance'.[3]

The raid had proved to be a tremendous success. Despite the threat of more reprisals by the Germans, the sabotage continued. The Germans even tried to infiltrate the group but those who tried were dealt with and their bodies dumped at the back of the Gestapo headquarters.

FARMER's saboteurs were now managing several derailments a week and disrupting the enemy's rail movements throughout the region. But it was not all straightforward. The increased number of attacks meant that large

---

3. Cookridge, op. cit., p.278.

quantities of explosives were required. These could not always be dropped from the air and so some had to come from other areas. Furthermore, transmitting from the region was never easy for Staggs. In fact, he was arrested at the end of the year, leaving Trotobas with no way of communicating except through neighbouring circuits, although the Germans never pinned Staggs down to the SOE. After two months of confinement and interrogation he would finally be released, but it had been a big enough scare for Staggs and so he decided to keep his head below the parapet until after the Allies had landed.

Michael Trotobas's luck eventually ran out in November 1943 when the Gestapo caught up with him. His sabotage expert, Michael Reeve (Olivier), had already been captured and this led to a large force of Germans, reported to be about 200, raiding the house where Trotobas was staying. But Trotobas was not prepared to be taken by the Gestapo and he eventually fell dead at his door after the last rounds of his revolver had gone.

Despite the loss of the energetic and most gallant Trotobas, FARMER's work continued under its new leader, Pierre Séailles, one of the circuit's former chiefs. Just days after the death of their leader, the circuit's saboteurs were at it again, this time destroying eleven locomotives at Tourcoing and putting one of the repair sheds out of action.[4]

Gustave Biéler's MUSICIAN had been hard at it too. By early 1943 he had made a sufficient enough recovery from his injury suffered during his parachute drop to continue his work and had established his circuit at Saint-Quentin. His saboteurs scored their first derailment, a troop train near Senlis, during February. Then, during May alone, they cut railway lines between Paris and Cologne thirteen times, and by the summer they were cutting the main line between Saint-Quentin and Lille every couple of weeks. In addition to blowing up the tracks, they destroyed points, signal boxes and shunting sheds between Saint-Quentin and Valenciennes, Maubeuge and other stations in Belgium.[5]

Besides its importance as an industrial and railway centre, Saint-Quentin was also at the heart of the waterway system of north-east France with

---

4. Foot, op. cit., p.239.
5. Cookridge, op. cit., p.272.

several canals passing through the area, many of which carried military and industrial material to aid the German war effort. The lock gates of Saint-Quentin, a route regularly used by the Germans for the transportation of naval equipment for vessels operating in the Mediterranean, were a favourite target for the RAF but even when its bombers did manage to damage the gates, they were quickly repaired again by German engineers and French forced labour.

The canal system was labelled a top priority target and the task for disrupting it was passed to the SOE. London, in turn, passed on the task to Biéler and he was dropped explosive limpet mines so that his saboteurs could finally block the Saint-Quentin canal.

Biéler gave the task to one of his chief saboteurs, André Cordelette, a farmer by profession and a rather frail looking middle-aged man. But Cordelette was an expert in his field. The plan was to attach the limpet mines to three of the main locks. With two assistants, he paddled out into the canal in a small boat loaded with timed explosives. They all lay flat as the boat appeared to be drifting empty on the calm water of the canal, passing right under the eyes of the German guards, until they came to rest alongside a line of barges. They quickly and silently made their escape before the boat, loaded with explosives, blew up, taking forty barges with it. This first attack against the canal caused havoc and succeeded in jamming the lock by destroying its gates and sinking dozens of barges, and putting the canal out of action for several weeks.

Biéler had long been requesting a radio operator and the success of his saboteurs meant that he finally got his wish. Yolande Beekman, codenamed 'Mariette', arrived by Lysander on the night of 17/18 September. A short, plump and dark-haired 32-year-old, with a cosmopolitan background, Yolande was an intelligent and immensely talented multi-linguist.[6]

Using her new identity of Yvonne de Chauvigny, Yolande set up her base in Saint-Quentin. She got on well with Biéler and it was now easier for him to set up more air drops to re-supply his circuit with explosives, arms and ammunition. But for the radio operators, transmitting in northern France

---

6. Escott, op. cit., p.121.

remained extremely hazardous work. Yolande even changed her identity and appearance after one particular scare during the winter months.

Biéler was now a wanted man and the Germans were on his tail. Finally, on 12 January 1944, Biéler and Yolande were arrested while meeting at a small café in Saint-Quentin. They had been betrayed and it was the beginning of the end for MUSICIAN.

One of those caught in the web was Paul Tessier (Théodore) who had only just been sent back into France. He had formed part of the DRESSMAKER sabotage team parachuted north of Escoussens the previous summer to attack tanneries at Mazamet and Tarn that were reportedly being used for the Germans. Tessier had returned for his second mission with MUSICIAN just two days before the arrests of Biéler and Yolande but was also arrested less than two weeks later. Although Tessier subsequently managed to escape, he decided against returning to England but went to work with the SPIRITUALIST circuit instead. It was a decision that would ultimately cost him his life as he would be killed in August during fighting in the eastern suburbs of Paris.

Meanwhile, Biéler and Yolande were both taken to the Gestapo headquarters in Saint-Quentin and subjected to the ghastly routine of interrogation and torture techniques that their captors seemed to revel in. Biéler was one of the few SOE officers who did not have to endure long imprisonment before his death. His countless acts of sabotage had so enraged the Germans that he was soon moved to the Flossenbürg concentration camp in Bavaria, where the brutal torture continued. But the Germans got nothing out of him and, on 5 September, Gustave Biéler, the man Maurice Buckmaster once described as the best student the SOE had, was executed by firing squad.

Poor Yolande Beekman would suffer a similar fate but not before the Germans had tried to make use of her. She was initially taken to the Avenue Foch where it was hoped the German wireless experts could get her to work with them. But it proved no use and Yolande was put into solitary confinement at Fresnes prison. She was later taken to the women's prison at Karlsruhe before being taken to the concentration camp at Dachau with three other women.[7] The following morning, 13 September 1944, Yolande

---

7. The other three women were Madeleine Damerment, Eliane Plewman and Noor Inayat Khan.

was taken out into a small courtyard next to the crematorium where her death sentence was announced to her and she was then made to kneel. Yolande's life then ended with a single shot in the back of her head, although it has also been reported that a second shot was required to end her life.[8] She was shot just a week after the death of her circuit organizer, Gustave Biéler.

Although the MUSICIAN circuit had lasted barely a year, it had achieved so much. To its south, another circuit, Ben Cowburn's TINKER, had also been actively involved in sabotage, although this group focused on disrupting the rail network. Cowburn had returned to England late in 1942 but was back in France for his third and most important mission. He had parachuted back into the field in April 1943 with his radio operator, Denis Barrett (Honoré), a former tailor in Paris and now an officer in the RAF.

TINKER was a small circuit in the Aube region of north-eastern France centred round Troyes. Amongst the active and trusted circle Cowburn put together was Charles Rechenmann (Julien), a French engineer and an excellent organizer of saboteurs, Pierre Mulsant (Paul), a former timber merchant, and Yvonne Fontaine, the circuit's courier.

The circuit quickly gained a reputation for being meticulously secure and its saboteurs achieving great success. On one night in early July, Cowburn and his team carried out a successful raid on the railway depot at Troyes. The mission is described in full in Cowburn's book *No Cloak, No Dagger*[9] but, in short, the railway marshalling yard at Troyes was the largest in eastern France. It had two large roundhouses where engines were parked like the spokes of a wheel. Cowburn had earlier carried out a reconnaissance of the site while posing as a manager of a local football team looking to fix up a game. From the railway football ground he could clearly see into the depot and, even better, he was then escorted to the roundhouses by a trusted railway official who gave him details about the German guards and willingly pointed out which of the many engines were the most valuable. He then led Cowburn out of the yard by a route that he recommended for entry at night.

---

8. Grehan & Mace, op. cit., p.52. (Statement made by the Karlsruhe Gestapo officer, Christian Ott, after the war).
9. Cowburn, op. cit., pp.169–79.

A few nights later, Cowburn returned to the depot alone and quietly wandered around unobserved. He had been told the job had been looked at before but had been considered too risky because of the strength of the German guard force at night. Cowburn felt it was possible for a small team, with just a handful of men, to enter the yard and cause significant damage. But rumours of a planned attack against the depot had already started to spread. Despite the fact the Germans may well have been expecting an attack of some kind, the raiders decided to go ahead with their plan and when news broke of a locomotive accidentally knocking a great gap in the outer wall of one of the roundhouses, they decided to take the opportunity of gaining easy access to the site.

Soon after midnight of 3/4 July, three pairs of saboteurs, each carrying explosives, entered the yard. They made their way up the track leading to the roundhouse and then entered through the gap in the outer wall. Each pair had been briefed to target five or six locomotives. It was as quiet as had been hoped and, having set their charges with the time pencils set at a one-hour delay, the men quickly made their escape. They had barely got out of the yard before the first charges went off, after which further explosions sounded at regular intervals.

The Germans had been expecting an attack but a few days before the raid took place they had arrested a number of suspects. Then, on the night of the raid, the saboteurs had more luck when a wagon had genuinely derailed at the yard. This had diverted the German guards, who believed this to be the act of sabotage they had been expecting, and there was a further stroke of fortune when the Germans carried out a search of the roundhouse the following morning. They found one of the charges had failed to explode and could see the explosive charges were of a British standard. Also, the charges had been expertly set and so the Germans concluded that the raid must have been carried out by some kind of Allied special force rather than by the local French Resistance. Any thought the Germans may have had of carrying out reprisals against workers at the yard disappeared, and so a number of Frenchmen being held in the aftermath of the raid were released.

Cowburn later described the operation as modest but it was anything but. Six large locomotives were destroyed and a further six severely damaged. From that moment on, the Gestapo had an even stronger presence in Troyes as their efforts to find the group of saboteurs increased. There had also been a number of arrests at the time, which now increased the danger to TINKER.

For Cowburn it meant that his third mission in France would soon come to an end before his luck would run out; he was simply too valuable for the SOE to lose. Cowburn handed over TINKER to Pierre Mulsant and was picked up by Lysander near Angers on the night of 17/18 September. But even after Cowburn had left, the Gestapo remained hot on the heels of his circuit and so, a few weeks later, Mulsant was also pulled out. So, too, were Charles Rechenmann, Denis Barrett and Yvonne Fontaine; they were all on the same November Hudson that took Francis Cammaerts back to England with another man, François Mitterrand, later to become the president of France. The evacuation of its key players meant, for the time being at least, that TINKER was in suspense.

Chapter 15

Stationers, Stockbrokers, Marksmen and Scientists

The urban circuits of SALESMAN, FARMER, MUSICIAN and TINKER had covered between them most industrial and transport targets of importance outside Paris. Meanwhile, by the summer of 1943 in central France, Maurice Southgate's STATIONER was busy carrying out a number of sabotage missions against targets such as power stations, aircraft factories and railway networks.

Southgate proved to be an extremely efficient and cautious organizer and rarely risked his brave courier, Jacqueline Nearne, who also proved to be an excellent radio operator, when conducting reception committees for incoming agents or supplies. He encouraged his groups, mostly communists, to appoint their own leaders and would never have more contact with them than needed.

With such a large area to cover, Jacqueline was constantly on the move and there were also calls on neighbouring circuits to be made. By now the circuit had received its own radio operator, René Amédée Maingard (Samuel), an unflappable Mauritian, and soon a number of agents were being received. Southgate was impressed by his Mauritian pianist, so much so that Maingard would soon become his second-in-command, organizing supply drops and delivering arms and ammunition to the resistance groups in the area.

Under Southgate's leadership, STATIONER proved to be a strong circuit. There was so much to do that in September another courier, 29-year-old Pearl Witherington (Marie), was parachuted into the region to help Jacqueline. The two then split the area from the Indre to the Pyrenees, with each travelling separately and using Maingard at Châteauroux as their hub.[1] The following month Southgate was recalled to London to report on

1. Escott, op. cit., p.126.

his circuit's progress and activities, and to be briefed on the months ahead, leaving by Lysander from a field near Tours in mid-October.

Elsewhere, Harry Rée had been moved to Belfort on the Swiss border to set up STOCKBROKER on his own. He had not been surprised to hear of John Starr's arrest and so it meant starting up his circuit from scratch. Under his new identity of Henri Rehman, a watchmaker from Alsace, Rée quickly set about recruiting new helpers and establishing several contacts, which all helped him prepare for the reception of arms and explosives.

The Maquis was strong in the Jura. It was an area where many young men had taken refuge in the mountains and forests from the threat of deportation and forced labour. For many weeks Rée had to make do without a radio link to London and so he had to rely on neighbouring circuits. But through various messages he was able to get supplies dropped at sites dotted around the landscape, and to store them in the many caves hidden in the surrounding mountains.

The Jura was a near-perfect location from which to run a circuit but it was not all success and there were severe setbacks for Rée along the way. The Germans were enraged by the increasing number of attacks and started to round up suspects in the area. Worried that the noose was tightening, Rée moved his headquarters to Vallentigney in the southern suburbs of Montbéliard at a house owned by a man called Barbier, an accountant at the nearby Sochaux works of the Peugeot motor company.

Like most good organizers, Rée rarely stayed at the same place for more than a couple of days. He was constantly out and about with his groups, usually using his bicycle to get around to avoid attracting attention. In August he was joined by Eric Cauchi (Pedro), a 26-year-old former tobacco grower, who parachuted into the Jura mountains as his sabotage instructor.

The two men immediately set about planning a raid that would cause significant damage without, hopefully, any loss of life. The raid planned was against the Peugeot car factory at Sochaux where Barbier worked, which was now being used to make turrets for tanks and engines for Luftwaffe fighters.

Like other major industrial families in France, the Peugeot family had been given little choice after the Nazi occupation but to co-operate with the Germans. They had been compelled to submit their factories to German control but while some French industrialists and businessmen had willingly

become collaborators, many secretly remained supporters of the French
Resistance. Amongst this latter group were the Peugeot family but it was
always a difficult situation for the French workers who had to do their job
or risk deportation or imprisonment. In the case of the Peugeot factory
at Sochaux, the Germans had also brought their own technicians in to
supplement the local workforce in order to increase production.

The factory at Sochaux had long been a priority target of the Ministry
of Economic Warfare and had been designated the third most important
industrial target in France. It had also been on Bomber Command's list of
targets, but bombing at night was never easy and an earlier air raid had been
ineffective. Even though every effort had been made to minimize civilian
casualties, by carrying out the attack from less than 10,000 feet after first
marking it by Pathfinders, the force of more than 150 Halifax bombers
missed the target. Less than 5 per cent of the bombs dropped hit the factory
and production had remained unaffected. Furthermore, French casualties
were reported as high as 123 civilians killed and 336 injured.[2]

The Peugeot factory was, once again, discussed between officials of the
Ministry of Economic Warfare and chiefs of RAF Bomber Command before
it was eventually suggested that SOE, and specifically F Section, should be
asked to do the job. It was then that Buckmaster asked Rée to plan an act of
sabotage to destroy, or at least hinder, production at the factory.

The factory was known to be heavily guarded, day and night, by a strong
German force. There was also a complicated system of passes in force and
workers were searched on entering and leaving the factory area. Instead of
trying to force a way in, Rée decided instead to make contact with Rudolphe
Peugeot to ask for assistance in carrying out an act of sabotage, pointing
out that his co-operation would prevent the RAF from returning to carry
out another attack, which, in all probability, would result in more collateral
damage and further loss of French lives.

It could not have been easy for a man who had been instrumental in building
up the factory before the war to become involved in its destruction, but not
only did Peugeot agree to the request, he also provided Rée with the plans of

---

2. Middlebrook & Everitt, *The Bomber Command War Diaries*, p.407.

the factory, pointing out the best place to lay explosive charges, and gave him the names of two of his trusted workers who would help with the attack.

On the night of 5 November 1943 a handful of saboteurs entered the factory grounds. The two workers inside the factory had hidden themselves in lockers when work had ended for the day and the plastic explosives had already been smuggled into the factory and hidden in a cleaner's cupboard. Having entered the factory with pass keys, the raiders freed the two workers from the lockers. Knowing their way around the inside of the factory meant they were able to avoid the sentries, and set the explosive charges in the transformer hall, assembly plant and steel presses, all key machines that would be difficult to replace. The raiders then let themselves out through the night watchman's room and made their escape. Then, just after midnight, the town was woken by the sound of heavy explosions. Fires soon raged and within minutes large parts of the factory lay in ruins.

The Germans began their investigations the following morning. A few suspects were rounded up but those who had carried out the attack somehow managed to avoid suspicion.[3] The factory was put out of action for at least three months and then three follow-up attacks, carried out between January and March 1944, effectively took it out of production for the rest of the war.[4]

Production at the Peugeot factory at Sochaux, which RAF bombers had found almost impossible to destroy, had been successfully sabotaged by a handful of men. Using a form of 'blackmail' against the factory's owners had been a novel method of getting inside the factory and gain valuable information about its layout and vulnerable points to attack rather than further risking the lives of circuit members.

The idea was fully supported by London for obvious reasons but it would not necessarily catch on elsewhere. When Maurice Southgate tried a similar method with the Michelin family, relating to their tyre factory at Clermont-Ferrand, which had already suffered an act of sabotage earlier in the year when over 300 tons of tyres were destroyed, there was no co-operation. Southgate's bluff had misfired and so Bomber Command carried out an air

---

3. Cookridge, op. cit., pp.190–3.
4. Foot, op. cit., p.256.

attack against the factory instead, causing far more widespread damage than would have have been caused by a small group of saboteurs.

The Germans tried hard to capture Rée. They nearly did, but he and Cauchi ended up making a hasty escape over the Swiss border later in the year, although Cauchi would return across the border early in 1944.

To the south of STOCKBROKER was Richard Heslop's MARKSMAN, also bordering on Switzerland and operating in the beautiful Jura and Savoy Alps. Again, it was ideal guerrilla territory with high mountains, deep valleys, pine forests and lakes. Not only was there the terrain, the vast area was home to isolated farms and hamlets to provide a number of safe havens for the Maquis as well as refugees and others trying to escape across the mountains into Switzerland.

Heslop had earlier been arrested with Denis Rake and Edward Wilkinson but, luckily for them, they were amongst many who benefited from sympathetic French prison officials when the Germans moved into the previously unoccupied south of France. Now Heslop was back, having arrived by Hudson during September. Although he was briefly recalled to England on the mid-October Hudson, he was back in France again two nights later, having been dropped in a Double Hudson into a field near Lons-le-Saunier, and bringing with him a courier, 25 year old Elizabeth Deveraux Rochester (Elizabeth), an American by birth, now working under the name of Elizabeth Reynolds.

The increase in the number of Maquis groups and their activity inevitably attracted interest from the Germans. Railway stations and factories became guarded and there were soon reprisals against the civilian population, such as burning down farms, making life during the winter months even harsher than before.

Also in the east, PIMENTO had become the largest circuit in the former unoccupied zone. It had been a quite remarkable effort by the young Tony Brooks. Since forming his circuit in July 1942 he had managed to steer his circuit around the troubles and debacles elsewhere. His group had received a number of large drops of weapons and explosives, and had carried out numerous acts of sabotage. The circuit also remained free from infiltration and betrayal as Brooks succeeded in sealing off his circuit whenever disaster struck nearby, in particular, following the earlier arrests of Maurice Pertschuk and Marcus Bloom leading to the demise of PRUNUS.

London could clearly trust Brooks. His reception committees always seemed to be in the right place and at the right time, and so he generally got the supplies he needed. He was so highly regarded that the SOE decided to pull him out of France for further training.

Leaving his deputy, André Moch, to run the circuit, Brooks left on one of two Hudsons sent to France during August 1943. Amongst the ten passengers on board the Hudson that night were Marie-Thérèse Le Chêne, Victor Gerson and Francis Basin, who had managed to escape from prison as the Germans moved south and would now spend the rest of the war back in England.

Another agent to return to England was Robert Boiteux, leaving SPRUCE dormant for the time being with its area covered by three separate organizers. One was Robert Lyon, who had arrived by Lysander at the end of June to set up ACOLYTE, but he soon found the area sternly policed and so could not carry out any meaningful sabotage. Another was Joseph Marchand, who set up NEWSAGENT but he found the same difficulties as Lyon, and the third was Albert Browne-Bartroli, Eliane Plewman's brother, who set up DITCHER with Jean Renaud (Jean).

André Moch had been left in charge of PIMENTO at a time when London was keen for the circuits in southern France – MONK and JOCKEY included – to raise the tempo against the rail and road links with Italy. With Italy now out of the war, it was left to the Germans to defend their southern flank and so reinforcements were piling across the border to counter the Allied advance.

In the south-west of France bordering the Pyrenees was WHEELWRIGHT led by George Starr who had picked up the surviving stragglers of PRUNUS. Starr had been joined by his radio operator, Yvonne Cormeau, who had parachuted into south-west France on the night of 23 August. Since WHEELWRIGHT covered such a large area, Yvonne was constantly on the move, taking her radio set with her everywhere as she travelled from the Dordogne to the Pyrenees. It was not unusual for her to cover up to 100 kilometres a day but she benefited from reliable connections who helped transport her heavy radio set or put her up overnight despite the risk. She did, however, at one point, transmit from the same remote location for several weeks. She had found an ideal spot in a village where she could see for some distance and its remoteness meant the Germans never searched there, even though a radio operator was known to be transmitting from the area.

By the end of 1943 Yvonne was making several transmissions a week as the air drops of equipment and agents increased. As the number of sabotage attacks increased, so did the number of drops, although she was kept away from the DZs to prevent her from being arrested. Yvonne was a perfectly unobtrusive and secure craftswoman who, during the course of a year, transmitted more than 400 messages for George Starr.[5]

Bordering WHEELWRIGHT to its east was a circuit that had been re-activated during the autumn of 1943. This was DETECTIVE, created in the Aude department and centred on the fortified town of Carcassonne. It was smaller than its neighbour and had been re-activated by its leader, Henri Sevenet, who earlier that summer had had a lucky escape to England. Sevenet parachuted back into France in mid-September and was joined two nights later by his pianist, Harry Despaigne, who arrived by Lysander after he had fortunately escaped the CARTE debacle.

While WHEELWRIGHT was big geographically, its neighbouring circuit to the north, Claude de Baissac's SCIENTIST was even bigger. Based in Bordeaux but stretching as far as Paris, its numbers had grown to more than 15,000, some of whom had migrated across to de Baissac following the downfall of PROSPER, while many more swelled its ranks in the belief that an Allied landing in north-west Europe was imminent. While they were, perhaps, somewhat over-optimistic, it was a remarkable fourfold increase since the beginning of the year. Furthermore, the number of air drops received had risen tenfold to more than a hundred during the year with its saboteurs achieving much success against a variety of targets, including a key communications establishment for the Atlantic U-boats and a power station supplying a Luftwaffe airfield.

But because of its large geographic area, which effectively stretched along the entire western side of France, SCIENTIST had become complex and unwieldy. It was made up of port saboteurs along its coastal stretch but the vast majority of the circuit were located inland and consisted of a miscellaneous mix of volunteers.[6]

---

5. Ibid., p.254.
6. Ibid., p.248.

As seen with other circuits elsewhere, SCIENTIST was snowballing out of control and things were about to get worse for de Baissac when details of circuit members were found by the Germans during a raid on an apartment in Bordeaux. Arrests soon followed and the noose started to tighten on those at the high end of the circuit. The earlier arrests of Suttill and others raised concerns that the Germans would be led to Bordeaux and, therefore, to Claude and Lise de Baissac.

Both de Baissacs were recalled to London during mid-August 1943 on board the same Lysander that took Nicholas Bodington back to England. SCIENTIST was left in the hands of André Grandclément, a retired army officer in his thirties, assisted by Roger Landes and Mary Herbert. But, just a month after Claude de Baissac had left, Grandclément was arrested while visiting Paris. His address had been given to the Germans and his house raided. Although fortunate to be out at the time, his photograph had been found amongst his belongings, after which he had been identified and arrested at a café.

Fearing for his wife's life, as well as being suspicious of increasing communist influence within the French Resistance, it did not take long for the right-wing Grandclément to reveal important information to the Gestapo. As well as betraying members of the circuit, he also gave away the location of arms dumps and this enabled the Germans to capture about one third of the group's arms.[7]

A number of arrests followed, including Charles Hayes (Victor) the circuit's sabotage instructor. But Hayes did not go down without a fight. At the house where he was staying, he and John Duboué, the son of the houseowner, managed to hold the Germans off for three hours before they were captured, along with two women at the house. Hayes would later be taken to the concentration camp at Gross-Rosen, a satellite camp of Sachsenhausen, and to his death.

After Grandclément's arrest, SCIENTIST had been taken over by Roger Landes, who had been suspicious of Grandclément from the start. Landes changed his identity to Roger Lalande, a real but absent person with authentic papers and registration,[8] but with the Gestapo crackdown and the

---

7. Ibid., p.250.
8. Obituary – Roger Landes MC & Bar – *The Times*, 17 July 2008.

142 Setting France Ablaze

number of arrests it was no longer safe for him to remain in France. He left for Spain.

Meanwhile, Harry Peulevé was back in France for his second mission. He had come in on the same September Lysander as Harry Despaigne and was due to make contact with Grandclément. But Peulevé had arrived in Bordeaux at the height of Grandclément's treachery, and at the point that SCIENTIST was about to collapse. At that point Peulevé could have given up and make his way back to England but he agreed to take over the surviving contacts around the port city and to set up AUTHOR in the Corrèze. And so, for now, it was the end of the great SCIENTIST circuit.

Chapter 16

The White Rabbit

While F Section was suffering the loss of so many of its agents, a British RAF officer working with RF Section, a man who would go on to become a legend within the SOE, parachuted back into France on 17 September 1943 for what was to be his second mission. This was Tommy Yeo-Thomas who operated under the codenames of 'Seahorse' and 'Shelly', but was to become better known as the 'White Rabbit'.

Although known as Tommy, his full name was Forest Frederick Edward Yeo-Thomas and, like many to become agents for the SOE, he had been born in England but raised and educated between his homeland and France. By the time he parachuted into France for his first mission in February 1943 he was already aged forty-one. Not a man who had ever looked for a quiet way of life, in 1920 he had fought with the Poles during the Polish-Soviet War but had escaped with his life after being captured by the Bolsheviks. Although sentenced to death he managed to escape the night before he was due to be shot by strangling a prison guard. Having then made his way back to France he worked in Paris between the wars but after the fall of France in 1940 he escaped to Britain where he enlisted into the RAF.

Yeo-Thomas was commissioned in the RAF but was considered too old for active operations and so his background made him an obvious recruit for the SOE. He joined RF Section in February 1942 and, after working in an administrative capacity, became a liaison officer with the BCRA. He was soon working with its head, André Dewavrin, the man known as Colonel Passy, and the gifted academic Pierre Brossolette, taken on by de Gaulle to bring political credibility to his campaign so that de Gaulle could be recognized by the Allies as the only credible leader of the Free French.

Between them, Dewavrin, Brossolette and Yeo-Thomas created a strategy for obstructing the German occupation of France, collating information from the French Resistance and working with the SOE to plan operations for agents inserted into France. All three had parachuted into France together in February 1943 for Yeo-Thomas's first mission. His task then was to accompany his two French colleagues during meetings with representatives of various resistance movements in Paris and northern France, and with Jean Moulin who had, by then, returned to France.

Moulin had succeeded in bringing resistance leaders and their groups together but was soon to die in horrific circumstances after being betrayed and arrested with a number of resistance leaders during a meeting in Lyons. Moulin was imprisoned and extensively interrogated by the Gestapo chief, Klaus Barbie. He was then moved to Paris but never revealed anything to his captors and died during a train journey just days later, either as a result of the horrific injuries he had sustained during torture or, as has also been suggested, suicide. Whatever the cause, Moulin's ability to withhold information from the Gestapo was extraordinary given the ferocity of the torture to which he was subjected. Jean Moulin is remembered today as an emblem of the French Resistance, owing mainly to his role in unifying the groups under de Gaulle and his extraordinary courage and death at the hands of the Gestapo.

After completing his first mission, Yeo-Thomas was picked up with Dewavrin and Brossolette in mid-April as part of a Double Lysander pick-up from a field near Rouen. Three passengers had made the journey from England, including Baron Emmanuel d'Astier de la Vigerie, soon to become de Gaulle's Minister for the Interior, and Jean Cavaillès, whom the BCRA had tasked with forming an intelligence network in northern France.

With Yeo-Thomas having returned safely to England, the BBC broadcast later that night the message 'le petit lapin blanc est rentre au clapier' – translated as 'the little white rabbit has returned to his hutch'. Although his first mission had lasted just a few weeks, the man now known as the White Rabbit had shown great courage and initiative during his time in France, particularly in one incident when he had enabled a French officer who was being followed by a Gestapo agent in Paris to reach safety and resume his work in a different area.

And so just five months after returning from his first mission, Yeo-Thomas was back in France. With him, once again, was Pierre Brossolette. Their task this time was to assess the state of the resistance network following the arrest, and subsequent death, of Jean Moulin, and to find out what was needed in the way of arms and ammunition.

Their arrival coincided with more arrests but undeterred they continued with their enquiries. Yeo-Thomas met with many resistance groups seeking Allied support but the Germans were now aware of the man called the White Rabbit and a price was put on his head. On six occasions he narrowly escaped arrest, including a close call when he reportedly had to make light conversation with the Gestapo chief, Klaus Barbie, on a train to Paris.

While Brossolette was to stay in France, Yeo-Thomas returned to England on 15 November after being picked up by a Lysander near Arras, taking with him further intelligence archives that he had secured from a house under surveillance by the Gestapo. He returned appalled by the apparent lack of logistical and material support for the resistance groups and even took his concerns direct to Winston Churchill, pleading with the prime minister to divert more aircraft for SOE operations to drop more agents and arms to the resistance.

Back in France, Pierre Brossolette had also become well known to the Germans. He was continuously hunted by the Gestapo but managed to escape arrest many times. He was eventually summoned back to London but a number of exfiltration attempts by Lysander during the hard winter months proved unsuccessful. Then, after attempting to escape from Brittany by boat, Brossolette was betrayed and captured, and imprisoned in Rennes.

When Yeo-Thomas heard about the arrest, he was determined to return to France to rescue Brossolette. But as RF Section's second-in-command, it was considered too much of a risk. Yeo-Thomas simply knew too much. If captured, he could be forced to divulge the names of all of the Section's agents and details of their operations.

But Yeo-Thomas remained determined to rescue Brossolette and, in the end, seemingly got his way to return to France. His mission, called ASYMPTOTE, included a number of tasks and amongst his instructions was general approval to carry out any investigations that he judged to be important to the prosecution of the war.[1]

---

1. NA HS 9/1458, Personnel File, F.F.E. Yeo-Thomas (Operational Instructions dated 15 February 1944) and Marshall, *The White Rabbit*, p.101.

This, effectively, would give him free licence once back in France. On the night of 24/25 February 1944, Yeo-Thomas again parachuted into France. His landing had been heavy and awkward, causing him to sprain an ankle, but he continued as planned and took a night train to Paris. But his plans to rescue Pierre Brossolette would never materialize. The White Rabbit had remained on top of the Gestapo's most wanted list and, despite Yeo-Thomas seemingly taking every precaution, he was also betrayed, reportedly by a newly-recruited sub-agent. On 21 March he was seized by the Gestapo on the steps of the Passy metro station in Paris.

Although Yeo-Thomas could not have known at the time, Pierre Brossolette would be dead in just a matter of hours. After capture he had been repeatedly tortured by the Gestapo at the Avenue Foch. Then, on 22 March, Brossolette was left alone as he recovered consciousness. What happened next may have been an unsuccessful attempt to escape or a decision to take his own life rather than implicate others under continuous torture, but he suffered fatal injuries after falling from a window several floors up. Pierre Brossolette died later that evening at la Pitié-Salpêtrière hospital.

Meanwhile, Yeo-Thomas was being held by the Gestapo. To preserve his true identity he made out that he was Kenneth Dodkin, a downed RAF pilot, but the Gestapo did not believe him. The Nazis rightly believed they had caught a jewel in the crown and, having taken Yeo-Thomas to the Avenue Foch, the same building where Brossolette had been detained, they interrogated him, beat him and then tortured him for four days.

Aware that he knew far too much, probably more than any one person at the time, Yeo-Thomas refused to crack. The Germans continued to try to break him by subjecting him to numerous physical beatings, applying electric shocks to his genitals and immersing him head down in ice-cold water while his legs and arms were chained, often to the point that he had to be revived by artificial respiration to bring him back to consciousness. He had all but lost an arm from blood poisoning as a result of the chains cutting his wrist.

The Gestapo were still unsuccessful but the questioning went on for two months. Yeo-Thomas was even offered his freedom on condition he gave up the information his captors so clearly desired. But still he did not break. He made two unsuccessful attempts to escape. He was then confined in solitude at Fresnes prison for four months, including three weeks in a darkened cell with very little food. Conditions were awful and many died there but throughout the torturous months Yeo-Thomas still refused to crack. His courage and inner strength inspired his fellow prisoners.

In July 1944 Yeo-Thomas was transferred to a prison at Compiègne. The Allies were now breaking out of Normandy and Paris was just days from being liberated. Again, he tried to escape – twice – after which he was transferred with a group of thirty-six other prisoners, mostly other SOE agents and captured members of the resistance, to Buchenwald. The journey took several days but there was still time for a further beating during a stopover at a transit camp at Saarbrücken.

Soon after their arrival at Buchenwald nearly half the group of prisoners were executed. It was clear to the others that the same fate awaited them and for most of the group that turned out to be the case. In early October, eleven more were executed but Yeo-Thomas had succeeded in hatching a daring and collaborative plan with one of the doctors, Erwin Ding-Schuler, a German surgeon and officer in the SS, who was responsible for carrying out medical experiments on prisoners in the notorious Hygiene Institute in the Experimental Station Block 46.

With the war entering its final phase, Yeo-Thomas had managed to get Ding-Schuler to agree to help him and two colleagues to switch identities with three of the doctor's subjects who had died from typhus. In return, Yeo-Thomas agreed to testify on Ding-Schuler's behalf at any war crimes trial after the war.[2]

In Yeo-Thomas's own words, he 'conveniently died of typhus on 13 October 1944'. It was an act which saved his life as his execution order arrived the following day. To maximize their chances of survival the three prisoners were then sent out to satellite camps. Yeo-Thomas, now living as Maurice Choquet, the dead Frenchman whose identity he had taken on, went to work at Gleina and then Rehmsdorf to the south of Leipzig, where he worked as a medical orderly in quite horrific and inhumane conditions.

Then, while the Allies continued to advance towards Berlin, the camp prisoners were evacuated east by train towards Czechoslovakia. During one of their stops Yeo-Thomas led a daring escape in broad daylight by twenty

---

2. Marshall, op. cit., p.209.

prisoners. Taking their chances the prisoners headed for the woods nearby but the German guards had been quick to react and half the group were killed. Yeo-Thomas was again lucky and was one of those to get away. After sleeping rough and evading capture for several days, he was eventually captured by a German patrol; he was within half a mile of the Allied lines.

Having taken on the role of a captured French officer, Yeo-Thomas was put in a French prisoner-of-war camp at Grunhainichen, just north of the Czech border, but two days later he escaped yet again, this time with ten French prisoners of war. They made their way through German patrols and a minefield before eventually reaching the American lines. Yeo-Thomas then made his way to Paris, arriving there on 8 May.

With the war in Europe over, Yeo-Thomas set about launching a mission to exact his own fierce retribution by assembling a small team and travelling to Germany to seek out former concentration camp guards now believed to be hiding in the American sector. He managed to persuade SOE to let him go but his request for sub-machine guns and pistols revealed his true intentions, as well as his psychological state. Fearing that his mission would 'degenerate with unpleasant repercussions', the mission was revised to one with a more peaceful outcome instead.

The story of Tommy Yeo-Thomas is best told by Bruce Marshall in his book *The White Rabbit*[3] but for his amazing exploits in France, Yeo-Thomas was awarded the Military Cross and Bar. Then, on 15 February 1946, came the official announcement of his award of the George Cross. He was just one of four SOE agents to receive this highest recognition and the only male of the four. His citation concludes:

> Wing Commander Yeo-Thomas thus turned his final mission into a success by his determined opposition to the enemy, his strenuous efforts to maintain the morale of his fellow prisoners and his brilliant escape activities. He endured brutal treatment and torture without flinching and showed the most amazing fortitude and devotion to duty throughout his service abroad, during which he was under the constant threat of death.

---

3. Ibid.

Chapter 17

Radio Games, Deception and Lies

A lthough there had been many successes during the past year, 1943 had also been a difficult one for F Section. Some of its misfortunes could not have been predicted but there had been mistakes as well. While those back in London cannot be held to blame for incompetence or lapses in security amongst the agents in France, or for the fact that some agents turned whilst under duress in captivity, the fact was that many smaller circuits had been allowed to become entangled with others and this had made some too big and unwieldy for organizers to manage.

There was also a shortage of trained radio operators in the field and this led to some pianists having to transmit for neighbouring circuits and sub-circuits. This would have always been done with the best intentions by those who worked hard to make things work but this had also brought radio operators into contact with far more agents than had been intended, and so the arrest of one radio operator could easily spiral into chaos. And then, of course, the Henri Déricourt situation had not been dealt with early enough and had been allowed to run on into 1944, by which time too many good agents had suffered as a result of the consequences.

While a finger could be pointed at those in London for certain aspects of the SOE's failings in France, there were also occasions when agents went against the training and advice they had been given before going into the field. For example, the expansion of PROSPER, with its many sub-circuits, meant there was a period when too many agents were in or around Paris at any one time. Furthermore, some circuit organizers met too often with their subordinates, some radio operators transmitted too often from the same location, making it easier for the German direction finders to locate their position, and some agents used the same address or safe house too many times.

The reasons for these lapses against all they had been taught before going into the field will vary. It may have been because of complacency or it may have been that some agents simply sought companionship in their world of secrecy and deception. But whatever the reason, the debacles of large organizations such as CARTE, PROSPER and SCIENTIST, and the downfall of circuits such as INVENTOR, were hugely costly and had cost the SOE some of its finest agents in the field.

Other circuits had fallen, too, during the latter half of 1943. These included CHESTNUT with the arrest of Charles Grover-Williams and his radio operator, Robert Dowlen (Richard). Dowlen had arrived in France by Lysander during March but lived away from the other group members in a villa in the north-western suburbs of Paris and it was there that he was caught by German direction finders, sometime around late-July or early-August. Although Dowlen had been caught, radio transmissions from his wireless set are known to have continued for a while, probably for at least two months. Whether it was Dowlen making these transmissions under duress or whether the Germans had replaced him and were using his radio set and codes is not known. Dowlen was later executed at Flossenbürg while Grover-Williams was taken to Sachsenhausen and shot.[1]

Another circuit to have fallen was Octave Simon's SATIRIST. The end of PROSPER had seen members of many circuits put at risk but probably none more than those of SATIRIST. A number of its members were arrested, although Simon managed to escape to Angers, despite some close shaves with the Gestapo, where he boarded the mid-August Hudson.

On board the same aircraft was Robert Benoist who, despite having been arrested during CHESTNUT's demise, had managed to escape while being taken for questioning in a car. It was an escape befitting a Hollywood movie. Benoist, seated between two Germans in the back of the car, was being taken away for questioning. Determined not to suffer like those before him, he patiently waited for his moment and when the car swung round a bend he shoved hard against his guard, forcing the door to open and both men to fall out into the road. Before the Germans could react, Benoist quickly scampered off into the distance and disappeared. Then, having found that

---

1. In their book *Unearthing Churchill's Secret Army*, p.76, Grehan and Mace include a suggestion that Grover-Williams may have actually survived the war and joined MI6 under the name George Tambal but later died in 1983.

all his friends' houses were under surveillance, he went into hiding for two weeks before managing to secure a flight home.

The end of CHESTNUT as an operational circuit, however abrupt, cannot be attributed to the demise of PROSPER. Other circuits, too, had successfully escaped the PROSPER vortex, usually because their leaders had managed to maintain an independence rather than looking to Francis Suttill for direction. Although most of them were in contact with Suttill, it tended to be through a system of couriers and mutual sub-contacts rather than there being any direct communication between the circuit leaders.

Some of the leaders deliberately kept a low profile by not living a lavish lifestyle, particularly those leading communist groups, and so they rarely visited Paris or frequented its bars and restaurants that were obvious playgrounds for the Gestapo. Amongst these was Jean Bouguennec, leader of the BUTLER circuit to the west of Paris and operating in the Sarthe. Although his group had overlapped with PROSPER territorially, it did not mix socially and BUTLER simply got on with its work. Arms were collected and the railway network disrupted, and so life had managed to go on through the summer of 1943, despite the disasters elsewhere.

So successful had Bouguennec been that one of his associates, Marcel Fox, managed to set up a new circuit, PUBLICAN, on the eastern side of Paris and centred on Meaux. His group were soon busy disrupting the rail network in the area between Lagny and Meaux, as well as carrying out sabotage at locomotive sheds at Vaires, Noisy-le-Sec and Faremoutiers.

Bouguennec and Fox had been so careful to avoid the chaos elsewhere but they still maintained contact with each other and this led to their own downfall during September 1943 when they were both arrested while having lunch together. It is thought they were betrayed by one of the circuit members but nothing was ever proved. Marcel Fox would end up in Flossenbürg where he was executed just weeks before the end of the war, six months after Jean Bouguennec's life had ended at Buchenwald.

Also arrested as part of this episode was Marcel Rousset, although he did what he could to deter his captors from learning about his radio transmissions. Rousset gave false information about his radio procedures and security checks, in the hope that London would spot the circuit had been compromised, but the Germans were able to continue operating as

BUTLER for a further nine months after Rousset's arrest, during which a number of air drops continued to be made.

Rousset was one of only a few to later escape captivity but the Germans were now playing a clever game. Not only had they succeeded in capturing a large amount of arms, explosives and ammunition, as well as hundreds of individuals on their most wanted lists, they had also succeeded in penetrating a number of SOE circuits in France while completely taking over the operation of others. Using a handful of captured radio sets and codes, the Germans managed to make London believe that a number of circuits were still in existence, so much so that air drops continued. The Germans even went so far as to ensure RAF aircraft delivering these supplies were left alone by the Luftwaffe so that they could make their drops.

It would take some time for London to realize what was going on and even in March 1944 half a dozen agents and a large amount of supplies were dropped straight into the arms of the waiting Gestapo.[2]

Three of those were captured on the night of 2/3 March. Two Americans, Maurice Lepage (Colin) and Edmond Lesout (Tristan), and their 20-year-old radio operator, David Finlayson (Guillaume), were to have set up a new organization called LIONTAMER to operate round Valenciennes. A fourth agent captured in the same drop, George McBain (Cecil), was to have joined ARCHDEACON; all four were later executed at Gross-Rosen.

Also dropped that night, 2/3 March, albeit at a different drop zone, was Adolphe Rabinovitch. He was returning to France after the SPINDLE debacle almost a year before to set up his own circuit, BARGEE, near Nancy. With Rabinovitch was a 21-year-old Canadian radio operator called Roméo Sabourin (Leonard), who was to join the PRIEST circuit in the Meuse. But their drop zone was also in the hands of the Gestapo and both were captured, but only after they had put up a fight.

All these unsuspecting operatives had fallen victims to yet another piece of German deception, the origins of which dated back to the previous summer and the arrests of the two Canadians, Frank Pickersgill and John Macalister, who had been sent into France to set up ARCHDEACON. Their arrests had triggered the chain of events leading to the whole PROSPER debacle and its

---

2. Foot, op. cit., pp.290–3.

disastrous aftermath. After the two Canadians had been beaten mercilessly at the Avenue Foch, the Germans were able to operate ARCHDEACON as a bogus circuit and formed a number of reception committees, often made up of genuine French resisters who, unknown to them, were loading trucks with supplies and agents that were being driven by collaborators or Germans posing as Frenchmen. Also captured under the same deception game was Alphonse Defendini who had been landed in Brittany to set up PRIEST. He had been given a list of railway targets to be sabotaged once the Allied landings were under way and should have been met by members of ARCHDEACON but he was arrested soon after his arrival and later hanged at Buchenwald.

For the Germans their scheme was working well but, with Rabinovitch and Sabourin captured immediately after landing, they had been unable to transmit a coded message to London indicating their safe arrival and so ARCHDEACON now came under suspicion. Drops to the circuit stopped and it brought an end to this small piece of the deception puzzle, although radio transmissions continued with the bogus circuit for some time afterwards to keep the Germans believing they were still in control. For Rabinovitch and Sabourin, though, they would meet the same end as so many others. Rabinovitch was deported to Germany and, being a Jew, was put to death in the gas chambers at Gross-Rosen, probably during the autumn of that year, while Sabourin was taken to Buchenwald and executed in September.

It was a similar story for Emile-Henri Garry's CINEMA-PHONO, which, after the arrest of its radio operator, Noor Inayat Khan, had also been taken over by the Germans. Using her radio set, her codes and her security checks, as well as knowing her transmission procedures and practices, which, as it turned out, they had gleaned from monitoring her transmissions over a lengthy period, the Germans managed to impersonate her transmissions for several weeks.

Although London had been suspicious of the transmissions coming from France for some time, it was eventually believed that it was probably Noor transmitting but a total of seven agents had dropped into two 'CINEMA-PHONO' reception committees of the Gestapo during February 1944. The first, a group of four, had dropped near Poitiers on the night of 7/8

February and amongst those captured was a 22-year-old Frenchman called Roland Alexandre, who was to set up a new circuit called SURVEYOR, and his American radio operator, Robert Byerly. Also captured that night were François Deniset, a French-Canadian who, had the circuit still have been in existence, was intended to be the arms instructor for Garry, and a 22-year-old Anglo-Frenchman, Jacques Ledoux, a promising young agent who was to set up ORATOR in the area of le Mans. All four were first imprisoned in Paris and then transferred to Gross-Rosen where they were believed to have been executed in the early months of 1944, although more recent information suggests that Ledoux might have escaped only to later die as a result of the appalling treatment he had received.[3]

Two more unsuspecting agents, also captured in February, were Julien Detal (Roderique) and 21-year-old Philippe Duclos (Christian). They were dropped into France to set up a new circuit, DELEGATE, and to prepare for the reception of twelve air drops, which would give them enough arms and explosives to disrupt communications between German units in Brittany and the rest of France. But the field they came down in was yet another in the hands of the Germans. They, like many others who had gone before them, would end up in a concentration camp, Detal at Buchenwald and Duclos at Gross-Rosen, where their lives were to end in September.

All these arrests meant that February 1944 was a particularly productive month for German intelligence, and a disastrous one for F Section, but the Gestapo's biggest catch of all was still to come – the capture of France Antelme. Antelme was described within the SOE as highly intelligent and one of the best of his type.[4] He had been fortunate to escape the PROSPER disaster and, after evading the Gestapo for a month, had been pulled out of France by Lysander. That close shave had almost destroyed him inside but he now felt refreshed and ready for his third mission in France.

Antelme had persistently made clear his desire to go back to France to find out, amongst other things, whether CINEMA-PHONO had fallen. He finally got his way and amongst the long list of tasks given to him was to

---

3. Grehan & Mace, op. cit., p.102.
4. NA HS 9/42-4, Personal file, J. F. A. Antelme (Comment by the Commandant of Arisaig dated 4 September 1942).

revisit any surviving BRICKLAYER contacts and help set up SURVEYOR anywhere to the south of Paris that he considered best. He was also to check on the security of BUTLER and establish the state of the PARSON circuit that had been operating round Rennes, which London now suspected of being in enemy hands.

Although London did not know at the time, PARSON had already been infiltrated by the Gestapo and had been in enemy hands since the end of 1943. Radio transmissions with London had continued but not by George Clement. He had been arrested and was in Rennes prison; he would later die at Mauthausen. Clement's arrest had meant that François Vallée and Henri Gaillot had gone to ground, but they, too, had later been arrested and their lives were to end at Gross-Rosen.

None of this was known in London and so, late in the evening of 28 February, Antelme and his radio operator, Lionel Lee (René), together with their French courier, 26-year-old Madeleine Damerment (Solange), took off from Tempsford. The drop was planned to take place into a park near the village of Sainville, to the south of Rambouillet in the Eure-et-Loire, with the aircraft due overhead the drop zone at 10.45pm.

An hour before the aircraft was due to arrive, the Germans cordoned off the entire area. While the SS swarmed all over the park, other German troops encircled the drop zone. The first drop was a number of containers and then came the agents with Antelme jumping first. The three agents stood no chance. They had jumped straight into the arms of the Gestapo. They were all taken to the Avenue Foch but none of them talked.

The Germans knew that in Antelme they had captured an extremely important agent but he continued to remain silent. He and Lee were later taken with others captured earlier in the month to the Gross-Rosen concentration camp where their lives were soon to end while Madeleine Damerment was shot on the morning of 12 September 1944 at Dachau alongside fellow SOE agents.

These losses suffered by F Section were particularly tragic. Agents were jumping straight into the waiting arms of the Gestapo before they could even get their mission up and running. Surely this could have been avoided? If there were already concerns about certain circuits being compromised, could the agents not have been dropped somewhere else, farther south for example where circuits were known to be secure or, equally, could they not have been dropped blind?

Whether some of those in Baker Street had become complacent, neglectful or gullible, or all three for that matter, is a matter of opinion. Since the war there have been direct or implied accusations made against the leadership within the SOE and suggesting that agents such as Antelme, Lee and Madeleine 'were deliberately sacrificed'.[5] Some will also argue that if F Section had treated every radio transmission received from France with utmost caution, then the SOE could never have got on with the war, a point made by M. R. D. Foot in his book *SOE in France*.[6]

It is important not to become involved in unfounded accusations, particularly with over seventy years of hindsight. There is no doubt that the situation regarding the Paris SOE outposts during early 1944 was an extremely confused one. But the fact also remains that agents continued to be dropped into France during February and March 1944, along with other supplies and large amounts of money, even though those in Baker Street may well have been aware that the Germans were playing clever radio games at the time.

These radio games, what the Germans called *funkspiel*, were being played out from the second floor of 84 Avenue Foch and run by Dr Josef Goetz, the Gestapo's radio and coding expert, and Joseph Placke, his assistant head of the wireless section. From there, the Germans were able to mimic SOE radio operators using captured wireless sets, codes and security checks. Transmissions from ARCHDEACON and CINEMA-PHONO, in particular, were part of the overall radio deception game being played and it is estimated that during this period as many as eighteen SOE agents fell straight into the arms of the Gestapo.

While this makes it look like the Germans had managed to gain the upper hand during the winter of 1943/44, it is more than likely that there was more to this period than at first meets the eye. The whole deception game was being cleverly played by both sides. In fact the tables had slowly turned as the SOE began to fight the Germans at their own game. Early in May 1944

---

5. Cookridge, op. cit., p.305.
6. Foot, op. cit., p.303.

London sent a false message to the fake Bertrand post of Frank Pickersgill saying that, to verify the security of his messages, an officer from F Section was due to fly over his area and speak to him from the aircraft by S-Phone, a short-wave radio telephone that had significantly improved the efficiency of air drops by enabling someone on board the aircraft to chat to the operator on the ground.

This caused the Germans in Paris a significant problem. At that stage Pickersgill was still alive but his exact whereabouts was unknown as he had already been sent off to a concentration camp. A later message from London revealed that the flypast and S-Phone conversation would take place over a field near Longyon and asked 'Bertrand' for confirmation that he would be there. With no option other than to try and play the impersonator game once more, the Germans used a man with a Canadian accent to stand in for Pickersgill.

The brave SOE officer on board the aircraft and taking part in the plot was Gerry Morel but in the end it turned out to be a somewhat farcical attempt by the Germans to convince Morel that it was Pickersgill on the ground. One voice first spoke in French and then a second in English. Morel listened to the voices for a short time but was astute enough not to reply. As it happened, it appears that the Germans had taken along John Starr to try to identify the voice of the agent on board the aircraft. But Morel was convinced the man on the ground was not Pickersgill and, just to be sure, another message was sent soon after with personal news concerning Pickersgill's family that required a reply.

At that point the game might easily have been given up by the Germans in Paris. Only Pickersgill could know the information needed in the reply but, instead of giving up on the game, the Germans managed to locate the emaciated and very sick Canadian agent at Ravitsch concentration camp on the Polish-Silesian border.

Pickersgill was then taken to Paris but, to give the Canadian the utmost credit, it would have been an easy option to go along with what the Germans wanted. They even told him they would keep him in Paris and that he would not have to return to the horrors of the camp, but so enraged was Pickersgill at the suggestion of playing their game that at one of his chats with the Germans he attacked his SS guard with a bottle, breaking it first and then stabbing the German in the neck and severing the man's jugular vein; the guard later died. Pickersgill then leapt out of the second floor window and made off down the road before he was cut down in a hail of bullets. Remarkably, Pickersgill survived, even though he had been hit twice and was also suffering from a broken arm suffered in his fall. He was taken to hospital but was later taken back to the horrors of a concentration camp. This time it was Buchenwald where the brave Canadian's life would soon end; he was executed on 14 September 1944 alongside his fellow Canadians, John Macalister and Roméo Sabourin.

The radio games had finally ended but they had cost many good agents their lives. But had it all been worthwhile? The answer to that question lies with those who were at the top at the time. But by the early months of 1944 the Allies were deep into the final planning phase for the forthcoming landings in north-west Europe, due to take place sometime soon and somewhere along the northern coastline of France, and so getting the enemy to spend time and resource focusing on a handful of bogus SOE circuits might help keep their attention away from the much bigger problem of the Allied landings. Furthermore, if this were to be true, then it would probably mean that valuable German resources would be diverted away from where the landings were actually due to take place.

It appears to have all been part of the game being played at the time but, nonetheless, it remains a truly wretched tale.

Chapter 18

An Economic Means of Achieving Strategic Success

Although the exact date and location of the Allied landings was not yet known, the SOE's role in support of it had been sketched in outline by a special planning group as early as the previous summer. The F Section circuits would be required to increase the tempo of sabotage and attacks on the enemy's lines of communication, and to harass the enemy occupying troops by any available means.[1]

The patient build-up by some circuit organizers was now paying dividends as some circuits were clearly beginning to flourish. In the Corrèze, for example, Harry Peulevé had successfully set up AUTHOR in the cultural town of Brive-la-Gaillarde. He had been helped by Maurice Arnouil, an engineer and local businessman in his early forties, who knew a number of reliable contacts in the area, including the anti-Fascist French novelist André Malraux, known as Colonel Berger, who helped form the backbone of the circuit.

AUTHOR had started receiving supplies in January 1944 and later that month Jacques Poirier (Nestor) arrived as Peulevé's assistant. This meant the circuit could now expand to the eastern Dordogne and it was not long before the circuit had received enough air drops to equip some 1,500 French communist members of the Resistance.[2]

AUTHOR's success was largely due to it being a rural circuit rather than a city-based one, where everyone knew everyone, making it easier to establish a secure network of contacts. Some 4,000 resistance fighters would be trained and armed before Peulevé was arrested at a safe house in March. An urgent message needed to be sent to London and so he had gone to the

1. Foot, op. cit., p.309.
2. Ibid, p.252.

hide of his radio operator, Louis Bertheau (Pelican), in Brive. It was mid-afternoon when two black Citroëns pulled up outside. Four men then burst through the front door and rushed upstairs to catch Peulevé, Bertheau and two others standing at the wireless set. By the time they had entered the room, Bertheau had already sent a rapid signal informing London they were being taken.

The four captured could consider themselves unlucky. It was not because the transmission had been detected but Bertheau's neighbour had seen people come and go at the house and so had reported the address, believing it to being used by a group of Jewish black marketeers.[3] Amongst others to be arrested at the house was Roland Malraux, André's half-brother, who had previously worked with the SALESMAN circuit in Rouen.

They were all taken to Tulle and then to Limoges before they ended up, inevitably, in Paris for interrogation at the Avenue Foch. Refusing to co-operate, Peulevé was tortured for several days before he was transferred to the Fresnes prison where he was put in solitary confinement. He later tried to escape, albeit unsuccessfully, before, in September, he was transported with thirty-six other prisoners to Buchenwald. It was at Buchenwald that Peulevé met up with Christopher Burney and the brothers Henry and Alfred Newton. Just a few days later, sixteen of the prisoners were hanged in the basement of the crematorium and it became apparent that the others would suffer the same fate. Peulevé was then involved in the same daring plan as Tommy Yeo-Thomas, along with a French BCRA officer, Stéphane Hessel, to switch identity with three camp prisoners who had died from typhus. Having assumed his new identity, Peulevé was transferred to the Junkers factory at Schönebeck and was later part of a working party on the River Elbe where, in April 1945, he managed to escape and was picked up by advancing American forces.

Meanwhile, Jacques Poirier had evaded capture and became the leader of a replacement circuit in the Corrèze called DIGGER. He was assisted by Peter Lake (Basil) and Ralph Beauclerk (Casimir), who both arrived soon after the arrest of Peulevé. They knew the Allied landings were imminent,

---

3. Grehan & Mace, op. cit., p.29.

although they did not know exactly where or when, and so there was little time to get as many of the local resistance fighters armed as possible.

The resistance groups of DIGGER were armed and ready for operations by early June. Lake's group, in particular, proved adept at guerilla warfare and he would later be awarded the Military Cross and the Croix de Guerre for his preparatory work and direction of the local Resistance in support of the Allied landings.[4]

DIGGER's neighbour, another new circuit called FOOTMAN, was even more successful. It was led by George Hiller (Maxime), a quiet and thoughtful 27-year-old English officer, assisted by his radio operator, Cyril Watney (Michel), a member of the famous brewer family. Hiller had also been sent into the Lot department of south-west France to support a rather elusive socialist resistance leader, Jean Vincent, better known to the French as Colonel Vény.[5]

Having found Vincent, Hiller and Watney were attached to his headquarters at Cahors. Moving his radio from place to place in a requisitioned van to avoid detection, Watney called for air drops of weapons to arm Vincent's followers. Although Vincent's organization was composed mainly of socialist partisans, they were not hard-line communists and, although centred on Cahors, its groups spread as far as Limoges in the north and Toulouse and Marseilles in the south.

Ten days after their arrival, Hiller and Watney were involved in one of SOE's major actions in France, the sabotage of the Ratier factory at Figeac, east of Cahors. The factory was turning out variable-pitch propellers for the Luftwaffe's Messerschmitts and Heinkels at the rate of around 300 per week.

On the night of 19 January 1944 a group of four saboteurs drove to the factory. Having obtained keys from a factory foreman, they entered the facility through a small back door. They then set about laying the charges against specifically targeted machines and presses. With the timers set for just thirty minutes they made off.

---

4. Obituary – Peter Lake MC – *The Times*, 14 July 2009.
5. Obituary – Cyril Watney MC – *The Times*, 31 March 2009.

Shortly afterwards Figeac was rocked by the sound of the explosions. Within minutes the whole factory was ablaze, resulting in several key machines that produced the precision blades being destroyed and bringing production to a halt for the rest of the war. But, inevitably, the sabotage of the Ratier works brought appalling acts of reprisals with the Gestapo carrying out brutal revenge attacks throughout the Lot and Corrèze.

Hiller and Watney had to split up and go to ground, although they would eventually surface and continue their work. Others, too, were sent to assist Vincent's group, including members of a small sub-circuit called FIREMAN, which operated in and around Angoulême and the neighbourhood of Limoges in the Haute-Vienne.

FIREMAN was led by two Madagascan brothers, Percy and Edmund Mayer, codenamed 'Barthelemy' and 'Maurice' respectively, who had parachuted into France in early March. They were joined two weeks later by a radio operator, a pretty 26-year-old Irish woman called Patricia O'Sullivan (Josette), who had trained with Cyril Watney. It soon proved to be a competent working circuit and covered a large area with Percy Mayer based in Argenton and Edmund often working as far away as the south Indre, while Patricia acted as pianist for them both. Once the Allied landings were under way, FIREMAN would play its part harassing enemy troops as they made their way to Normandy and then they would continue to hinder their withdrawal as they retreated towards Germany.

It was also important for F Section to recover its efforts where circuits had been dormant for some months. The arrests of Gustave Biéler and Yolande Beekman at the beginning of the year had led to the downfall of MUSICIAN, just at a time that F Section had hoped to expand its operations. These arrests had left an important part of the country open and so F made a number of attempts to cover it. The most successful of these was SPIRITUALIST, led by a cunning and extremely well connected 35-year-old businessman, René Dumont-Guillemet (Armand), who had left France the previous October to undergo training in England.

Dumont-Guillemet had parachuted into the Eure-et-Loir on the night of 5/6 February with his radio operator, Henri Diacono (Blaise). Their task was to resume contact with FARMER in Lille and to look at carrying out audacious attacks against targets such as Fresnes prison so that its prisoners could make a mass escape. They would also hatch a daring plan to capture a leading German engineer and a rocket designer known to be working on the V-weapons but, as things were to turn out, the engineers were too well protected and so the idea was dropped. The attack against the prison was also aborted after the leader of the group that was to carry out the attack was arrested.

These were setbacks but Dumont-Guillemet did manage to establish contact with members of FARMER and soon created an effective counter-intelligence network. Reasonable supply lines were established and the groups were soon receiving a number of air drops to equip reliable bodies of saboteurs near the Belgian border.

The combination of SPIRITUALIST's railwaymen and the saboteurs of FARMER seemed to work well. Having successfully got things moving with his neighbouring circuit, Dumont-Guillemet then decided to take things beyond the brief he had been given in London. He was keen to re-establish an F circuit in Paris and felt that enough time had passed since the PROSPER and INVENTOR disasters of the previous year. Despite finding barriers amongst some, particularly the communist members of the Resistance, who were wary of him because he had been sent by F Section, Dumont-Guillemet succeeded in creating a force of more than 5,000 men in the suburbs of Paris.

Meanwhile, Henri Frager had returned to France, arriving by sea near Morlaix at the end of February 1944. He had been sent back into the field to revive DONKEYMAN and develop resistance groups in the Yonne and the Côte d'Azur. During the coming weeks his group would receive thirty-five air drops of arms and equipment, enough to arm 700 men in the Yonne, 300 in the Joigny area and a further 700-plus in the surrounding areas.[6]

In the far south of France there had also been a move to pick up the work of Jean Meunier (Mesnard) who had set up DIRECTOR from the ashes of CARTE. The circuit had operated round the city of Arles in the Bouches-du-Rhônes and was probably unique in that none of its members had been trained in England. Nonetheless, the SOE had been keen to support its work and so set up communications with the circuit through a courier in

---

6. Grehan & Mace, op. cit., p.67.

Switzerland. However, although a number of re-supply drops took place, the circuit had seemingly been snuffed out in early 1944.[7]

And so a young French nobleman, the Baron Marie Joseph Gonzagues de Saint-Geniès (Lucien), was parachuted in during March to resurrect the DIRECTOR circuit in the Jura mountains under its new name of SCHOLAR. With him was 22-year-old Yvonne Baseden (Odette), a slim, dark-haired and attractive English radio operator, working under the identity of Marie Bernier.[8] They arrived to find that Meunier had been arrested but it did not take long to re-establish many of the contacts and so they quickly set about finding suitable drop zones for air drops to be made.

Nearby in the Lyonnais, Tony Brooks's PIMENTO was still active in the railway yards. Brooks had returned to France after just two months back in England, although his return was saddened soon after by the death of his trusted friend, André Moch, who was killed in a gun battle with the *Milice*.[9]

Meanwhile, Robert Lyon's ACOLYTE, Joseph Marchand's NEWSAGENT and Albert Browne-Bartroli's DITCHER all had sabotage groups under training in the country. Their efforts had been boosted by the arrival of Jean-Marie Régnier, a long-time activist in his early thirties, and a former assistant of Marchand during their days with SPRUCE. Régnier had parachuted into France near Roanne on the night of 3/4 March with his radio operator, Marcel Jaurant-Singer, to set up MASON and to work alongside NEWSAGENT in and around Lyons. Their task was to sabotage German road and rail movements around Chalon-sur-Saône.

There was also Charles Rechenmann's ROVER in and around Tarbes. He had escaped the previous November with his colleagues of TINKER and returned to France by sea in late March with instructions to sabotage factories and railroads. His group had great success in the Haute-Pyrenees before Rechenmann had the ill fortune to be betrayed and trapped during May while meeting with a sub-agent, René Bochereau, in Angoulème;

---

7. Foot, op. cit., p.228.
8. Escott, op. cit., p.153.
9. The *Milice* was the French collaborative police, effectively a French Gestapo, set up by the Vichy French to assist the *Abwehr* and Gestapo in their campaign against the French Resistance.

Rechenmann then followed the trodden path to Fresnes and Buchenwald and did not return.

The circuits and resistance groups had now stepped up their effort to disrupt as much of the enemy's war effort as possible. At Decazeville in the Midi-Pyrenees, a commune built on coal, there were numerous acts of sabotage, many of which were minor, but all had an impact on the production of coal. The first recorded attack took place in August 1943 when the destruction of lifting gear resulted in a halt in production of ten days. But it was during early 1944 that the facility suffered the most. Three attacks during January, each seemingly quite minor in their execution, resulted in damage to a winch, cut off the power to the plant and blocked a shaft, which, all combined, succeeded in bringing production to a halt for a total of three days and caused a reduction in production on two more. This success was followed up the following month when a transformer was destroyed and stopped production for four more days. In fact, the disruption of the facility would continue until mid-June by which time there had been ten separate acts of sabotage against the plant.

The Aubert and Duval facility at Ancizes in the Puy-de-Dôme, a major producer of steel, was also on the receiving end of several attacks. The first, in May 1943, resulted in a cessation of output for three months after causing damage attributed to defective coal, and production at the end of the year was then reduced considerably for a month after a second attack in November. Three more attacks followed in 1944. The first, in February, badly damaged a water reservoir before the second, in April, halted output for two days. But it was the third attack of the year, at the beginning of May, that stopped production altogether until after the liberation of France.

There were other industrial targets too, all feeding the German war machine. One example was Air Liquide, a leading company in the production of gases and services for industry. The company had two major facilities in the north of France, at Roubaix and at Boulogne-sur-Seine, producing compressed air and liquid oxygen. Two attacks were made against the facility at Boulogne-sur-Seine. The first took place in November 1943 with minimal success; the charges had not been well laid and caused only slight delays in production. The second, however, in March 1944, was far more successful and brought a halt to general output for two weeks and thereafter a reduction of 25 per cent for the rest of the war; it also brought a permanent halt to the production of liquid oxygen. With the severe hampering in output of this facility, the second at Roubaix was later attacked twice, making the facility useless to the Germans for the rest of the war.

Similarly, an attack against the chemical plant at Bordères-Louron in the Hautes-Pyrenees, carried out in early February 1944, brought production to a halt for six weeks. There were also attacks against the facility at Lannemezan, involved in the production of various metals and chemicals. Four major attacks were made against the facility during the first five months of 1944, all disrupting the facility to one degree or another.

Many more acts of sabotage were carried out by the resistance groups in the same department in south-west France during the first quarter of 1944. Facilities producing aluminium, copper and hydro-electricity were all targeted, mainly the transformers, and achieved varying degrees of success, ranging from minimal to bringing output to a complete halt and causing severe disruption across the area for weeks on end.

Hydro-electricity was also a popular and comparably easy target for the saboteurs with attacks against at least fourteen separate hydro-electric plants during the year prior to the Allied landings. Some of them were hit several times and resulted in severe disruption for the enemy.

There were other attacks, too, against anything that was considered to be helping the German war effort. The Renault factory in Boulogne-sur-Seine, involved in the construction of tanks, the Phillips factory at Brive-la-Gaillarde in the Corrèze (wireless valves) and the Hispano-Suiza facility at Tarbes in the Hautes-Pyrenees (aircraft engines) would all be targeted several times during the early months of 1944. The Dunlop factory at Montluçon, too, which had only resumed its production of tyres in September 1943 after a devastating air raid, would suffer three setbacks during 1944, two of them major, with output halted for two weeks in April before the destruction of a transformer brought production in parts of the factory to a complete halt. Then there were attacks against oil refineries, ball-bearing factories and there was even the destruction of an alcohol plant in Grenoble. And so it went on.

Although the results of industrial sabotage in France, in terms of damage achieved and delay to the enemy's war effort, might be summed up as only moderate at best, the fact that they were carried out across the country and were, at times, quite diverse in their nature, caused repeated disruption to the enemy and continuously placed a strain on the German war economy. The attacks also succeeded in diverting the enemy's valuable resources away from conducting more conventional forms of warfare against the Allies. The SOE had provided an exceptionally economic means of achieving strategic aims.

Chapter 19

Maximum Effort

For F Section the early months of 1944 proved to be a period of ups and downs. One new circuit, called LACKEY, which was to be established in the Saone-et-Loire department near Lyons to reinforce DITCHER, never really got off the ground. Its elderly leader, Jules Lesage (Cosmo), and his Canadian radio operator, Alcide Beauregard (Cyrano), struggled from the start.

They arrived by Lysander near Tours in February 1944 but it seems that Lesage had very few friends from his earlier days of operating in Lyons and none of his former colleagues were prepared to co-operate with him. Nonetheless, Beauregard worked on, but he would later be caught by German direction finders and taken to the Montluc prison in Lyons where his life came to an end early one Sunday morning in August. The Germans and *Milice* selected 120 of the inmates and drove them out to an abandoned fort to the south-west of Lyons. Once inside the fort the Germans opened fire. For three-quarters of an hour the executions continued; just one man survived the massacre to tell the tale. The dead, including Beauregard, were buried three days later in the presence of the local population and in front of the Germans.[1]

There were other disasters too, including LABOURER sent into France during the early days of April 1944 only for its three agents – Marcel Leccia (Baudouin), Elisée Allard (Henrique) and Pierre Geelen (Pierre) – to be arrested just days later. They had been parachuted into central France to set up their circuit around Touraine and Paris. Having made their way to the capital, they were arrested after being betrayed by a so-called friend of Leccia; all three were later taken to Buchenwald and, in September, were amongst a group of sixteen agents hanged without trial. For one young

---

1. Grehan & Mace, op. cit., p.24.

woman, though, there was a lucky escape. Odette Wilen had just joined the circuit as a courier but had not been with the others at the time of their arrest and so later returned home via the Pyrenees.

There was also the end of MONK around Marseilles. The betrayal and arrest of its leader, Charles Skepper, towards the end of March, had triggered its downfall. The day after Skepper's arrest, the circuit radio operator, Arthur Steele, and the courier, Eliane Plewman, were also arrested. They had heard there had been a raid and so had gone to Skepper's residence to see if he was still there. When they arrived at his apartment they found the entrance guarded by two Germans and, believing Skepper to still be inside, they tried to force their way in with guns but were both overpowered and captured.[2]

Their capture was just the start of MONK's downfall, as more arrests followed. Steele and Eliane faced the same outcome as their leader – death. Steele was executed at Buchenwald in September at the age of just twenty-three. Eliane also suffered a terrible end to her life. She was first cruelly treated to the point that she was unrecognizable, and she then followed the same dreaded and, sadly, well-trodden path to death: Fresnes prison, Karlsruhe and finally Dachau where her extreme suffering, and her life, came to an end on the morning of 13 September 1944, alongside Madeleine Damerment and Yolande Beekman, with a single bullet to the back of her head.

Although MONK had been destroyed, its work was about to bear fruit. The circuit had provided vital intelligence about the deployment of German forces and the coastal fortifications in the south of France. Indeed, it would be no exaggeration to say that when the Allies later landed in the south, their swift advance northwards was at least partly because of the intelligence received from Skepper and his circuit during its time in existence.

Surviving as a circuit was tough but one widespread circuit to have managed to escape largely unscathed into 1944 was Francis Cammaerts' JOCKEY, despite great efforts by the Gestapo in Cannes to get captured members to betray its leader. Cammaerts had returned from London to pick up his work with the circuit and from his groups a force of 10,000 men

---

2. Ibid, p.141.

would emerge, made up of many strong and well-disciplined units of Free French.

Cammaerts, like Brooks with PIMENTO, had always taken great care to keep his address secret from his circuit members; no one knew where to find him. Another exceptionally secure circuit was GARDENER at Marseilles run by Robert Boiteux, the former head of SPRUCE, who had returned to France by parachute in early March to link up with MONK. With him had come Gaston Cohen, a radio operator who had earlier been fortunate to escape the collapse of JUGGLER by crossing the border into Switzerland. Boiteux had arrived back in France just at the time that MONK was at the point of destruction and so incorporated into his own plans the work previously done by Charles Skepper.

Meanwhile, in the Aude, Henri Sevenet had built his DETECTIVE into an efficient group of saboteurs, totalling some 600 well-armed men, and, in Gascony, George Starr's WHEELWRIGHT was not only flourishing but was so successful that the Germans would never succeed in breaking it up. Starr's circuit had become so big that two more agents had been dropped in earlier in the year, an explosives expert, Jean-Claude Arnault (Neron), and a young courier, 20-year-old Anne-Marie Walters (Colette).

Anne-Marie had been sent into the field to help Yvonne Cormeau in what had become an extensive network in south-west France. It was an extremely busy part of the country and Starr was now receiving more containers than anyone else; over a thousand were dropped in a hundred or so sorties during the final months leading up to the Allied landings.

In addition to carrying out sabotage, WHEELWRIGHT also supported the local resistance groups and provided assistance to the escape line across the Pyrenees. Anne-Marie, in particular, proved extremely popular and was helped in every way possible; she was even able to celebrate her twenty-first birthday in the field amongst friends. Unlike so many stories of brave young women in France, which so often ended in tragedy, Anne-Marie would survive her eventful few months in the field as, after the Allies landed, Starr would get her out of danger and across the Pyrenees, and eventually back to England, before her luck could so easily have run out.

Meanwhile in the east, STOCKBROKER had also quietly gone about its business despite its leader, Harry Rée, remaining across the border in

Switzerland having beaten a hasty retreat six months before. His assistant, Eric Cauchi, had continued the good work through the winter but when he failed to stop at a street check of papers in Montbéliard on 5 February he was pursued by Germans and then surrounded at the Café Grangier in Sochaux. During the firefight that followed, the gallant Eric Cauchi was gunned down and died in the street two hours later. The gun battle had also cost the life of Jean Simon (Claude), a man locally recruited by Rée when the circuit had first formed.

To replace Cauchi, London sent the Comte de Brouville (Théodule) during April to set up TREASURER with an American radio operator, Edwin Poitras (Paul). Another developing connections with Rée's contacts was a young French-Canadian, 20-year-old Paul Sarrette (Louis), with his new circuit, GONDOLIER, round Nevers in the Nièvre department on the upper Loire in east-central France. Sarrette had been recruited in the field and had earlier worked as the leader of RODOLPHE between Marseilles and Lyons under the codename of 'Contrand'. He had then gone to England to become fully trained by the SOE and was now given his own mission under the alias of Paul Sawyer.

Also sent into the Doubs were Ernest Floege and André Bouchardon, both of whom were parachuted back into France for their second period of activity with SACRISTAN and to take over the work of Rée. They had both been forced to flee France the previous winter after Bouchardon had escaped his captors following his arrest on Christmas Eve. Bouchardon had been shot while resisting arrest but had not subsequently been searched and while being driven to the SD's headquarters in Angers, he pulled his revolver and shot all three of his captors before making his escape. For a while he hid with Floege before the two were put on the Vic escape line and crossed the Pyrenees to safety during a harsh winter blizzard, Bouchardon with the bullet still in his lung. But now they were back in France.

Also back in France was Roger Landes. He had earlier escaped France across the Pyrenees and, after a period in a Spanish prison, reached Gibraltar and eventually arrived back in London. There was a period when he came under suspicion for the number of arrests within the great SCIENTIST network but it was soon realized that he was not the betrayer and he was instead awarded the Military Cross.

Landes had parachuted back into the field near Auch in early March 1944 and had made his way to Bordeaux to create ACTOR, a circuit to be built from the remnants of SCIENTIST, in time for the Allied landings. He soon made contact with the surviving members of the once great network and begun to call for arms drops. But one who had not survived capture during the time Landes had been away was Mary Herbert. She had been arrested by the Gestapo just a few weeks earlier but would later be released after the Germans were taken in by her story that she was a Frenchwoman from Egypt; she would later marry Claude de Baissac in London.

Landes knew that his task could not be accomplished without first dealing with the treacherous André Grandclément and his wife. Having been informed that they and Grandclément's adjutant, Marc Duluguet, had all fallen into the hands of the Resistance near Arcahon, Landes went there to take charge.[3] The three collaborators were taken to a farmhouse at Belin where Grandclément was tried by a court martial of the Free French, with Landes in attendance. Having confessed to his treachery, which has been estimated to have cost the lives of some 300 men and women, Grandclément, his wife and Duluguet were all sentenced to death. They were then shot and buried in a wood near the farm.[4]

Another to return to France during this period was Charles Corbin, a police inspector in his fifties, and one of Claude de Baissac's most reliable friends. He was to set up CARVER with his radio operator, Allyre Sirois (Gustave), who had jumped with Landes in early March. With Corbin's former turf of Bordeaux being considered too risky, he was sent into the field slightly farther to the north to operate between Angoulême and Rochefort on the Bay of Biscay.

Also back in France was Virginia Hall, the American heroine of SOE's early days and known to the Gestapo as 'The Limping Lady'. Virginia had narrowly escaped to England via Spain after the Germans had moved into Lyons and occupied the previously Vichy south, but she was now back for her second mission. Her artificial limb prevented her from parachuting in

---

3. Obituary – Roger Landes MC & Bar – *The Times*, 17 July 2008.
4. Cookridge, op. cit., p.326.

and so she was landed along the Brittany coastline by a Royal Navy patrol boat.

Codenamed 'Diane', Virginia had been given a new identity of a French social worker, Marcelle Montagne. She made her way to the Nièvre in central France and, acting on her own in a mission called SAINT, she made contact with the French Resistance groups. She singlehandedly organized drop zones for supplies and for Allied special forces soon to arrive in France. The hilly terrain, combined with the fact that she had to be constantly on the move, made it extremely hard work for Virginia. Furthermore, some resistance groups seemed reluctant to take direction from her, but she worked tirelessly during her time in the field and even though the Gestapo knew she was back in France they were unable to get close to her.

In addition to René Dumont-Guillemet's SPIRITUALIST, there was also a smaller circuit working in Paris. This was called WIZARD, a name taken from the codename of its leader Jean Savy, a 36-year-old solicitor in the city. Savy was a pseudonym (his real name was Millet) and he had been working undercover with the SOE for some time. A friend of France Antelme, he had a lucky escape the previous year when he narrowly avoided the downfall of PROSPER and, after two aborted flights, he finally arrived back in France by Lysander in early March 1944.

Travelling with him was his young radio operator, 22-year-old Eileen Nearne (Rose), the younger sister of Jacqueline Nearne. Having made their way to Orleans, Savy and Eileen went on to Paris where they arrived in the middle of the winter snow. Eileen assumed the identity of Jacqueline du Tertre and soon found suitable digs to set up her wireless set.

Operating in Paris was about as dangerous as it got, as anyone in the city at the time would testify. The Gestapo were well versed at the whole SOE game and were constantly on the lookout for agents and their activities. With Eileen left in Paris to establish herself in the capital, Savy set about finding his friend Antelme, who he knew had parachuted into France just a few days before.

At that time Savy was unaware that Antelme had already jumped straight into a Gestapo trap as part of the radio games and ARCHDEACON debacle but, having soon found out that his friend had already been arrested, Savy then stumbled across some vital information. He found out that the

Germans were hiding a large stockpile of V-1 weapons in a quarry at St Leu d'Esserent, near Creil. Considering his information to be too sensitive to transmit, he decided to take the news personally to London.

RAF Bomber Command would later attack the V-1 site and, in one of those strange coincidences of war, the Lysander that picked Savy up near Châteauroux on the night of 9/10 April also took his radio operator's sister, Jacqueline Nearne, back to England. With Savy back in England, Eileen Nearne remained in Paris. She had already been introduced to Dumont-Guillemet and so, for the time being, worked for SPIRITUALIST instead.

On the same night that Savy and Eileen Nearne had arrived in France, another Lysander landed near Chartres to bring in two more agents. These were Robert Benoist, no stranger to life in the field, and his beautiful 26-year-old radio operator, Denise Bloch (Ambroise). They had been sent to revive CLERGYMAN around Nantes, which Benoist had set up a few months before.

Benoist had been back and forth between France and England. Having escaped his captors in France the previous summer by the skin of his teeth, he had returned to the field in an October Hudson to set up CLERGYMAN with his radio operator, Albert Dubois (Hercule). But just two weeks later the German direction finders had caught up with Dubois, which, ultimately, led to his death, after which Benoist had returned to England in early 1944. But now he was back in France yet again.

Denise Bloch was also no stranger to life in the field. She had been living in France during the early years of the war and had been drawn into the French Resistance. She had then been the courier for Henri Sevenet's DETECTIVE but as soon as some of its members were arrested she hastily left for Marseilles. She later had a further narrow escape in Lyons and so went into hiding until early 1943, after which she worked for George Starr as his courier for WHEELWRIGHT. Denise had then been sent to England for training to prepare her for a return into the field as a radio operator. Now, with the rank of ensign in the FANY, she was working under her new identity of Micheline Claude de Rabatel.

CLERGYMAN was to operate as a small team with their main task being to destroy vital high tension pylons over the river Loire carrying electricity generated in the Pyrenees to Brittany. Then, once the Allied landings were under way, their task would be to cut lines of communication, including the railway, leading to Nantes. But, sadly, Benoist and Denise would not survive in the field for much longer; Benoist was arrested in Paris in June during a visit to his dying mother while Denise was arrested the following day at a villa near Rambouillet in the suburbs of Paris. She happened to be in the wrong place at the wrong time. Neither would survive their captivity; Benoist was executed at Buchenwald during the September massacres, while Denise's life was to end at Ravensbrück shortly before the end of the war.

There was also another arrival during March 1944 worth a mention. This was Pierre Mulsant, a colleague of Octave Simon and former member of Ben Cowburn's TINKER, who was dropped back into France with his radio operator, Denis Barrett, to set up MINISTER around Troyes. They were soon joined by their colleague Yvonne Fontaine who had also worked with TINKER and was now to be their courier. All three had earlier been pulled out of France following a series of arrests and, after receiving some training (neither Mulsant nor Yvonne had been trained by the SOE before), now returned into the field to operate between Meaux and Provins in the Seine-et-Marne department on the eastern side of Paris, specifically to disrupt lines of communication in north-eastern France.

Octave Simon, incidentally, would return to France four nights after Mulsant and Barrett when he parachuted with his radio operator, 23-year-old Marcel Defence, to resume SATIRIST around Beauvais. Tragically, though, instead of being met by members of Jean Bouguennec's BUTLER circuit as had been the plan, the pair had jumped straight into the arms of the waiting Gestapo. It was one of the many sad consequences of the radio games debacle, and both were to die at Gross-Rosen.

It was not long before MINISTER was receiving air drops and carrying out a number of attacks. These ranged from cutting telephone cables and overhead wires to disrupting enemy vehicle movements by road, as well as attacking the canals and barges used for transportation. They also received more agents during April and May 1944, including a three-man team called BEGGAR, to work to the north of Paris, and DIETICIAN, a lone saboteur sent to disrupt rail and canal traffic around the area of Nangis.

To the east in the Aube, Yvon Dupont (Abelard), had now kick-started his DIPLOMAT into life. A former member of George Starr's

WHEELWRIGHT, the young Parisian had taken over the work of TINKER, training more than a hundred men to attack lines of communication in the Champagne-Ardennes and to isolate the town of Troyes. He was joined by the former FARRIER radio operator, André Watt (Geffroi), to relieve the amount of work placed on the hard working and efficient Denis Barrett during the previous weeks.

Barrett had, in fact, been operating two radio sets, one in Troyes and the other hidden in the surrounding countryside. It was extremely hazardous work. The Germans knew someone was transmitting from Troyes and had direction-finding vans circulating in the town but Barrett decided to transmit only from outside the town, using his second set.

In this game of cat and mouse, the Germans had stepped up their efforts to make it harder for pianists to move freely around the countryside by increasing the number of paid informers and by infiltrating the resistance groups operating in the area. As the weeks counted down to D-Day, the number of RAF air drops significantly increased but many deliveries were being intercepted by the Germans, often as a result of treason or indiscretion that had given them advance information of a drop.

As the Germans nervously waited for the expected Allied landings to come the horrific reprisals against the local French continued. But despite this, the circuits and resistance groups were getting on with their work all across France. The landings were imminent and had given a new impetus to all that they did.

Chapter 20

Towards Liberation

The Allied landings in France were now just weeks away and more agents were being sent into the field. One was Lilian Rolfe (Nadine), a tall and dark-haired woman soon to celebrate her thirtieth birthday. Lilian could have stayed at home in South America but she chose instead to make her way to Britain where she joined the WAAF. Her fluency in languages had duly brought her to the attention of the SOE and, after training as a radio operator, she arrived in France by Lysander near Tours on the night of 5/6 April 1944.

Lilian was to join up with her circuit organizer, George Wilkinson (Etienne). He had arrived the night before to set up HISTORIAN, another new circuit in the area of Orléans, bordered by HEADMASTER to the west and DONKEYMAN to the east.

Being so close to Paris meant that it was a dangerous part of France in which to work. It would, in fact, take Lilian several weeks to join up with Wilkinson and so she spent her early days in France becoming familiar with the area in which she was to operate and make herself known in her new identity of Claudie Irene Rodier. There was so much to do, particularly with organizing air drops and then ensuring that the arms dropped were distributed amongst the circuit that had now significantly swelled in its number. Lilian's radio work was always accurate and clear, and often carried out under extremely difficult and hazardous conditions.

But, like so many others, Lilian's luck, and that of George Wilkinson, was soon to run out. First, Wilkinson was trapped and captured near Orleans just days after the Allied landings; his life would end in the September massacres at Buchenwald. Then, in July, Lilian was unfortunate to be in the wrong place at the wrong time. She was lodging at a house in Nangis, to the south-east of Paris, when a final Gestapo sweep in search of someone else took her by surprise. Lilian was duly arrested and, after time at the Avenue Foch and

Fresnes prison, she was shackled and put on a train to Germany where her life came to an end at Ravensbrück shortly before the end of the war.

To the south of HISTORIAN had been a revived VENTRILOQUIST led by Philippe de Vomécourt. He had returned to France in April 1944 to re-establish his contacts in the Sologne. Using the codename of 'Major Saint-Paul', he was joined by his radio operator, Muriel Byck (Violette), a small and dark-haired 25-year-old former London secretary. Being the daughter of Russian Jews, Muriel had an understandable and abiding hatred for the Nazis and so the SOE had been just right for her. With her new identity of Michèle Bernier, Muriel had parachuted into France the night before de Vomécourt.

It was not long before de Vomécourt was leading his group in acts of sabotage, the most notable being a combined air and ground raid on the large German weapons dump near the small town of Salbris to the south of Orleans. The dump stored heavy munitions – artillery shells, tank ammunition and bombs for the Luftwaffe – for the garrisons in north-western France and along the defensive Atlantic Wall.

The site had been kept under observation for some time but it was considered all but impossible for saboteurs to enter unobserved and lay explosives. But when de Vomécourt learned that goods trains were due to arrive at Salbris to collect large supplies of munitions from the dump during a weekend in early May 1944, he immediately contacted London and requested that the railway yards be bombed. His men could then mine the roads and set up ambushes.

On the night of 6 May the trains arrived and munitions were seen to be loaded on board. A signal was sent to London and late the following night a force of more than fifty RAF Lancasters bombed the dump. There was chaos on the ground. Some of the trains packed with explosives blew up and, as the Germans fled the inferno, they fell victims to the mined roads in the surrounding area and ran into the many roadblocks and ambushes set up by de Vomécourt's men. At least 200 Germans were killed with relatively few casualties amongst the local French population, who had been forewarned to keep clear of the area as much as possible.

This was just one of a number of attacks by de Vomécourt's group and many more soon followed against enemy troops moving towards Normandy.

Tragically, though, Muriel's life as an agent in the field was to be short-lived. Six weeks after arriving in France she was dead, not as a result of any failing or enemy action but due to, of all things, meningitis, which she had apparently suffered from as a child.

Also on the same Lysander insertion as Philippe de Vomécourt was Lise de Baissac, now to undertake her second mission. Since arriving back in England she had become a training officer for the SOE but an injury to her leg, suffered during a parachute descent, meant she could not risk jumping back into France.

Having landed near Châteauroux, Lise made her way to Toulouse to become a courier for PIMENTO. But it was not easy for her. The socialist views of many circuit members were at odds with her own and so she requested a move. Lise then made her way under the new identity of Janette Bouville, codenamed 'Marguerite', to Normandy to join up with her brother, Claude, who had parachuted back into France two months earlier to re-establish old contacts around the area of Chartres under his circuit's new title of SCIENTIST II.

The de Baissacs were at the heart of where the Allied landings were due to take place. Their mission was to amalgamate, arm and energize the resistance groups stretching from Caen to Laval. To help them were two young men, 20-year-old Jean Renaud-Dandicolle (René) and a powerfully-built Mauritian radio operator, 22-year-old Maurice Larcher (Vladimir). They all worked well together and SCIENTIST II soon spread over a large part of Normandy, although operations were always going to be hazardous given this key coastal area was densely populated with Germans.

Meanwhile, RF Section launched two operations in France during April 1944, CITRONELLE in the Ardennes, with the task of seeking out and supplying resistance groups along the Franco-Belgian border, and BENJOIN in the Massif Central to make contact with a larger group of the Maquis known to exist in the mountainous Auvergne region. Making contact with these groups would connect them with London so that they could be supplied with arms and weapons. While CITRONELLE's progress was slow, BENJOIN managed to achieve success more quickly, mainly because it took place in a part of France where it was much easier to move around and because there were fewer Germans watching every move.

BENJOIN had been organized by Maurice Southgate, the leader of STATIONER. He had returned from London at the beginning of the year and his network had spread to include a large resistance group in the Auvergne. The group was made up largely of communists headed by their socialist leader, Émile Coulaudon, better known as Colonel Gaspard and a rather unpredictable character to the SOE but, nonetheless, one of the principal leaders in the Auvergne who was soon to become head of the Free French in the region.

Southgate and Coulaudon met at Montluçon where the two leaders discussed creating a large hideout in the Auvergne for the weapons soon to be received through a number of air drops; machine guns, anti-tank weapons and light artillery – enough to wage war on the Nazis when the Allies came.

The meeting was followed by a conference of leaders at a farm near Paulhauget where it was decided to set up a 'Grand Council'. It was agreed to concentrate Maquis groups in the mountains and forests of Margerides, between the valleys of the rivers Loire and Allier, which were to converge in three main areas during the weeks ahead in preparation for the Allied landings, forming a total force of up to 20,000 maquisards.[1]

Arrangements were made to step up the number of air drops in the region and detailed plans were drawn up for the mobilization of units. Those on the ground were also to prepare to receive BENJOIN's leader, Freddy Cardozo, and members of a new F Section circuit, called FREELANCE, which would operate to the south of BENJOIN.

The first to arrive were two members of FREELANCE. These were John Farmer (Hubert), the organizer, and his 31-year-old courier, Nancy Wake (Hélène), who both parachuted into a field near Montluçon on the night of 29/30 April. They had been briefed to meet with Southgate as soon as possible and take direction from him.

But Southgate was not there when they landed and there would, in fact, be no meeting. On 1 May Southgate was caught in a Gestapo trap in Montluçon. He had missed the security check and was captured; it was probably his only mistake during his time in the field. Southgate had been a wanted man for some time and, given the number of arrests during the

---

1. Cookridge, op. cit., pp.353–4.

past few weeks, there had been plans for him to return to England before the Allied landings took place. But his luck had run out. He was deported to Germany and eventually taken to Buchenwald where, for almost a year, he managed to cheat death until the camp was liberated by the Americans just before the end of the war.

Although the capture of Southgate had been a grievous blow, STATIONER remained in good hands. René Maingard and Pearl Witherington simply split the responsibilities and carried on. She took the north of the Indre and Cher valley, operating to the north of Châteauroux with her group called WRESTLER, while Maingard worked to the south-east of her with his group called SHIPWRIGHT, in an area bordering FIREMAN and expanding its operations to cover the area between Poitiers and Montluçon.

John Farmer and Nancy Wake, meanwhile, had settled in to their new home above a radio shop in Cosne-d'Allier. They hung around for several days waiting to meet with Southgate or get news of the arrival of their radio operator, Denis Rake, who had earlier managed to escape the prison camp at Chambaran.

With no sign of any progress, Nancy finally bucked up the courage to wander round the village but was shocked to find that all the locals seemed to know who she was and why she was there.

After it had become obvious there was to be no meeting with Southgate, Nancy used all her charm to arrange a meeting with Coulaudon. When they did finally meet she found him arrogant, surly and a bully, and felt he was a bluffer. He was evasive in his answers to all their questions and intuitively she decided that he had no intention of co-operating with London at all. She believed he was a man who would try to trick her into giving him huge sums of money and obtain for him powerful supplies of arms, and who would then use them for his own private war.[2]

Nancy could see that Farmer's reaction to Coulaudon had been the same as hers. She was not impressed but she was a strong character and managed to get Coulaudon to agree to send her to the leader of another group who proved easier to get on with and far more organized.[3]

2. Braddon, *Nancy Wake*, pp.146–7.
3. Escott, op. cit., p.188.

Rake arrived by Lysander on the night of 9/10 May, the night after BENJOIN's leader, Freddy Cardozo, parachuted on to the snow-clad Mont Mouchet to the south of Clermont-Ferrand. A few days later, Farmer met with Cardozo. The two men agreed to work together and with Rake having arrived as the circuit's radio operator, FREELANCE had a vital link with London and so air drops could be arranged with Nancy, as the courier, allocating arms and equipment that were parachuted in.

Cardozo's first challenge was to overcome the suspicions of Coulaudon. Coulaudon's doubts, however, would soon dissipate after Cardozo arranged for a mass air drop involving nearly thirty aircraft loads of arms and ammunition to be parachuted in during a two-week period covering the end of May and early June. As Coulaudon gradually become amenable to reason, Nancy passed on to him a list of targets given to her prior to her leaving England and he, in turn, delegated the various tasks to groups situated conveniently to them.

Now convinced the Allied landings were imminent, Coulaudon issued his first order announcing the time had come to rise up and asking all the Maquis leaders of the Auvergne to converge with their men on the plateau of Mont Mouchet. He called it his Army of Liberation and by the time the Allies landed in Normandy more than 12,000 maquisards had assembled. They came from all the adjacent departments, as far as the Lyonnais and Boubonnais, and from all walks of life: railway workers, steel workers, firemen, policemen, farmers, landworkers, miners, tradesmen, shopkeepers and schoolteachers. They brought with them everything they could carry that might be useful: tents, blankets, guns of all types and shovels. They were organized into companies and groups: logistics, caterers, intelligence and saboteurs. And so it went on. It was, indeed, a magnificent army.

Elsewhere, Henri Frager's DONKEYMAN had spread far and wide beyond its original strongholds of the Yonne, Brie and the Aube, and had expanded as far as the Ardennes, Lorraine and Burgundy, and as far south as the Savoy mountains. Frager had set up his headquarters in Aillant-sur-Tholon, while his deputy, Jacques Adam, had set up the largest camp in the Forest of Othe. But Frager would always be hampered by the fact that his two subordinates, Roger Bardet and Raoul Kiffer, continued to work for the Germans.

With the landings just a matter of days away, DONKEYMAN was joined by a radio operator, Henri Bouchard (Noel), and a petite young 24-year-old courier, Marguerite Knight (Nicole), known as 'Peggy'. They had jumped into the Côte d'Or in early May but they had jumped into a circuit of chaos, deceit and lies. Bouchard was separated from his radio set on landing and so would not be able to transmit for some time, and Peggy felt uncomfortable about some of the members, particularly Roger Bardet, from the outset. But with no experience and minimal training there was little she could do. She simply got on with her work as DONKEYMAN received a number of air drops and succeeded in arming and training a large number of Maquis in the area. Peggy was a tough little fighter and after the landings had taken place she was often at the heart of attacks with groups of maquisards to prevent German reinforcements from reaching Normandy.

Frager, meanwhile, had remained on the German's most wanted list. Despite Hugo Bleicher's best efforts to capture the man he only knew as 'Paul', the Frenchman had eluded him. Bleicher continued to rely on Bardet for information about Frager and his networks but Bardet had now become rather elusive. Bleicher, therefore, suspected the Frenchman of betraying him to the French Resistance. He was right. With the tide of war changing, Bardet was already thinking more about his own self-preservation after hostilities had ceased and so started siding more with his Maquis colleagues to safeguard himself.

But despite Frager's qualities and courage, he was gullible and his weakness was that he still believed the man known as 'Colonel Henri' to be genuine and anti-Nazi. The two men had even met in the past and it had been during that meeting several months before that Frager had disclosed his sister's address on the outskirts of Paris, suggesting to 'Colonel Henri' that he could use this should the Allies enter the city, and it was there, in early August 1944, that Henri Frager was finally arrested; his life ended at Buchenwald just weeks later. Hugo Bleicher would be arrested at the end of the war and handed over to the French authorities but was found not guilty of war crimes and released. He went back home to Germany but returned to France for the first time in 1949 when he appeared as a witness in the trial of his two wartime informers Roger Bardet and Raoul Kiffer. Both were sentenced to death but later reprieved with their sentences commuted to a lengthy imprisonment.

In addition to Claude de Baissac reviving his SCIENTIST II, Sydney Hudson also revived his HEADMASTER during the early months of 1944. Hudson had earlier managed to escape captivity as part of a mass breakout of prison and, after making his way back to England, he had been given a second mission with his former radio operator, George Jones.

They had been sent back into France to kickstart HEADMASTER into life in the area of le Mans. At the end of May, they were joined by three new arrivals who parachuted in to a remote field to the west of le Mans. They were Raymond Glaesner (Alcide), a colleague of Hudson who had escaped with him from captivity; a 38-year-old sabotage instructor and former French soldier called Francisque Eugene Bec (Hughes); and a young 20-year-old courier, Sonya Butt (Blanche).

Being an agricultural area, it did not prove easy to recruit new members. The local population had, in the main, managed to avoid the hardship of Nazi occupation and some had even profited from it. Not only was it difficult to recruit, but it was also difficult to find safe places where arms and equipment could be dropped and stored, despite it being a rural area.

The capture of a container the same night as the three agents had dropped indicated to the Germans that a female agent was operating in the area. The search was on from the start but Sonya, posing as Suzanne Bonvie, chose not to go into hiding. She decided instead to use her youthful looks and charm to integrate fully into the local population, and so she managed to avoid any suspicion and quickly set about delivering whatever was needed to the resistance groups scattered around her area.

HEADMASTER and SCIENTIST II worked closely together with Hudson's circuit supporting de Baissac's larger network, which now included a second radio operator, Phyllis Latour (Geneviève). She was a partially-trained 23-year-old WAAF who was rushed into the field due to the imminence of the Allied landings to work alongside Lise de Baissac.

But SCIENTIST II was expanding so quickly that it was in danger of becoming too unwieldy and so de Baissac split his circuit. While he would lead one group in the Orne and Eure-et-Loire, Renaud-Dandicolle and Larcher would lead a sub-circuit, VERGER, in Lower Normandy, specifically in the departments of Calvados and Manche.[4] Sadly, though, these two young and very brave men were to die before France was liberated. During July they were both staying at a house at Saint-Clair in Calvados when a neighbour reported suspicious activity to the Germans. Larcher was killed during the ensuing fight but Renaud-Dandicolle managed to escape, although he was soon captured and it is thought that it was then he was killed.

As the SOE boosted its numbers yet further in this vital region of France, another circuit, HERMIT, led by Roger Henquet, was created in late May to support de Baissac in southern Normandy; Henquet's area of responsibility was between Chartres and Blois. There was another new circuit, too, formed in Brittany called RACKETEER and led by a Belgian, Maurice Rouneau (Adolphe), whose task was to try to pick up where PARSON had left off. Rouneau was to try to get things moving in that part of north-west France ahead of the Allied landings but, in reality, it would prove almost impossible, given the location and the fact that he had no radio operator and hardly any time at all to make anything happen.

It was also during May that another new circuit, SILVERSMITH, led by Henri Borosch (Girard), was set up to work alongside ACOLYTE in the lower Saône valley. Borosch was assisted by his courier, Madeleine Lavigne (Isabelle), a divorced mother of two in her early thirties, who parachuted back into France on the night of 23/24 May. She had earlier worked for the SPRUCE circuit and knew Borosch well, and had only been in England a few weeks after leaving France on the first Hudson of the year when the Gestapo had become too close.

It was another example of F Section agents being rushed into the field prior to D-Day. In addition to working alongside ACOLYTE, part of SILVERSMITH, including Madeleine Lavigne, was established in Reims to the north. Using her new identity of Mariette Delormes, she soon met up with former colleagues and associates, establishing a number of safe houses in the area and busily delivering messages and ferrying around whatever needed to be moved. In what seemed like no time at all, both parts of SILVERSMITH were firmly established and waiting for the Allies to land.

---

4. Ibid., p.192.

Even more F agents were sent into the field in the final hours before the Allied landings in one last effort to prepare the ground. These included René Guiraud, bound for the Haute Marne as GLOVER, and George Millar (Emile), who parachuted into France near Besançon just four days before D-Day to set up CHANCELLOR to the east of Dijon close to the Swiss border. Their task was to delay the movement of German reinforcements from the south of France to the battlefields in the north once the Allies had landed.

During the five months leading up to D-Day, forty separate F Section circuits were in operation across the country.[5] It was the zenith of SOE's activities in France. Between them all they would disrupt and delay German forces reinforcing northern France immediately prior to, and then after, the Allied landings.

The huge expansion of agents and circuits had meant that tons of weapons and explosives were received, with the disruption of the rail network being particularly successful. It was impossible for the Germans to defend the lengthy railway lines across France and so the maquisards were able to pick and choose, with relative ease, the parts of the network they would attack. In the ten months leading up to D-Day, 1,822 locomotives were destroyed or badly damaged, 200 passenger carriages were destroyed with a further 1,500 damaged, and 2,500 freight wagons were destroyed and a further 8,000 damaged.[6]

Much of this effort had occurred during the first three months of 1944 when the supply of explosives had been stepped up a gear. Furthermore, a report by the Vichy Ministry of the Interior covering just one month towards the end of 1943 reported that, during the period, there had been more than 3,000 separate attempts by resistance saboteurs to disrupt the rail network, of which 427 resulted in very heavy damage while 132 caused derailments of trains with serious losses to German troops.[7]

The air effort to supply the Maquis had been immense, with the number of sorties flown by the RAF in support of the SOE having risen

---

5. Foot, op. cit., p.324.
6. Cookridge, op. cit., p.313 (Quoted from *Les Résultats de l'Action de la Resistance dans la SNCF* (History of the FFI) p.1364).
7. Ibid., p.313 (Quoted from Report of the Vichy Ministry of the Interior).

tremendously since 1941 when only twenty-two air sorties had been carried out successfully from airfields in England. This figure had risen to ninety-three by the following year and 712 during 1943, but the big effort had come in 1944 when 4,589 sorties were carried out (65 per cent of more than 7,000 sorties planned). Of all the air drops from airfields in England during 1941–44, a total of 5,416 sorties (3,733 for F Section and 1,683 for RF), the overall sortie success rate was 64.5 per cent (8,394 were planned). From the sorties that did take place, more than 71,000 containers and 20,000 packages were dropped, containing nearly 600,000kg of explosives, 200,000 Sten guns, 20,000 Brens, 127,000 rifles and 58,000 pistols. Among the heavier weapons dropped during the later months were more than 9,000 mines, 1,200 portable anti-tank weapons, 2,400 bazookas and 285 mortars.[8]

The SOE circuits and Maquis groups had been able to attack an impressive list of targets: hydro-electric power stations and high-tension sub-stations; the aircraft and motor industries; the electrical and radio industries; coal mines; the rubber industry; the steel, aluminium and general engineering industries; the chemical, liquid oxygen and synthetic oil industries; the ball-bearing industry; the precision and optical instrument industry; waterways; and railways. In addition to the containers and packages containing weapons and explosives, 1,200 agents and other personnel had been dropped into the field.[9]

On D-Day, 6 June 1944, Allied landings took place along a front stretching fifty-six miles (ninety kilometres) along the Normandy coast. By then, it is estimated the SOE had armed about 125,000 of the French Resistance, although there was still a substantial shortage of ammunition with only about 10,000 resistance fighters having enough ammunition to last for more than a day.[10]

With troops and equipment piling ashore along the Normandy coastline, more SOE operatives went into France. One pair, Gérard Dedieu (Jerome), a French schoolmaster and resister since 1942, and his radio operator, Ginnette Jullian (Adèle), were to form PERMIT, intended to operate in

---

8. NA HS 7/135, SOE Activities in France, 1941–44 (Appendix C).
9. Ibid.
10. Foot, op. cit., p.314. (Foot also quotes that of the 125,000 resistance fighters armed, it
    is estimated that about two-thirds had been armed by F Section and one-third by RF).

the Somme area and based at Amiens. However, they ended up working in the south of Normandy, centred on Chartres, to fill the gaps for Claude de Baissac's SCIENTIST II, which was now being pulled off to the Orne close to the Allied bridgehead, Sydney Hudson's HEADMASTER, George Wilkinson's HISTORIAN and Roger Henquet's HERMIT. Together, they made a formidable group.

Chapter 21

Violette

Since Philippe Liewer's recall to London earlier in the year, SALESMAN, the network he had created in and around Rouen, had seemingly broken up. F Section had received word that several members had been arrested and so, determined to find out what had happened to his friends, Liewer returned to France in early April 1944 during the Easter moon, taking with him a young, petite and very attractive courier, 22-year-old Violette Szabo (Louise).

Liewer and Violette had met during training and got on very well, and so it had been a natural choice for them to go into the field together. Born in Paris, the daughter of a British soldier and French mother, Violette was fluent in French having spent much of her early life in France. Although she was still so young, she was already a widow with a young daughter of nearly two. Her husband, a French officer of Hungarian descent, had been killed in North Africa and, seeking revenge, Violette had joined the SOE. Her training at Wanborough Manor had gone well but an accident during a parachute jump at Ringway resulted in an injured left ankle and a period convalescing before she was considered fit enough to go into the field.

It was far too risky for Liewer to go to Rouen and so he took Violette to Paris first. Knowing that he was a wanted man, Liewer arranged for Violette to stay with an aunt while he made his own arrangements. Then, after a day in the city, Violette boarded the morning train to Rouen using her new identity of Corinne Reine Leroy, a company secretary.

The train was full, mostly with Germans. Violette's striking looks and charm meant she was instantly accepted by the German officers on board the crowded train. The journey would take a couple of hours and there were no spare seats and so she was grateful to be invited to sit with them in a reserved compartment.[1]

---

1. Minney, *Carve Her Name with Pride*, p.109.

No one seemed to find her suspicious in any way. There were just admiring looks. Violette must have been feeling hatred towards those she was travelling with, but she had been trained well. She simply made the usual simple and courteous comments, giving no hint of what she felt inside. Besides, she knew not to push her luck. A good agent should avoid drawing attention and remain as inconspicuous as possible, not easy for an attractive female in a compartment full of soldiers.

After the initial pleasantries, it proved to be a long and fairly quiet journey to Rouen. Once there, Violette stuck to her brief when it came to the places she should go. She soon found that most of Liewer's friends had gone, and the city to be full of Germans looking to make more arrests. She also saw posters spread across Rouen looking for two French terrorists whom she instantly recognized as Liewer and Maloubier.

Violette was in no doubt that a traitor was at work and after discreetly trying to find out what had happened to a number of people, she came to the conclusion that the circuit had been decimated and was beyond repair; nearly a hundred members had been arrested but what had become of them she could only fear.

Among her forged papers was a permit to enter the prohibited coastal zone, a vital part of the German's Atlantic Wall defences and out of bounds to all except the residents and those with a pass. During the course of her travels over the next two weeks, Violette gathered much useful information, particularly regarding coastal batteries and the strengthening of German defences along the Atlantic Wall, and she even managed to find out some useful information about V-1 sites in northern France. Her papers had stood the test of several inspections and everything so far had held together. Armed with valuable information, and without wishing to push her luck any further, she made her way back to Paris to meet up with Liewer once more.

The once great SALESMAN no longer existed. Many had been arrested, including Liewer's deputy, Claude Malraux, and the radio operator, Isidore Newman. Malraux had been arrested while meeting with a man claiming to want to join the Resistance but, worst of all, Malraux had been carrying two suitcases full of documents containing lists of names and details of sabotage. That same night, thirty to forty members of the circuit were arrested. Malraux was later shot at Ravitsch while Newman was executed at Mauthausen.

Having sent their report to London, Buckmaster ordered Liewer and Violette back to London. There was nothing more the two could do for now and so they both returned to England by Lysander at the end of the month, after just three weeks in the field.

Back in London, Liewer was more determined than ever to return to the field but the weather was bad during May and so he would have to wait for the June moon. Then, with the Allies embedding themselves in Normandy, Liewer and Violette were sent back into the field to resurrect SALESMAN.

It was just two days after D-Day, during the night of 7/8 June, when they parachuted back into France from an American B-24 Liberator near Sussac in the Haute-Vienne in west-central France. The large reception committee came as something of a surprise. They had been expecting a handful to greet them, but around thirty locals had turned out, all wishing to give a welcoming hug and to embrace them. The Allied landings had clearly brought a change in mood. It was as if victory itself had come, and there was certainly a feeling of elation, complacency even, amongst the maquisards who were there to greet them.

The local Maquis had already been swelled by new members since news of the landings had been received. The leader of the group was the young but quite formidable Jacques Dufour (Anastasie), known to the Germans as 'the biggest bandit of all the Maquis in the Limoges area',[2] who had amassed some 600 men, a mix of farmers, landworkers, gendarmes and communist workers from Limoges.

News that an SS Panzer Division was moving from Toulouse to reinforce Normandy, and that its advanced units were now just a few kilometres away, had sprung the group into action. At several points along the way the division was being attacked by maquisards in a series of ambushes and skirmishes. Bent on vengeance for these attacks, there followed well-publicized atrocities by the Germans at Tulle and Oradour-sur-Glane on 9-10 June with the massacre of hundreds of innocent French civilians.

Knowing that the poorly-armed maquisards could not tackle such a force on their own, Liewer decided to call on reinforcements from other Maquis groups in the Corrèze and Creuze. He was particularly keen to make contact with Jacques Poirier of the neighbouring circuit DIGGER but, because

---

2. Ibid. p.134.

Poirier was an hour's car journey away, Liewer decided to send Violette instead.

Violette would normally have used her bicycle for travelling around but because of the distance involved for this journey she was to be driven part of the way by Dufour. On the morning of 10 June they set off. The journey was expected to last around an hour but it would not be an easy one because at some point they would have to cross the main road from Toulouse that headed north to Limoges, and it was there that they would most likely come across the Panzer division heading for Normandy.

Having picked up another passenger, a young boy, Dufour decided they would cross the main road at Salon-la-Tour and it was there that he spotted Germans ahead. It was either a roadblock or an ambush but he could not take a chance. He immediately stopped the car near a farm and, using the vehicle as a shield, they all jumped out. But they had been spotted by the Germans who quickly opened fire.

A fierce gun battle soon raged. Hopelessly outnumbered, Dufour and Violette made off together, firing as they went, while the young boy dashed off into a field and to safety. They continued to hold off the Germans while withdrawing across the neighbouring fields.

More Germans had arrived but Dufour and Violette continued to keep them at bay. The chase continued for a couple of kilometres before they reached a cornfield and it was there that Violette fell as her weakened ankle gave way. Going immediately to her aid, Dufour tried to help her, part supporting her and part carrying her, but it was no good. The Germans were now getting too close.

Taking up a position next to some trees, Violette continued to fire on the Germans as they closed. She managed to gain enough time for Dufour to get away until, eventually, she ran out of ammunition and could fight no more. She was then captured, but this time there would be no exchange of pleasantries with the Germans.

It was an outstanding act of courage by the young Violette but, like many great accounts of extreme heroism during the Second World War, there has been post-war scrutiny amongst some historians and authors about whether a gun battle actually took place. However, versions of the incident by those who have studied Violette the most,[3] and that of her daughter, Tania, are clear that it did happen.

Whatever the truth, Violette was first taken to the SD's headquarters in Limoges, where she was interrogated. There was a plan put together by Liewer to try to rescue her but she had by then been moved. Violette was taken to Fresnes prison and, ultimately, to the Avenue Foch but she remained silent throughout.

With the Allies advancing, the Germans decided to move their prisoners to Germany. On 8 August Violette was one of thirty-seven SOE operatives moved from Paris. They were bound for different destinations but, sometime in late August, Violette eventually arrived at the concentration camp at Ravensbrück.

Being English and potentially useful to the Germans as a political prisoner for any future settlement in the latter stages of the war, Violette's life was briefly spared. She was used in various working parties and she even spent time at another camp at Königsberg. By early 1945 she was back at Ravensbrück and it was there that the life of this exceptionally brave young woman came to an end; she was still only twenty-three at the time of her death. Although it is believed that Violette's life ended with a single bullet through the back of her neck, there remains some uncertainty about how she died. Whether it was in this way or whether she was hanged is not known for certain; such were the cover ups by the Nazis during the final days of the war.

By the time Violette died, the battle for France had long been won. She could never have imagined that she would leave behind such a legacy. Few, if any, stories of gallant young female agents have captured the British public's imagination more than hers. In 1958 a film titled *Carve Her Name with Pride*, based on the book by R. J. Minney, took the story of Violette Szabo into the home. Both the book and the film tell her story after she had become the second woman to be awarded the George Cross for her immense courage after capture. Information available in London at the time makes no

---

3. Including Violette's biographer, Susan Ottaway, in *Young, Brave and Beautiful* and Minney in *Carve Her Name With Pride*.

reference to the incident at Salon-la-Tour but refers instead to an incident at a house where members of her group were surrounded by Germans. It reads:

> Madame Szabo volunteered to undertake a particularly dangerous mission in France. She was parachuted into France in April, 1944, and undertook the task with enthusiasm. In her execution of the delicate researches entailed she showed great presence of mind and astuteness. She was twice arrested by the German security authorities but each time managed to get away. Eventually, however, with other members of her group, she was surrounded by the Gestapo in a house in the southwest of France. Resistance appeared hopeless but Madame Szabo, seizing a Sten-gun and as much ammunition as she could carry, barricaded herself in part of the house and, exchanging shot for shot with the enemy, killed or wounded several of them. By constant movement, she avoided being cornered and fought until she dropped exhausted. She was arrested and had to undergo solitary confinement. She was then continuously and atrociously tortured but never by word or deed gave away any of her acquaintances or told the enemy anything of any value. She was ultimately executed. Madame Szabo gave a magnificent example of courage and steadfastness.

Those who had met Violette during the final weeks and months of her life, and who survived the war, testified just how brave and inspirational she had been. During her train journey to Ravensbrück in the heat of August 1944, an air raid had brought the journey to a temporary halt. While the guards took cover, Violette and Lilian Rolfe, to whom she was shackled to, crawled along the corridor to take water from the lavatory to the parched men in the next compartment. One of those men happened to be Tommy Yeo-Thomas who reportedly commented 'that girl has guts'.[4]

Whatever the circumstances regarding Violette's death, she almost certainly suffered the same fate as Lilian Rolfe and Denise Bloch. They both died at the same camp and at the same time. It is only hoped that when they

---

4. Escott, op. cit., p.174.

went to their deaths, whatever their state physically and mentally, all three knew that the France they had all fought so gallantly for had, by then, been liberated.

Violette has, arguably, become the most famous SOE agent and epitomizes the courage of all those who went into the field in France. In 2009, on a patch of grass on Albert Embankment in London, between Lambeth Palace and the River Thames, and overlooking the Houses of Parliament where decisions are made to send the nation to war, a monument to the SOE was unveiled by the Duke of Wellington. It is fitting that the design is a sculpture of Violette on a plinth to represent the agents of the SOE and those who did not survive.

As a final word about Violette Szabo, there can be few more poignant and worthy compliments than those of her fellow agent, Odette Sansom, who described Violette as 'the bravest of us all'.

Chapter 22

To Victory

The D-Day landings had, understandably, increased the workload of the circuits in and around the Normandy area. As the Allies attempted to break out of the Normandy beachhead, enemy lines of communication, such as the telephone wires and the road and rail networks, were disrupted, damaged or destroyed in any way possible.

Sydney Hudson's HEADMASTER, for example, was constantly carrying out acts of sabotage against the enemy troop concentrations as they passed through the Sarthe. From their two large bases, one in the Forêt de Charnie and the other in the Forêt de Bercé, the groups were able to mount their attacks in and around le Mans. Unfortunately, though, there were losses too. After capturing a group of maquisards, the Gestapo had learned of the base in the Forêt de Charnie and, during a heavy attack on 16 June, Francisque Dec was killed.

Meanwhile, in the Auvergne, FREELANCE had continued to cause havoc amongst the Germans. On D-Day they had set about demolishing the list of targets John Farmer and Nancy Wake had been given before leaving London: underground cables; factories at Clermont-Ferrand and Montluçon; a synthetic petrol plant at St Hilaire; and a railway junction at Moulins. All were destroyed except the petrol plant at St Hilaire as the maquisards chose to seize the entire output of fuel instead.

Using Denis Rake's radio link with London, more and more air drops were arranged by Farmer and Nancy. The Germans reacted by bringing up reinforcements and between 18 and 20 June, some 20,000 German troops, with strong artillery and air support, attacked the Mont Mouchet redoubts in great strength.

The battles in the heart of the Auvergne would last for several weeks. During July the Maquis attacked enemy convoys, wrecked electrical installations and arms factories and even carried out an attack against the

Gestapo headquarters at Montluçon, during which the raiders left behind a scene of utter devastation and several Germans dead.

Nancy always seemed to be at the midst of these attacks and even led some of them, although she was now seen more as a leader within the organization and so could not be risked too often. She also became instrumental in recruiting more members and helping turn the various resistance groups into a formidable force. To the *Maquis d'Auvergne*, she had quickly grown from a seemingly useless female agent, with a handbag full of coveted money, into probably the most powerful individual among 7,000 fighting men.[1] Nancy seemingly had no fear. One Maquis leader, Henri Tardivat, once said of her, 'She is the most feminine woman I know until the fighting starts. Then she is like five men.'[2]

Nearly a thousand acts of sabotage were made against the rail network in the first twenty-four hours after D-Day as the Germans desperately tried to reinforce Normandy. PIMENTO, for example, succeeded in closing all rail movements between Toulouse and Montauban, and constantly isolated Marseilles and Lyons. Its young leader, Tony Brooks, would later lead his units in bitter streetfighting to help liberate Lyons during September and by the time the war was over he was the longest surviving circuit organizer with the rank of major and a well-earned Distinguished Service Order and Military Cross to add to the Croix de Guerre and Legion d'Honneur awarded to him by the French; he had only just celebrated his twenty-third birthday.

Disruption of the rail network occurred all across France. For example, the rail saboteurs of Francis Cammaerts' JOCKEY made sure that every train leaving Marseilles and heading northwards for Lyons after D-Day was derailed at least once, while DIPLOMAT disrupted the rail network around the important junction of Troyes. Furthermore, the combined efforts of Pearl Witherington's WRESTLER and René Maingard's SHIPWRIGHT resulted in more than 800 rail disruptions in the Indre during the month of June alone.[3]

---

1. Braddon, op. cit., p.157.
2. Ibid. p.195 (Quote of Tardivat) and Escott, op. cit., p.189.
3. Foot, op. cit., p.344.

In the Cluny area of eastern France, Albert Browne-Bartroli and Jean Renaud had turned DITCHER into a highly effective force, converting their men from single saboteurs into a strong fighting unit. In the days following the Allied landings they blew several key bridges between Villefrance and Tournus, and carried out several attacks from three main bases at Cluny, Charoles and Saint-Genoux.

Renaud, in particular, would stop at nothing to get back at the enemy. His wife and three children had been taken by the Germans earlier in the year and were now in a concentration camp in Germany. Renaud must take great credit for turning the resistance in and around Cluny into the fighting force that it had become. But, sadly, his war of revenge came to an end just five days after the Allies had landed in Normandy. His group had managed to divert a German re-supply train and was unloading it at Cluny station when the Germans attacked. Renaud was hit in the leg and could not get away. He was captured and, being well known to the Gestapo, tortured; his exact date of death is not known.[4]

No matter where the Germans set off from to make their way to Normandy, there were circuits and saboteurs just waiting to hamper every move. And when the Germans did manage to get anywhere near the battlefields in north-west France, there was Philippe de Vomécourt's VENTRILOQUIST to get through, even before the enemy could see the Loire. Then, once north of the river, there was HEADMASTER in the Sarthe and finally, when approaching Caen, the scene of where much of the heaviest fighting was taking place, there was Claude de Baissac's SCIENTIST II to contend with.

It was a monumental effort by all the circuits involved. Between them they caused chaos, delay and casualties amongst the German forces that had been forced to run a gauntlet of irregular warfare before they even reached the Normandy area where their 'real' battle was to begin.

With the main Allied landings having taken place, SOE sent into France a number of three-man teams, all of whom went into the field in uniform and wearing the rank and insignia of their nation and service. These were the Jedburghs, known as Jeds, consisting of a mix of British, American and French volunteers, formed and trained by the SOE.

---

4. Grehan & Mace, op. cit., p.151.

The Jeds were to act as a broker between military operations and those of the French Resistance. Each team parachuted behind enemy lines in a key part of France to organize, arm and train the Maquis, and co-ordinate various acts of sabotage and guerrilla warfare to assist the advance of the Allied forces on the ground. They were also required to work closely with other Allied uniformed forces operating behind enemy lines, such as the British Special Air Service (SAS) and the American Operational Groups.

The first two Jedburgh missions were inserted behind enemy lines in western France immediately after D-Day. Two more teams were inserted into Brittany soon after, while two others went into central France, one to the department of Nièvre and the other to the Vienne. Jed teams were also inserted across southern France from Blida in Algeria and by the end of June there were two teams operating in the south-west (in the Lot and Haute-Pyrenees) while another was operating in the department of Cantal in south-central France. Four more teams had been inserted in the south-east, one in the Hautes-Alpes, two in the Drôme, and one in the Ardèche.

By the end of July the number of Jed teams operating across France had risen to twenty-six and, by the time the last volunteers went into France during September, nearly a hundred teams had been inserted. But not everything went according to plan and it would cost the lives of many. There were also mix-ups and confusion along the way, and there was probably no greater disaster than what happened during July in the upland district of Vercors in the south-east of France.

The importance of the Vercors had seemingly not been grasped by those back in London. Little attention had been paid to warnings by men such as Francis Cammaerts who was concerned that his groups were not suitably armed. Despite organizing and training more than 6,000 men, Cammaerts had warned that the *Maquis du Vercors*, a rural resistance organization led by Colonel François Huet (Hervieux), and using the Massif du Vercors (Vercors Plateau) as a refuge, needed heavier weapons, such as artillery, mortars and anti-tank guns.

With German troops now in the area to counter the Maquis, the SOE finally sent in a mission, called EUCALYPTUS, led by an English officer, Major Desmond Longe. Longe's mission did not get off to a good start due to a series of misunderstandings with Cammaerts and the leader of the Jed team operating in the area, Major Neil Marten. The root of the problem hinged on the fact that London had failed to tell Cammaerts that EUCALYPTUS was coming and had also failed to brief Longe who Cammaerts was.

But there were other differences too. Cammaerts had always believed that his men should operate in small units, behaving like mosquitoes, hassling enemy troop convoys, blowing up bridges and destroying lines of communication, and generally being a thorn in the enemy's sides, and so he had always trained his men to avoid large-scale or heavy engagements. Longe, however, had little experience in the field and no great understanding of the French language. His task was to organize the arming of the Maquis with Stens, rifles and grenades to conduct larger-scale warfare but there was no mention of heavy weapons. There was the odd half-promise here and there that some heavier weapons might be dropped at a later date, but the reality was that Vercors was not a high enough priority at the time.

At that stage the plateau was free of Germans, although there were occasional skirmishes with the enemy on the edges as the Germans increased their probing patrols. But many of Huet's leaders were no longer able to control their impatience for action. There had been an increasing number of examples where his men's patriotic imprudence got the better of prudence and this led to an uprising in the Ubaye valley, a department in Cammaerts's region of the Alpes de Haute-Provence.

In early July 1944 the 'Free Republic of Vercors' was proclaimed as the first democratic territory in France since the German occupation. Huet called up more of his volunteers and within days there were more than 3,000 maquisards on the plateau. They were armed with the vast quantities of supplies that had recently been received, including the contents of a thousand containers dropped in just one day alone, and there was also a landing strip at Vassieux prepared for the arrival of American Skytrains, but there was still no sign of any heavy weapons.

But the Free Republic of Vercors was to be a short-lived regime as, by the end of the month, it would cease to exist. The enemy's strength had built to an estimated 10,000 and on 18 July the Germans launched an all-out assault on the plateau. The fight lasted for several days due to the rugged terrain and bravery of the maquisards but, when the Germans landed gliderborne troops on the landing strip that had been prepared for the Americans, the maquisards lacked the heavy firepower to remove them; they were simply mown down in large numbers by the more heavily armed Germans.

Huet gave the order for his men to disperse and the battle, since known locally as 'the hell of Vercors', ended in tragedy for the French. As the Germans overran the plateau they committed the kind of atrocities that have long since been associated with the horrors of the Nazi occupation, burning farms, raping and looting, as well as torturing and slaying those who stood in the way.[5]

The bloody suppression at Vercors served as a warning to the Maquis that the war was far from won. It had also proved they were not suitably armed, or organized enough for that matter, to directly confront the enemy in a large-scale conflict until the Allies arrived. And so the maquisards returned to their more traditional style of waging war, in smaller numbers, rather than trying to engage the Germans in large-scale tactical operations.

One role that SOE operatives were not specifically trained to do was to provide tactical intelligence for the Allied forces but one new circuit, HELMSMAN, led by Jack Hayes, ended up doing just that. Hayes had dropped into a reception near Avranches organized by Claude de Baissac in mid-July. Advancing American forces reported they were short of tactical intelligence and so Hayes's task was to provide it. In just a matter of days he had pulled together a dozen or so local volunteers whose task was to carry messages from him through the lines to give the Americans vital details of the enemy's dispositions. De Baissac did the same for the British, using members of his SCIENTIST II. Similarly, in the Marne, Nicholas Bodington, who had returned to France during July to re-activate the old PROFESSOR circuit under its new name of PEDLAR, provided useful intelligence leading to a number of targets being bombed by the RAF.

But it was dangerous work. Eileen Nearne, WIZARD's young radio operator, had also been busy transmitting intelligence to London as well as supporting René Dumont-Guillemet's SPIRITUALIST by organizing air drops. So much had been asked of Eileen but in late July she was finally caught at her radio set in the house she had been using at Bourg-la-Reine.

---

5. Foot, op. cit., p.346.

The Gestapo raid was so quick that there was no time for her to hide the wireless set or destroy her codes. Eileen was eventually taken to Ravensbrück and may well have suffered the same fate as so many others had she not have managed to escape just days before the end of the war while being moved to another camp; she was later picked up by the Americans.

It was also at the end of July when Ben Cowburn parachuted into France in an attempt to rescue his two MINISTER friends, Pierre Mulsant and Denis Barrett. Both had reportedly been arrested by the Gestapo after going to the aid of an SAS group in the forest of Fontainebleu. Their arrests had left the circuit leaderless but responsibility for its work had been taken over by Yvonne Fontaine, the extremely competent courier.

It was Cowburn's fourth mission. His task was to also include setting up a resistance cell near Amiens but, as things were to turn out, the city was liberated just days later and Cowburn never found his friends; Mulsant and Barrett were both on their way to Buchenwald, where they were executed in early October.

Having broken out of the Normandy beachhead, the Allies were now reaching many cities, towns and villages, their arrival bringing obvious joy to those now liberated. But for some the war was far from over, particularly those far away from the advancing Allied units. In the Jura mountains, SCHOLAR had been busy cutting all lines of communication and organizing air drops but one large drop, which had seen some 400 containers dropped by American B-17 Flying Fortresses in what was the USAAF's first mass daylight drop of weapons and supplies, led to a rather bizarre end for the circuit's leader, Baron Gonzagues de Saint-Geniès.

While celebrating the circuit's success with his leaders at Faubourg de Chalon in Dole, a sudden warning was received that Germans were coming. The group then scattered to various hiding places, with de Saint-Geniès hiding in the loft. A search of the building had discovered a number of the group but then, quite by chance and more as a warning than anything else, random shots were fired into the ceiling. One hit de Saint-Geniès in the head, killing him instantly. There are two slight variations to the exact circumstances behind his death, although both relate to the same location and at the same time: one says that he was seen and shot while the other states he was shot while trying to escape. It makes no difference. The brave young French nobleman was dead.

Amongst many others captured that day was Yvonne Baseden, the circuit's young radio operator, who had been found hiding beneath the floorboards. But the Germans seemingly never worked out who she was, or her role, and, although she ended up at Ravensbrück, Yvonne somehow cheated death and was one of the few F agents to survive the camps.

There were other parts of the country, too, where liberation did not come quickly enough and some of F's great agents were to die during the final desperate weeks of the struggle for France. These included Henri Sevenet, who was killed near Carcassonne during July. His little army had come under attack from a strong German column estimated to be about 4,000 strong and supported by tanks, artillery and aircraft. During the main engagement on 20 July, Sevenet's group suffered heavy losses and had to disperse, and it was during the evening that the gallant Henri Sevenet was killed.[6]

Another to lose his life during the final days before liberation was Paul Sarrette who was killed in the hills of Nièvre during early September. The life of this quite remarkable young man came to an end in a tragic accident during a firing practice when a mortar tube blew up, killing him and six others; Paul Sarrette was only twenty-one.

The final struggle for the liberation of Paris took place during August 1944 when the combination of the advancing Allies and Free French forces, assisted by a tumescent Maquis, triggered an uprising in the capital. The German garrison surrendered on 25 August, soon after the Allies had landed in southern France.

Paris had finally been liberated after more than four years of Nazi occupation. Just how much the SOE had contributed to its liberation is yet another of those post-war debates. But the courage of those who had opposed the Nazi occupation, and then helped to pave the way for victory, cannot be in any doubt.

Elsewhere in France, battles were still being fought before the whole country could be free. In the Auvergne, the Germans had underestimated the strength and capability of the Maquis, Coulaudon's so-called 'Army of

---

6. Grehan & Mace, op. cit., p.170.

Liberation', but when they did realize just how powerful it had become they sent in an SS battalion and more. John Farmer, Denis Rake and Nancy Wake were continuing the battle to drive the occupiers out, and from the forests of Tronçais, the Maquis blew up bridges across the River Allier and cut off the enemy's line of retreat towards the Belfort Gap and back into Germany.

Coulaudon's army soon liberated Montluçon before turning south towards Clermont-Ferrand as he was determined to be the first Free French commander to enter Vichy, known to some as the 'capital of shame'. On 17 August Coulaudon received an emissary from Marshal Philippe Pétain offering to surrender. Pétain would have surrendered himself but he was whisked away to Germany while the SS troops, Gestapo and *Milicens* committed further atrocities before fleeing the town.

As Paris was being liberated, so, too, was Vichy. By 25 August order was restored by the resistance groups within the town, after which more than a thousand *Milicens* and collaborators were rounded up. Feelings were understandably running high and a number of those rounded up were killed.[7] But amongst the carnage of the past few months, there was decency as well. The Maquis had held a small group of German prisoners in the forest of Tronçais. Now that the enemy had gone, and the Allied forces were soon to arrive, there was no longer the need to keep on with the killings and so Nancy Wake went to considerable lengths to ensure their German prisoners were handed over safely to the Americans when they arrived.[8]

Marseilles had also been liberated at the end of August, although it had cost 4,000 French lives with thousands more wounded. The JOCKEY circuit of Francis Cammaerts, who had managed to escape the disaster of the Vercors Plateau, had played a vital part. The main route of the Allied advance from Cannes to Grenoble was kept open, allowing the Allies to get clear of the lower Rhône valley. Also, in the Jura, Richard Heslop's men had helped liberate a vast area of several thousand square kilometres, long before the first Allied armour appeared north of Grenoble.

But Cammaerts was arrested during this final phase of the German occupation and taken to the Gestapo prison at Digne. Fortunately for him,

7. Cookridge, op. cit., pp.360–4.
8. Braddon, op. cit., p.237.

the Germans did not appear to realize who they had captured and it took the intervention of the circuit's tough but highly intelligent new courier, Christine Granville (Pauline), to save him.

The radiantly beautiful Christine Granville was, in fact, an alias. She had been born in Poland as Maria Krystyna Skarbek and had become a British agent even before the SOE had formed, helping compatriots in occupied Poland from her base in Budapest. After withdrawing to Palestine and Cairo, she came under the aegis of the Middle East branch of the special forces, and had been parachuted into southern France from SOE's base in Algiers. She had only been in France for just a few weeks when she found herself intervening to save the life of her organizer. Cammaerts was duly released by two former collaborators after Christine had threatened them with being turned over to the advancing Americans, whose arrival was imminent, should they not co-operate.

For a man who had started the war as a conscientious objector, Francis Cammaerts had proved to be an outstanding SOE agent and was awarded the Distinguished Service Order at the end of the war while Christine Granville was awarded the George Medal.

Lyons was liberated in September while, in the south-west of France, Roger Landes, later to receive a Bar to his Military Cross, had helped to liberate departments without the help of the Allies, while George Starr had led his units towards Toulouse. The bulk of France had now been cleared of the German occupiers, although there would still be pockets that would remain under occupation for several months. The circuits in eastern France, STOCKBROKER and CHANCELLOR, for example, were still very much in action in the Franche-Comté region, laying ambushes against the retreating Germans, and, in Brittany, the Atlantic port of Lorient had been designated by Hitler as a fortress to be defended to the last man. The Americans simply surrounded it until the German garrison surrendered at the end of the war.

For many the battle was over. People like Denis Rake and Nancy Wake could now go home; their job was done. Rake, who had continuously managed to maintain a radio link with London under difficult and perilous conditions for several months, was awarded the Military Cross while Nancy received the George Medal. Her citation includes:

Ensign Wake's organization ability, endurance, courage and complete
disregard for her own safety earned her the respect and admiration of
all with whom she came in contact. The Maquis troop, most of them
rough and difficult to handle, accepted orders from her, and treated her
as one of their own male officers.[9]

After the war Nancy chose to stay in France for a while, although she would
eventually return to England. In his book *Nancy Wake*, the author Russell
Braddon describes her as 'SOE's greatest heroine'. Few could argue.

For the French it would take some time for life to return to normal.
Figures vary considerably but anywhere between 125,000 and 200,000
French men and women were deported to German concentration camps,
of whom, perhaps, only 40,000 returned home. It has also been reported
that the French Resistance lost around 24,000 men and women executed by
the Germans in France[10] and a further 20,000–30,000 maquisards killed in
action.[11]

The French patriots had paid a terrible toll for their freedom. There would
also be a power struggle in post-war France between those who expected
to govern and lead the nation and those who had led the resistance effort
against the enemy during the occupation. But that was not for the SOE to
resolve, although there was the business of clearing up its circuits in France
and this was conducted from Paris with F and RF Sections sending an
investigation mission round the country to report to Maurice Buckmaster
and Harry Thackthwaite respectively.[12]

On the SOE monument in London, situated on the Albert Embankment
and overlooking the Houses of Parliament, it states the SOE sent a total of
470 agents into France. According to SOE records, 325 of these had been
sent into the field by F section: 172 British; ninety-two French; forty-six
American; and fifteen from other nations. Of the total of 325, the number
listed as casualties is 125 (twelve killed in action, forty-five executed, thirty
prisoners of war and thirty-eight listed as missing). Of the 172 Britons sent

9. Ibid. p.278.
10. Cookridge, op. cit., p.389.
11. Michel, *Histoire de la Résistance*, p.124.
12. Foot, op. cit., p.372.

into the field, 108 became casualties of whom eighty-eight never returned. In addition to those agents of F Section, RF Section and the Free French also sent agents into the field and 279 Jeds dropped into France. [13]

It has been estimated that around 200 men and women from F and RF Sections were sent to concentration camps. Few would return; maybe thirty at best. In Buchenwald, for example, there had at one time been forty SOE operatives held at the camp. These included great men such as Tommy Yeo-Thomas, François Garel, John Macalister, Frank Pickersgill, Alphonse Defendini, Denis Barrett, Robert Benoist, Pierre Culioli, Henri Frager, Emile-Henry Garry, Julien Detal, Marcel Leccia, Elisée Allard, Pierre Geelen, Charles Rechenmann, the Newton 'Twins', Christopher Burney, Harry Peulevé, Maurice Southgate, Arthur Steele and George Wilkinson. By the time the camp was liberated by the Americans only four had survived (Christopher Burney, Maurice Southgate and the Newton brothers), although a handful had cheated death in other ways.[14]

Many had also perished at the other concentration camps, including Dachau, Sachsenhausen, Ravensbrück, Natzweiler, Mauthausen, Ravitsch and Gross-Rosen, to name but a few. In the case of the female agents, only three of the fifteen who fell into German hands survived the horrors of the camps (Yvonne Baseden, Eileen Nearne and Odette Sansom). As for the rest, some had succumbed to the appalling conditions in which they were held but most had their lives cut short by being hanged, or a lethal injection, or a bullet in the back of the neck. And all this after they had first suffered torture, indignity and interrogation. Such was the evil tide of Nazi policy for those who were caught.

While some agents would later be recognized with awards and decorations bestowed upon them by both the British and the French, the stories of many went unheard. There were certainly thousands who had been recruited locally in France, and had worked tirelessly in the face of almost certain death if caught, who went unrecognized. But the fact was that many of the most deserving men and women could not be recognized for their outstanding

13. NA HS 7/135, SOE Activities in France, 1941–44 (Appendix A - Number of agents sent to the field – F, RF and Jedburgh).
14. Foot, op. cit., pp.373–4.

achievements because those circuit leaders, who would willingly have brought their names to the attention of the British, were dead.

And so, for many, they would have to take comfort from knowing that they had done their bit, although the end of the war would bring new problems for some as they struggled to adjust to normal life once more. Their physical or mental scars, or both, meant they faced a lifetime of uncertainties; their families and friends could not even start to imagine what they had been through.

As those fortunate to survive arrived back home, wherever home was, they must have all spared a thought for those left behind. Not only those who had never lived to see the liberation of France, having been killed during the course of their duties, but also those who had died in the camps during the final days of the war. Sadly, they were so close to making it through to the end but never got to see the freedom that they had all fought so valiantly for.

Bibliography and References

Published Sources

Appleyard, J. E., *Geoffrey* (Blandford Press, London, 1947)
Basu, Shrabani, *Spy Princess* (Sutton, Stroud, 2006 and The History Press, Stroud, 2008)
Binney, Marcus, *The Women who lived for Danger* (Hodder & Stoughton, London, 2002)
——*Secret War Heroes* (Hodder & Stoughton, London, 2006)
Bleicher, Hugo, *Colonel Henri's Story* (Kimber, London, 1954)
Boyce, Frederic & Everett, Douglas, SOE: The Scientific Secrets (Sutton Publishing, Stroud, 2002 and The History Press, Stroud, 2009)
Braddon, Russell, *Nancy Wake* (Cassell, London, 1956 and The History Press, Stroud, 2013)
Buckmaster, Maurice, *They Fought Alone* (Odhams Press Ltd, London, 1958)
Burney, Christopher, *Solitary Confinement* (Clerke and Cockeran, London, 1952)
Carré, Mathilde-Lily, *I was 'The Cat'* (Souvenir Press, London, 1960)
Churchill, Peter, *Duel of Wits* (Hodder & Stoughton, London, 1953)
Clark, Freddie, *Agents by Moonlight* (Tempus Publishing, Stroud, 1999)
Cookridge, E. H., *Inside SOE* (Arthur Barker Ltd, London, 1966)
They Came from the Sky (Heinemann, London, 1965)
Cowburn, Benjamin, *No Cloak, No Dagger* (Jarrolds, London, 1960 and Pen & Sword, Barnsley, 2009)
Crowdy, Terry, *SOE Agent: Churchill's Secret Warriors* (Osprey, Oxford, 2008)
Dodds-Parker, Douglas, *Setting Europe Ablaze* (Springwood Books, Windlesham, 1983)
Escott, Beryl E., Sqn Ldr, *Mission Improbable* (Patrick Stephens, Wellingsborough, 1991)
The Heroines of SOE (The History Press, Stroud, 2010)
Fitzsimons, Peter, *Nancy Wake* (Sydney, 2001 and Harper Collins, London, 2002)
Foot, M. R. D., *SOE in France* (HMSO, London, 1966)
—— *SOE: The Special Operations Executive 1940–1946* (Pimlico, London, 1999)
Ford, Roger, *Fire From the Forest* (Cassell, London, 2003)
—— *Steel From the Sky* (Orion Publishing, London, 2004)
Fuller, Jean Overton, *German Penetration of SOE: France 1941–44* (William Kimber, London, 1975)
Gleeson, James, *They Feared No Evil* (Corgi Books, London, 1978)
Grehan, John
& Mace, Martin, *Unearthing Churchill's Secret Army* (Pen & Sword, Barnsley, 2012)
Helm, Sarah, *A Life in Secrets* (Little Brown, London, 2005 and Abacus, London, 2012)
Heslop, Richard, *Xavier* (R. Hart-Davies, London, 1970)
Howarth, Patrick, *Undercover: The Men and Women of the SOE* (Routledge and Keegan Paul Books, London, 1980)

Hudson, Sydney, *Undercover Operator* (Leo Cooper, Barnsley, 2003)

Irwin, Will, Lt Col (Retd), *The Jedburghs* (Public Affairs, Cambridge MA, 2005)

Keene, Tom, *Cloak of Enemies* (Spellmount, Stroud, 2012)

Lett, Brian, *The Small Scale Raiding Force* (Pen & Sword Military, Barnsley, 2013)

Mackenzie, William, *The Secret History of SOE* (St Ermin's Press, London, 2000)

Marks, Leo, *Between Silk and Cyanide* (Harper Collins, London, 1998 and The History Press, Stroud, 2007)

Marshall, Bruce, *The White Rabbit* (Cassell, London, 1952)

Middlebrook, Martin

& Everitt, Chris, *The Bomber Command War Diaries* (Viking Books, London, 1985)

Minney, R. J., *Carve Her Name with Pride* (George Newnes Ltd, London, 1956 and Pen & Sword, Barnsley, 2013)

Nicholas, Elizabeth, *Death Be Not Proud* (White Lion Publishers/Cresset Press, London, 1958)

Oliver, David, *Airborne Espionage* (Sutton Publishing, Stroud, 2005 and The History Press, Stroud, 2013)

Ottaway, Susan, *Sisters, Secrets and Sacrifice* (Harper, London, 2013)

Violette Szabo (Pen & Sword, Barnsley, 2002 and Thistle Publishing, London, 2014)

Perrin, Nigel, *Spirit of Resistance: The Life of SOE Agent Harry Peulevé DSO MC* (Pen & Sword, Barnsley, 2008)

Richards, Brook, *Secret Flotillas: Clandestine Sea Operations to Brittany 1940–44* (Pen & Sword, Barnsley, 2012)

Rochester, Deveraux, *Full Moon to France* (Robert Hale, USA, 1978)

Ruby, Marcel, *F Section SOE* (Leo Cooper, London, 1985)

Saward, Joe, *The Grand Prix Saboteurs* (Morienval Press, London, 2006)

Starns, Penny, *Odette* (The History Press, Stroud, 2009)

Thomas, Jack, *No Banners* (W. H. Allen, London, 1955)

Tickell, Jerrard, *Moon Squadron* (Allan Wingate, London, 1956 and Endeavour Press Ltd, Kent, 2013)

Verity, Hugh, *We Landed by Moonlight* (Ian Allan Ltd, London, 1978 and Crécy Publishing Ltd, Manchester, 1998)

Walker, Robyn, *The Women Who Spied for Britain* (Amberley Publishing, Stroud, 2014)

Walters, Anne-Marie, *Moondrop to Gascony* (Macmillan, London, 1946 and Moho Books, Wiltshire, 2009)

West, Nigel, *Secret War: The Story of SOE* (Hodder & Stoughton, London, 1992 and Teach Yourself Books, UK, 1993)

Wilkinson, Peter

& Astley, Joan Bright, *Gubbins & SOE* (Leo Cooper, London, 1997 and Pen & Sword, Barnsley, 2010)

Yarnold, Patrick, *Wanborough Manor, School for Secret Agents* (Hopfield Publications, 2009)

The National Archives, Kew – File and Document References

ADM 179/227	SSRF - Operation AQUATINT
ADM 202/399	Operation FRANKTON
DEFE 2/109	SSRF – Operations BARRICADE, DRYAD, BRANFORD, AQUATINT, BASALT, BATMAN

DEFE 2/842	Folbot/Goatley/Cockles
HS 7/121	Personnel Dropped by F Section
HS 7/135	SOE Activities in France 1941–44
HS 7/244	France F Section Diary, July-September 1942
HS 7/245	France F Section Diary, October-December 1942
HS 7/246	France RF Section Diary, July-December 1942
HS 7/247	France RF Section Diary, January-June 1943
HS 7/249	France RF Section Diary, July-September 1943
HS 7/250	France RF Section Diary, October-December 1943
HS 8/895	MEW & SOE Casualties in the Field, January 1943 - December 1945
HS 8/896	MEW & SOE Casualties in the Field, January 1943 - December 1945
HS 8/1002	British Circuits in France by Major Bourne-Patterson
HS 9/42	Personnel File – Joseph Antoine France Antelme
HS 9/59/2	Personnel File – Vera Atkins
HS 9/127	Personnel File – Robert Marcel Charles Benoist
HS 9/183	Personnel File – Christine Granville
HS 9/314	Personnel File – Peter Morland Churchill (Vol 1)
HS 9/315	Personnel File – Peter Morland Churchill (Vol 2)
HS 9/355/2	Personnel File – Pearl Witherington
HS 9/422	Personnel File – Henri Alfred Eugene Déricourt
HS 9/648/4	Personnel File – Odette Sansom
HS 9/836/5	Personnel File – Noor Inayat Khan
HS 9/1089/2	Personnel File – Eileen Nearne
HS 9/1089/4	Personnel File – Jacqueline Nearne
HS 9/1096/8	Personnel File – Alfred Willie Oscar Newton
HS 9/1097/1	Personnel File – Henry George Rodolfo Newton
HS 9/1110/5	Personnel File – Gilbert Maurice Norman
HS 9/1287/6	Personnel File – Diana Rowden
HS 9/1289/7	Personnel File – Yvonne Rudellat
HS 9/1395/3	Personnel File – Maurice Southgate
HS 9/1430/6	Personnel File – Francis Suttill
HS 9/1435	Personnel File – Violette Szabo
HS 9/1458	Personnel File – Forest Frederick Edward Yeo-Thomas
HS 9/1545	Personnel File – Nancy Wake
KV 2/927	Mathilde Lucie Carré, alias Victoire, La Chatte
WO 106/4417	Early Planning of the SSRF

Index

The index below lists the people and circuits (in capitals) included in this book.